The Routledge Guide to Modern English Writing

In 1963 President John F. Kennedy was shot, Sylvia Plath published *The Bell Jar*, and the Beatles were in their prime. This was a changing world, which British and Irish writers both contributed to and reflected in drama, poetry and prose.

The Routledge Guide to Modern English Writing tells the story of British and Irish writing from 1963 to the present. From the first performance of Tom Stoppard's *Rosencrantz and Guildenstern Are Dead* in the 1960s to lad novels and chick lit in the twenty-first century, the authors guide the reader through the major writers, genres and developments in English writing over the past forty years. Providing an in-depth overview of the main genres and extensive treatment of a wide range of writers including Philip Larkin, Ted Hughes, Angela Carter, Benjamin Zephaniah and Nick Hornby, this highly readable handbook also offers notes on language and cultural issues, quotations from selected works, a timeline and a guide to other works.

Drawing on the prize-winning *The Routledge History of Literature in English* (second edition 2001) by the same authors, *The Routledge Guide to Modern English Writing* is essential reading for all who are interested in contemporary writing.

John McRae is Special Professor of Language in Literature Studies at the University of Nottingham, and has been a Visiting Professor and Lecturer in over forty countries. **Ronald Carter** is Professor of Modern English Language in the School of English Studies at the University of Nottingham. He has published widely in the fields of English Language and Literary Studies.

D0315736

The Routledge Guide to Modern English Writing

Britain and Ireland

JOHN McRAE and RONALD CARTER

Routledge
Taylor & Francis Group

LONDON AND NEW YORK

First published 2004 by Routledge
11 New Fetter Lane, London EC4P 4EE

Simultaneously published in the USA and Canada
by Routledge
29 West 35th Street, New York, NY 10001

Routledge is an imprint of the Taylor & Francis Group

Typeset in Futura and Goudy by
Keystroke, Jacaranda Lodge, Wolverhampton
Printed and bound in Great Britain by
TJ International, Padstow, Cornwall

British Library Cataloguing in Publication Data
A catalogue record for this book is available from the
British Library

Library of Congress Cataloging in Publication Data
A catalog record for this book has been requested

ISBN 0–415–28636–0 (hbk)
ISBN 0–415–28637–9 (pbk)

my Bala, your Jaan

Contents

Acknowledgements

The editors and publishers wish to thank the following for permission to use copyright material:

Anvil Press Poetry Ltd for material from Carol Ann Duffy, 'A Valentine' from *Mean Time* by Carol Ann Duffy (1993);

BBC Worldwide Ltd and PFD on behalf of the author for material from Alan Bennett, 'A Chip in the Sugar' from *Talking Heads* by Alan Bennett. Copyright © FORLAKE LTD 1993;

Carcanet Press Ltd for Edwin Morgan, 'The Welcome' from *Collected Poems* by Edwin Morgan; and Eavan Boland, 'Beautiful Speech' from *In a Time of Violence* by Eavan Boland;

Curtis Brown on behalf of the author for material from Grace Nichols, 'The Fat Black Woman Goes Shopping' from *The Fat Black Woman's Poems* by Grace Nichols. Copyright © Grace Nichols 1983;

David Godwin Associates on behalf of the author for Simon Armitage, 'Xanadu' (1992);

Faber and Faber Ltd and Grove Weidenfeld, Inc for material from Tom Stoppard, *Rosencrantz and Guildenstern Are Dead* by Tom Stoppard (1965), and Harold Pinter, *Silence* (1969); and with Farrar, Straus and Giroux, LLC for Ted Hughes, 'Fulbright Scholars' from *Birthday Letters* by Ted Hughes. Copyright © 1998 by Ted Hughes; and for material from Thom Gunn, 'In Time of Plague' from *Complete Poems* by Thom Gunn. Copyright © 1994 by Thom Gunn; Seamus Heaney, 'Digging', 'North' and 'The Rain Stick' from *Opened Ground: Selected Poems 1966–1996* by Seamus Heaney. Copyright © 1998 by Seamus Heaney; and Philip Larkin, 'Annus Mirabilis' from *Collected Poems* by Philip Larkin. Copyright © 1988, 1989 by the Estate of Philip Larkin;

Tony Harrison for material from 'The Pomegranates of Patmos' and 'Y' from *The Gaze of the Gorgon* by Tony Harrison, Bloodaxe Books (1992);

Nick Hern Books for material from Caryl Churchill, *Cloud Nine*. Copyright © Caryl Churchill 1979, 1980, 1983, 1984, 1985;

James & James (Publishers) Ltd on behalf of the Executors of the Estate of James MacGibbon and New Directions Publishing Corporation for Stevie Smith, 'Not Waving But Drowning' from *Collected Poems of Stevie Smith*. Copyright © 1972 by Stevie Smith;

Tom Leonard for material from 'Intimate Voices' and 'Report from the Present';

Methuen Publishing Ltd for material from Patrick Marber, *Closer* (1997), and Sarah Kane, *Blasted* (1995); with Grove Weidenfeld, Inc for material from Joe Orton, *Loot* (1966); and with Casarotto Ramsey & Associates Ltd on behalf of the authors for material from Edward Bond, *Bingo*. Copyright © 1974 by Edward Bond; and Howard Brenton, *The Romans in Britain*. Copyright © 1980, 1981 by Howard Brenton;

The Orion Publishing Group for R. S. Thomas, 'Love' from *Collected Poems* by R. S. Thomas, J. M. Dent (1978);

Penguin Books Ltd with Houghton Mifflin Company for Geoffrey Hill, 'XXII' from 'Mercian Hymns' from *New and Collected Poems 1952–1992* by Geoffrey Hill, Penguin Books (1985). Copyright © 1971, 1985, 1994 by Geoffrey Hill; and with Scribner, an imprint of Simon & Schuster Adult Publishing Group, for material from Peter Shaffer, *Equus*, Penguin Books (1977). Copyright © 1973 Peter Shaffer;

PFD on behalf of the authors for Roger McGough, 'No Surprises' from *Defying Gravity* by Roger McGough, Viking Press. Copyright © 1991, 1992; and Andrew Motion, 'Close' from *Love in a Life* by Andrew Motion, Chatto (1991); and material from Andrew Motion, 'Scripture' from *Natural Causes* by Andrew Motion, Chatto (1987);

Althea Selvon for Samuel Selvon, 'Brackley and the Bed' from *The Ways of Sunlight* by Samuel Selvon (1957);

Benjamin Zephaniah for 'As a African' from *City Psalms* by Benjamin Zephaniah, Bloodaxe Books (1992).

Every effort has been made to trace the copyright holders but if any have been inadvertently overlooked the publishers will be pleased to make the necessary amendment at the first opportunity.

Introduction

What is 'modern' writing anyway? The *Harry Potter* series and *The Lord of the Rings*, *Bridget Jones's Diary*, and *4.48 Psychosis* by Sarah Kane have all recently reached worldwide audiences – and they range from the 1950s, when Tolkien first wrote about his fantasy world, to fantasy created forty years later, and to the totally different torments of end-of-the-century female characters.

In some parts of the world English literature is still seen as '*Beowulf* to Virginia Woolf'. For many audiences, recent theatre in English comprises plays by writers such as Edward Bond and Sarah Kane, even though their work is not necessarily much staged or well known in their own country. For others, 'performance theatre' has taken over from the traditional text-based canon of drama; and in poetry, performance or dub poetry and rap have brought the genre full circle from its ancient origins to a new oral tradition.

For many readers it is modern poetry that best represents the current flowering of writing in English. With Seamus Heaney from Ireland and Derek Walcott from St Lucia winning the Nobel Prize for Literature, poetry in English has moved offshore, away from its traditional roots, while both these great voices acknowledge their deep links to the canonical traditions of English and European poetry.

It is one of the most striking features of recent writing in English that the centre has shifted. Most titles are still published in London. But they are written in different voices, from different centres, from what used to be thought of as the fringes, in voices which used to be thought of as 'outsiders'. In political terms devolution has become significant, and a sense of cultural devolution, of local assertion and affirmation, is a feature of literature too.

Television and cinema have created their own ways of writing and reading. Cinema has been the shaping mode of fiction in the twentieth century. It is ironic, therefore, that it has now become the ideal mode to transform a novel and take it to the widest possible audiences: the movie of the book frequently consolidates the novel's success, at least temporarily. A writer such as Andrew Davies has made an art form of adapting classic, canonical novels for television, bringing Jane Austen, George Eliot, Anthony Trollope and other writers to audiences and readers in greater numbers than ever before.

Every year more and more novels are published. Books targeted originally to children now not only reach adult readers but win major 'adult' prizes, thanks to writers such as J.K. Rowling and Philip Pullman – this would have been astonishing only ten years ago. Detective fiction is a staple of television, and the original books have achieved literary 'respectability' through the works of P.D. James, Ruth Rendell, Reginald Hill and Ian Rankin, to name only a few. Fiction is just one of the modes of prose: cookery writing, travel writing, biography and autobiography, memoirs, diaries, journalism and critical writing: recent years have seen best-sellers, masterpieces and glowing reputations in all these areas.

Fashions change and return, writers go in and out of favour, reputations rise and fall. 'Chick lit' and 'lad lit' have reflected the tastes of the times in the late 1990s. Scotland in the 1980s and 1990s rivalled Ireland in its literary renaissance. Writers of all accents, colours and ethnic origins now contribute to the ever-richer mix that is writing in English. It is no longer surprising to find names from all continents, accents from every part of the world, voices from all viewpoints writing and making themselves heard in English. Many of these writers do not consider themselves British, or want to be considered as such: in the 1980s Seamus Heaney famously repudiated his inclusion in a book of modern English poetry, affirming his Irishness, and his distance from that kind of canonical categorisation, while never denying his close bonds with the traditions implied. Writers from different continents, from Salman Rushdie to Buchi Emecheta, from Derek Walcott and Wilson Harris to David Dabydeen and Anita Desai, illustrate how there is a less and less clear concept of what Britishness might be. Is it language, domicile, education, upbringing? It is certainly not just a question of citizenship, and as for language – it is even debatable whether there is such a thing as English nowadays, with the growth of new Englishes all over the world.

'Best-sellers' is a term we have used to indicate books of their moment: books which move a lot of copies in a short period of time. In our present-day world of instant success and sales figures, this is the kind of indicator which gives a book and an author a very high profile. But yesterday's best-sellers are often today's forgotten remainders. Every year has its splurge of self-help books, television tie-ins, 'lifestyle' guides, cookery and gardening best-sellers. Popular fiction from Cartland and Cookson to Follett and Forsyth always sells in vast quantities. On the other hand, poetry and drama books hardly ever make the best-seller lists. Although we are concerned with readership and audiences, and frequently do use that as a criterion of success, there is also the need to signal longer term critical impact.

So can there be a 'mainstream'? Or is it only possible to make a subjective list to answer the question 'Have you read any good books lately'? Every choice is subjective in some ways. It depends on what we, the authors, two white male European writers of Scottish and English origin, one gay, one straight, have read and reacted to. We have listened to many friends, colleagues, critics and pundits. We have put in everything we consider vital, and many other things we consider significant, a lot we like, and some we don't like that much. Some writers have been given more extended consideration; and there are many quotations, selected to give a taste, however brief, of what makes that author or text distinctive, without going into textual analysis or commentary. We have left out lots of writers and books we would have liked to include. In five or ten years' time we will want to change some of the choices, as well as add many new ones.

It is a rich and bubbling, lively and exciting world, the world of modern writing in English. This is a glimpse into that world, one which we hope readers will enjoy, which will tempt them to read further, to make judgements, to challenge us and our choices and opinions, and decide for themselves the books and writers that matter.

Setting the scene

1963 AND ALL THAT

The year 1963 was when President John F. Kennedy was shot. And it was the year in which Sylvia Plath published her only novel, *The Bell Jar*. It begins, 'It was a queer, sultry summer, the summer they electrocuted the Rosenbergs.' In Britain it was the high summer of the Beatles and the Great Train Robbery. In the autumn the golden age of the Kennedy Camelot ended in Dallas. Forty years on Camelot is the name of the company that runs the National Lottery.

Philip Larkin summed up the start of things when he wrote that 'sexual intercourse began in 1963/ Between the *Lady Chatterley* ban and the Beatles' first LP'. From the 1960s to the present the shape, the taste, the social, economic and racial mix of Britain and of what is English has changed completely. The language is now more multicultural and socially varied than it has ever been. Attitudes and priorities have changed. The novels, plays and poetry of the past forty years reflect these changes, and in some ways encapsulate them. Where Shakespeare's Hamlet could speak of 'the form and pressure of the time' there are now a multitude of forms, media and modes of cultural production that illustrate the times. Movies and television are just as significant as creative modes as have been the more traditional forms.

The 'swinging sixties' were seen as a time of liberation, especially in sexual terms. The 1970s seemed duller, the 1980s were a time of materialism, the 1990s the consolidation of that boom, and the big decade for multiculturalism. And in the new millennium there has been something of a disillusion with that materialism, and, as yet, no new direction has emerged. Challenge has been the mode of the past few years.

In every decade, every single year, best-sellers emerge: some of these are successes of the moment, others have a lasting impact. And there is no way of telling what might be the lasting contribution to literature and what might be no more than incidental.

But looking back now over the past forty years, we can see trends and fashions, books that were not necessarily widely noticed when they were first published but which have achieved more lasting status, and, of course, we can find a few works which may yet come to be seen as representative of their age. We are not looking for what is 'the best' – that would be too subjective a judgement. But we will be looking at impact, influence and inspiration. These should be enough to give us an idea of what has been happening in writing in Britain and Ireland since the early 1960s.

SEX AND THE MARKET-PLACE

Of course in the sense of endings and beginnings that 'sexual inter-course began' line was just Larkin's little joke, in a poem called 'Annus Mirabilis', written in 1967 and published in the 1974 collection High Windows.

But what he was getting at is important – until the early 1960s Britain had been living in the shadow of the Second World War, and the subsequent period of recovery, rationing and regrouping. In the 1960s the country started to enjoy itself, and to look forward to the future. New voices had already begun to be heard in the novels and poems and plays of the 1950s: working-class 'kitchen-sink' drama, angry young men (yes, they were still usually men) in novels and plays, and poetry that celebrated motorbike gangs – the tastes of the 1960s had been emerging quite distinctively for a few years.

Sex became a subject that was talked about, rather than a taboo, when a novel by D.H. Lawrence, Lady Chatterley's Lover, first published in 1928, was taken through the courts in 1960 and cleared of all possible charges of obscenity. Sex, as Michel Foucault memorably put it, 'became discourse'. The taboos and restrictions faded gradually over the years – censorship of the theatre, which had dated back to 1737, ended finally in 1968; homosexual behaviour became legal between consenting adults in 1967. Lady Chatterley's Lover, when it was published in paperback, became one of the biggest selling books of all time, and certainly the biggest best-seller of the 1960s. It took some time for sex to become as all-pervasive a subject as it is nowadays and there was a lot of resistance, especially on television.

It is easy to see the 1960s as the decade when all the writing was therefore about young people, sex and music, and the breaking down of old ideas about class, taboos and society. That was what it may have felt like at the time, but of course the reality now seems rather different.

The move from taboo to explicit was seen as liberation and the new freedoms remain something of a keynote in folk memory of the time – hippies, the political upheavals in various countries in 1968, the boom in pop music and culture, fashion and media. Satire and new forms of comedy, new attitudes towards politics and institutions, sex and drugs and rock'n'roll – the writings of the 1960s reflect all that.

But despite all the knowingness, there is perhaps a note of innocence, ingenuousness, to be seen now in that age before the Internet, before mobile phones and digital television. The 'peace and love' generation was also the generation shaken by the assassinations of popular American heroes such as John F. Kennedy, Robert Kennedy and Martin Luther King. The first of these has been depicted as the end of Camelot, a golden age that lasted for only a couple of years. The 1960s was the beginning of a brave new world, but a reaction soon set in, a loss of innocence, and along came the 1970s and different priorities. Money became the new sex.

CHAPTER 1

Drama and the theatre

Old anger, new violence

'INCEST TO ADULTERY'

The biggest influences on modern British theatre have come from Europe. The influence of the Norwegian playwright Henrik Ibsen and the Russian Anton Chekhov lasted throughout the twentieth century. Later it was the political theatre and style of the German Bertholt Brecht, and the minimalist theatre of the Irishman Samuel Beckett whose influence was all-pervasive. Samuel Beckett, born in Ireland but based in France for most of his life, was the author of *Waiting for Godot*, staged in French in Paris in 1953 and in English in London in 1955, which remains one of the single most important, influential and performed plays of the twentieth century. *Rosencrantz and Guildenstern Are Dead*, by Tom Stoppard, first performed at the Edinburgh Festival in 1965, took off from Godot, returned to Hamlet, and changed the face of modern British theatre.

Stoppard's plays bring a new level of intellectual comic gymnastics to the theatre, and make new uses of old, familiar texts and forms – he brings intertextuality to theatrical life. *Rosencrantz and Guildenstern Are Dead* makes two minor characters in Shakespeare's *Hamlet* the leading players in a comedy of identity, and lack of it, with Hamlet as a very minor character. Like Beckett's characters, Vladimir and Estragon, who are waiting for the non-existent (or is he?) Godot to come or not to come, Rosencrantz and Guildenstern are waiting for something to happen, to give them a reason for existing. They exist, however, in a play where the main character is Hamlet, where 'an exit in one place is an entrance somewhere else', and they live in 'the irrational belief that somebody interesting will come on in a minute', finding their justification in what happens around them, over which they clearly have no control. Here they comment on what has happened to Hamlet:

ROS [*lugubriously*] His body was still warm.

GUIL So was hers.

ROS Extraordinary.

GUIL Indecent.

ROS Hasty.

GUIL Suspicious.

ROS It makes you think.

GUIL Don't think I haven't thought of it.

ROS And with her husband's brother.

GUIL They were close.

ROS She went to him –

GUIL – Too close –

ROS – for comfort.

GUIL It looks bad.

ROS It adds up.

GUIL Incest to adultery.

ROS Would you go so far?

GUIL Never.

ROS To sum up: your father, whom you love, dies, you are his heir, you come back to find that hardly was the corpse cold before his young brother popped onto his throne and into his sheets, thereby offending both legal and natural practice. Now why exactly are you behaving in this extra-ordinary manner?

GUIL I can't imagine!

[*Pause.*]

But all that is well known, common property. Yet he sent for us. And we did come.

Tom Stoppard, *Rosencrantz and Guildenstern Are Dead*

This kind of two-character banter, full of clever word-association, in-jokes and literary references, moves on from the kind of silent-movie clowning which Beckett's characters had perfected. It appealed to the young generation of playgoers, who were more likely to be university educated than their predecessors, and to be at least familiar with the intellectual terms of reference. This change of audience focus is significant: people who would have been cut off from *Lady*

Chatterley's Lover and even *Hamlet* were now theatre-goers who wanted their intellectual pretensions to be flattered, and their new attitudes and standards catered for.

A logical development of this kind of intelligent, indeed intellectual humour, combined with a context of what in the 1950s had been called absurdity, would be the epoch-making television comedy series *Monty Python's Flying Circus*. Where 'dumbing down' of culture has been an accusation in more recent times, the 1960s gave a boost to intelligence, commitment and a degree of cultural sophistication.

Stoppard's other plays also use tried and tested formulae, and then twist them in what comes to be seen as a postmodern way. *The Real Inspector Hound* (1968) is a one-act farce, parodying the genre of detective fiction. *Jumpers* (1972) moves into the world of philosophical speculation, with real gymnasts as a visual counterpoint to mental acrobatics. *Travesties* (1974) makes high comedy out of the simultaneous presence of Lenin, James Joyce and Tristan Tzara in Zurich during the First World War, and involves them all in rehearsals for a performance of Wilde's *The Importance of Being Earnest*.

Stoppard, like many writers of the period, is also a significant writer for radio and television. His more recent plays for the theatre have extended his idiom into the love comedy (*The Real Thing*, 1982), and spy intrigue (*Hapgood*, 1988). *Arcadia* (1993) moves back and forth between the Romantic era and the present day, bringing together a literary mystery story, reflections on landscape and the emotional involvements of the characters. *Indian Ink* (1995) examines conflicts of cultural identity in postcolonial India. Stoppard also co-wrote the successful film *Shakespeare in Love* (1998), which has strong resonances of *Rosencrantz and Guildenstern Are Dead*.

Stoppard's 2002 trilogy of plays under the general title *The Coast of Utopia* is an ambitious presentation of nineteenth-century European politics from the 1830s to 1870, looking at Russian radicalism and the forces of what might now be known as democracy: rebellion against authority is the keynote. The three self-standing plays, *Voyage*, *Shipwreck* and *Salvage*, show something of the difficult progress of political change, finding echoes in modern history, and indeed show the ambitious scope of the plays, which audiences have found both enthralling and ambiguous. Critics and audiences seem to be undecided whether they are magnificent or magnificent failures, but they demonstrate yet again Stoppard's intellectual inventiveness and theatrical power. The title echoes Oscar Wilde's line that a map of the world is worth nothing if it does not show Utopia on it – a line which David Hare also used for the title of his play A Map of the World.

ICONOCLASM AND CONTROVERSY

The other major dramatists who even now give us a taste of the theatrical excitement of the 1960s are Joe Orton and Edward Bond. They could hardly be more different: Orton was gay, sacrilegious and iconoclastic, and his plays were farcical sexual comedies. Bond was heavily political, and his plays were socially committed and deeply serious. Both caused controversy, and both remain significant and influential now. Indeed, many would argue that there has not been such an exciting and controversial outpouring of theatre since the 1960s, when the necessity to end censorship provoked some very deliberately controversial writing: after the Theatres Act of 1968 the ways in which censorship worked would become more commercially based.

The English tradition of social comedy exemplified over the centuries in writers such as Congreve, Sheridan, Oscar Wilde and Noel Coward reaches a high point in the subversive farces of Joe Orton. Often the writers of these comedies were outsiders: Irish in the case of Wilde, as well as gay. Orton allowed his sexual viewpoint to determine much of the satiric attack on society's hypocrisies and revelled in the scandal his 'outrageous' comedies caused. Satire was very much a vehicle of the 1960s, in cabaret, theatre, radio and television: targets were political and sexual, challenging the taboos of the time.

Loot (1966) is a black comedy, involving the taboo subject of death, hilariously mixed up with sex and money. Entertaining Mr Sloane (1964) is a comedy of forbidden sexual attraction, older man and younger boy, a theme expanded and developed in Orton's last play What the Butler Saw (1969), which takes sexual and psychological subversion to new heights of farcical exploration. The climax of this play takes comedy back to its original Greek roots, of the God Pan, and the panic which comic chaos can create, and many British taboos, from

Winston Churchill's cigar (and its possible phallic symbolism) to incest, adultery and nudity, are exploited to full comic effect.

In this scene from *Loot*, Truscott, the corrupt police authority figure, is trying to obtain information from one of the two young guys involved in a bank robbery and the concealment of a corpse (which gives rise to the line 'Whose mummy is this?' when the wrapped up body is found. Of course the answer Hal gives is 'Mine' – and it is). Here the traditional friendly image of the British bobby is totally overturned, and the hiding place of the stolen money in Hal's mother's coffin is about as sacrilegious as it can be:

TRUSCOTT Understand this, lad. You can't get away with cheek. Kids nowadays treat any kind of authority as a challenge. We'll challenge you. If you oppose me in my duty, I'll kick those teeth through the back of your head. Is that clear?

HAL Yes.

[*Door chimes.*]

FAY Would you excuse me, Inspector?

TRUSCOTT [*wiping his brow*] You're at liberty to answer your own doorbell, miss. That is how we tell whether or not we live in a free country.

[FAY *goes off left.*]

[*Standing over* HAL] Where's the money?

HAL In church.

TRUSCOTT Don't lie to me!

HAL I'm not lying! It's in church!

TRUSCOTT [*shouting, knocking* HAL *to the floor*] Under any other political system I'd have you on the floor in tears.

HAL You've got me on the floor in tears.

TRUSCOTT Where's the money?

Joe Orton, *Loot*

Orton's life and death became the subject of the successful movie *Prick Up Your Ears*, and he remains one of the icons of the 1960s lifestyle, as well as a playwright whose works, at first seen to be controversial and iconoclastic, have become a mainstay of English comedy.

Edward Bond's *Saved* (1965) caused considerable controversy when censorship was still in force, because of the staged stoning to death of a baby, but *Saved* emerges as a key play in the recent political development of the theatre. Its depiction of the casual cruelty of a gang of young men, and its final image of life continuing silently and uneventfully, are both shocking and disturbing, but clearly real, both in the social context of the 1960s and of more recent times. Although his plays are staged more in Europe than in Britain, where 'political' theatre has never been very popular, in the late 1990s Sarah Kane acknowledged Bond as one of the major influences on her plays.

When we move on to how Bond developed in the 1970s, after a play about Queen Victoria called *Early Morning* in 1968 (with the fashionable fantasy of a lesbian relationship with Florence Nightingale, which was worthy of Orton), we find his major play *Lear* (1971), which takes Shakespeare's tragedy as a starting point for an examination of human cruelty. Where Samuel Beckett had taken despair as his keynote of the human condition, Bond examines the geography of the human soul in a different way, concentrating on cruelty as the expression of frustration and despair – here with direct and indirect intertextual reference to the Shakespearean tragedy which critics have always seen as his most pessimistic. This is a reflection of the rediscovery of the power of the theatre as a vehicle for the deeper examination and discussion of issues. It is a different use of theatrical tradition and intertextual reference from Stoppard's, but very much part of a similar pattern of re-evaluation of traditional genres, forms and readings.

Bond's *Bingo* (1973) actually puts the character of Shakespeare on stage, in an examination of the clash between artistic and capitalist values. The play shows Shakespeare in his retirement in Stratford, as a property owner rather than the cultural colossus history has made him. Bond's Marxist viewpoint makes Shakespeare a class enemy, an enemy of the people, in his support for the enclosures of common land. On the cultural level, an encounter with Ben Jonson also undermines the traditional ideas of Shakespeare, the man and the playwright:

JONSON What are you writing?

SHAKESPEARE Nothing.

[*They drink.*]

JONSON Not writing?

SHAKESPEARE No.

JONSON Why not?

SHAKESPEARE Nothing to say.

JONSON Doesn't stop others. Written out?

SHAKESPEARE Yes.

[*They drink.*]

JONSON Now, what are you writing?

SHAKESPEARE Nothing.

JONSON Down here for the peace and quiet? Find inspiration – look for it, anyway. Work up something spiritual. Refined. Can't get by with scrabbling it off in noisy corners any more. New young men. Competition. Your recent stuff's been pretty peculiar. What was *The Winter's Tale* about? I ask to be polite.

Edward Bond, *Bingo*

Edward Bond was a questioner, politically outspoken, who cast his net wide for his range of theatrical subjects: from the Japanese poet Basho in *Narrow Road to the Deep North* (1967), the English poet John Clare in *The Fool* (1975), to country society in *The Sea* (1973). In the 1980s he expanded his range with *Restoration* (1981), a historical drama in the style of Brecht, with episodic scenes, and songs commenting on the action. *Summer* (1982) takes a post-war eastern European state as its setting to explore capitalism, injustice and social conflict. Bond has never been fashionable in Britain: political drama has never been attractive to London West End audiences, but his appeal in Europe is considerable, and he is regarded very highly as a voice of commitment and international perspectives.

'SUCH A SILENCE' – BECKETT AND PINTER

Samuel Beckett always worked towards minimalism: after full-length plays and the shorter monodrama *Krapp's Last Tape*, his work in the

1960s becomes shorter and shorter. In his later plays, Beckett reduces his theatre to its essentials: from two acts in *Waiting for Godot* and *Happy Days* (1961), to one, starting with *Endgame* (1957); from five characters to four, then three, then two, then one, and finally – in *Breath* (1970), which lasts only about thirty seconds – there are no characters at all.

Beckett's 1964 play, entitled *Play*, has three characters, out of a traditional love triangle, buried up to their heads in urns, condemned endlessly to repeat their torments, addressing an interrogating spotlight. The final stage direction, after the first time through, is 'REPEAT PLAY' – it comes to be an endless circle of memory and recrimination. *Not I* (1972) reaches a new limit of theatrical imagery and expression: on stage we see a Mouth, vivid, mobile, eloquent, and the voice speaks to an almost invisible listener, both affirming and denying her existence: the events narrated never happen to 'I', but to a third-person pronoun. The character almost elides herself, but exists in sight and sound through the rambling torrent of her memories.

Throughout the 1970s Beckett continued to produce thrilling short dramas: *Footfalls* has its character pace out her memories in a repeated pattern of sound trying to make sense; *Rockaby* sits an old woman in her rocking-chair as she repeats her memories; *Ohio Impromptu* presents reading, interruption and rereading in its characters' attempts to find a story; *Catastrophe* (1982) is a theatrical and meta-theatrical attempt to question the nature of staging and representation, trying to call a performance up out of nothing, to make something of nothing. Theatre and existence make the metaphor of all representation, the transitory yet endless 'lines to time' which Shakespeare spent his writing life exploring.

The move towards minimalism in Beckett's writing is a *reductio ad absurdum*, which can perhaps allow the term 'absurd' to be reclaimed in a theatrical context. The setting of *Breath* is reduced to a 'stage littered with miscellaneous rubbish', and only the sounds of birth, breath and death are heard. This is the ultimate image of the wastelands of twentieth-century literature, where 'we are born astride of a grave' and 'the light gleams an instant, then it's night once more', as Vladimir says in *Waiting for Godot*.

Beckett took drama to new extremes, and pushed his characters to the limits of solitude, non-communication and hopelessness. Yet they all survive, and any thoughts of suicide are always dispelled. Hamlet's age-old question, 'To be or not to be', is answered in the affirmative, even though Beckett takes his characters closer to the extremes of despair and hopelessness of *King Lear* than any other writer since Shakespeare. Critics have tended to see close parallels between *King Lear*, in particular, and the plays of Beckett – citing this as proof of Shakespeare's modernity. Equally, it might be evidence for Beckett's universality in the face of seemingly tragic situations. Yet in Beckett there is no resort to the melodrama of a tragic climax: continuing the struggle to remain alive is offered as the unavoidable and necessary conclusion. His novel *The Unnamable* (1958) had summed up the paradox of the 'absurd' life humankind leads in the words, 'Where I am, I don't know, I'll never know, in the silence you don't know, you must go on. I can't go on, I'll go on.' Beckett's novels and prose pieces in the 1960s continued the move towards reduction, as we will see (p. 187).

It is a characteristic of the language of postmodernity that it aspires towards silence. The critic who coined the term 'postmodern', Ihab Hassan, sees it in rather Nietzschean terms as 'a dual retreat from language . . . language aspires to Nothing' and, in a contrary excess, 'it aspires to All'. But it is always 'conceived in the interests of life'. 'Both are manners of silence, formal disruptions of the relations between language and reality. It is these two modes . . . that account for the development of antiform in modern literature from Kafka to Beckett.' This 'roar on the other side of silence' had been identified by George Eliot in *Middlemarch* in the late Victorian era. It becomes ever more noticeable in modern writing, as Hassan suggests. And no writers use it more effectively than Beckett and Harold Pinter. Language is both adequate and inadequate, life and art become expressible and inexpressible.

Harold Pinter's plays have many superficial resemblances to Beckett's, and critics, especially early on, tried to emphasise the similarities. As time has gone on, however, Pinter has emerged as a much more political writer than Beckett. The two men were friends, and Beckett is certainly a major influence on Pinter, as he is on many writers of the past fifty years. All the same, Pinter is more concerned with the dangers inherent in the silences between characters, the menace in the meaning of what is said and not said. His characters do not have the resources and capacity that Beckett's characters have, to fill their time with memories, wordplay, chat or tortured reflections. They are much less self-sufficient and more dependent on the unstable ties that bind them to each other.

The Caretaker (1960) and The Homecoming (1965) are full-length plays of menace, ambiguity and unfulfilled ambitions. Like Beckett, Pinter developed the one-act play into a major theatrical form. The year 1969 saw the first production of Silence, arguably his most fully realised and innovative work, in which three characters rehearse their interlinked memories without ever relating directly to each other. Their words resemble a kind of musical fugue, in which silence becomes – ever more clearly – the dominant presence.

> [ELLEN *moves to* RUMSEY.]
> ELLEN It's changed. You've painted it. You've made shelves. Everything. It's beautiful.
> RUMSEY Can you remember . . . when you were here last?
> ELLEN Oh yes.
> RUMSEY You were a little girl.
> ELLEN I was.
> [*Pause.*]
> RUMSEY Can you cook now?
> ELLEN Shall I cook for you?
> RUMSEY Yes.
> ELLEN Next time I come. I will.
> [*Pause.*]
> RUMSEY Do you like music?
> ELLEN Yes.
> RUMSEY I'll play you music.
> [*Pause.*]
> RUMSEY Look at your reflection.
> ELLEN Where?
> RUMSEY In the window.
> ELLEN It's very dark outside.
> RUMSEY It's high up.

ELLEN Does it get darker the higher you get?
RUMSEY No.
[*Silence.*]
ELLEN Around me sits the night. Such a silence.

Harold Pinter, *Silence*

In a speech in 1962, Pinter had underlined the importance of silence:

When true silence falls we are still left with echo but are nearer nakedness. One way of looking at speech is to say that it is a constant stratagem to cover nakedness.

Since *Old Times* (1971), *No Man's Land* (1975) and *Betrayal* (1978), Pinter has himself moved closer to silence. His more recent work, such as *Mountain Language* (1988), is a powerful examination of language, power and freedom, which brings a directly political dimension to his writing – introducing a new focus of concern, not obviously present in early Pinter. *Ashes to Ashes* (1996) explores similar territory to *Old Times*, but Pinter continues to write and explore new themes. In this play he uses images of Nazism and the Holocaust, bringing together the political and the personal: 'I'm not simply talking about the Nazis; I'm talking about us, and our conception of our past and our history, and what it does to us in the present.' *Celebration* (2000) is a social comedy about the new rich of the present day. It was first staged together with his very first play *The Room* (1957), showing the similarities and differences between his early and later works. He continues to use a small group of characters in an enclosed space and to explore the tensions and conflicts between them.

Pinter's political commitment has always been a major part of his life and work, but his reputation as a dramatist has centred on the plays of menace, silence and lack of communication. However, more recently, he has come to be recognised as a writer of very serious political views, which do not give rise to the kind of post-Brechtian political theatre of Edward Bond, or the more English-based concerns in the plays of Howard Brenton and David Hare. He is outspoken, and does not follow any kind of politically correct fashions. He uses language and silence in the context of the widest political themes. To quote him again, from 1989, at the end of the Cold War: 'For the last forty years, our thought has been trapped in hollow structures of language, a stale, dead but immensely successful rhetoric. This has represented, in my view, a defeat of the intelligence and of the will.'

Pinter's political views are worth quoting at length, especially since they reveal a deep personal concern with language and how it works, as he said above. In another, later context he said,

> We are in a terrible dip at the moment, a kind of abyss, because the assumption is that politics are all over. That's what the propaganda says. But I don't believe the propaganda. I believe that politics, our political consciousness and our political intelligence are not all over, because if they are, we are really doomed. . . . I'm going to retain my independence of mind and spirit, and I think that's what is obligatory upon all of us. Most political systems talk in such vague language, and it's our responsibility and our duty as citizens of our various countries to exercise acts of critical scrutiny upon that use of language. Of course, that means that one does tend to become rather unpopular. But to hell with that.
>
> **cited in John Pilger's essay in *Harold Pinter: A Celebration***

The National Theatre staged Pinter performing his own most recent work, *Press Conference*, in 2002, just after he had been diagnosed with throat cancer – critics remarked on his courage in the face of adversity, but, as always, did not respond too positively to the political content of the play, which, in its form, title and content, is just about as far from silence as he could go: it is speaking out. 'Our political consciousness' is at the heart of all of Pinter's work, and a critical re-evaluation of his place in theatre must now begin to take that into fuller account.

POLITICAL THEATRE: THE DISCONTENTS OF THE 1970s

A move away from politics and confrontation has meant that writing over the past forty years has tended to become more accommodating than challenging, often more concerned with being commercially viable rather than with taking risks. There are always exceptions to this, of course, but Alan Ayckbourn (see pp. 23–24) will always be more popular than Edward Bond. The politically charged and inventive early David Hare play *Fanshen* (1975) was described by the critic Kenneth Tynan as 'the first native offshoot of the Brechtian tradition that seems to me to stand comparison with the parent tree'. But a quarter of a century later Hare has toned down the political thrust of his drama and now enjoys much greater commercial and critical success with a star vehicle like *The Breath of Happiness* than with any of his earlier, more overtly political pieces.

However, it is the political drama rather than commercial British plays that has achieved success in Europe, where politically committed writers of old and younger generations such as Arnold Wesker, Edward Bond, Howard Brenton and Sarah Kane have achieved much more frequent success than they have in their own country.

Theatre in the late 1970s and 1980s moved away from the centre, which, as with publishing, was London and its theatrical West End, and several companies developed and toured their productions to parts of the nation which rarely if ever had been exposed to modern theatre. These plays often evolved through improvisation and company work, rather than always through the hand of one single author.

The Joint Stock Company had close links to the Royal Court in London, and John Godber's Hull Truck Company enjoyed wide success, but it was John McGrath's 7:84 Company which toured furthest. Its name derives from the fact that 7 per cent of the British population owns 84 per cent of the wealth, and this political tone resonates through all the company's works, which toured, especially in Scotland, to the furthest reaches of the country. *The Cheviot, the Stag, and the Black, Black Oil*, written by John McGrath and developed with the company of actors, was the company's most successful show, tackling the subject of Scottish oil revenues, land clearances, and the historical and cultural dimensions of Scottish identity in relation to English exploitation. More recently, playwrights such as Howard Barker and Mark Ravenhill have worked with small touring companies rather than concentrating on the London centre, and have taken their works around Britain and Europe, reaching a much wider range of audiences than London's West End would have given them.

Political clashes of values are the basis of several of the plays of David Hare, from *Knuckle* (1974) through *Plenty* (1975) to *Racing Demon* (1989), which is a satirical portrayal of the relationship between the church and the state, the second part of a trilogy of 'state of the nation' plays; the third – *Murmuring Judges* (1992) – examines the judicial system. The first play of the trilogy, *The Secret Rapture* (1988), is a family tragedy, where politics and pragmatic financial policies – echoing the concerns of the Thatcher years – are seen as no solution to the eternal human questions of emotional truth and lasting values. This is the type of conflict which David Hare dramatises best; where contemporary political ideas and ideals are set against more basic human characteristics.

Skylight (1995) has been Hare's most popular play to date. It brings together a successful businessman (a very 1990s figure), and a socially conscious schoolteacher who has rejected his lifestyle to live and work in an economically deprived area of London. *Skylight* is a social debate play, in the tradition of George Bernard Shaw, but with constant reversals of sympathy, shifting of standpoints and theatrical surprises. In the final scene, the younger generation (the businessman's rejected son) provides a Ritz-style breakfast in Kyra Hollis's cold flat: this is one of Hare's recurring scenes of celebration (a huge wedding scene in his earlier co-written play *Brassneck* is equally memorable). *Skylight* is very much a play of 1990s issues and is perhaps Hare's most direct reflection on the decade. As Kyra says, 'there is this whole world I'm now in. It's a world with quite different values. The people, the *thinking* is different . . . it's not at all like the world which you knew.' The characters reflect on 'what extraordinary courage, what perseverance most people need just to get on with their lives'.

Amy's View (1997) then became Hare's most successful play. Written as a star vehicle for Dame Judi Dench it is a play of an actress's memories and fantasies. *Via Dolorosa* (1998) was a one-man play which Hare performed himself in London and New York, recounting his experience of a visit to Israel retracing the steps of Christ through Jerusalem. *The Judas Kiss* (1998) was a different kind of play again, about Oscar Wilde's tragedy and reputation. Hare continues to explore the atmosphere of contemporary Britain in *My Zinc Bed* (2000) which brings together the contrasting world of an Internet entrepreneur and a poet he commissions to write about him.

Having written one very successful star vehicle, Hare went on to write *The Breath of Life* (2002), which brought Dame Judi Dench and Dame Maggie Smith together on stage. The lives of two ageing women intertwine in the course of a single night as they talk through their related pasts. Hare's familiar themes of past and present, together with the quality of the performances, assured the play considerable success, although it is somewhat leaden in structure and content.

Peter Shaffer's concern has been less with the political situation of the present than with universal mysteries. He wrote several epic dramas with a historical or psychological basis. *The Royal Hunt of the Sun* (1964) is set at the time of the Spanish conquest of the Inca Empire; *Equus* (1973) is a probing psychological drama of sexual deficiency; and *Amadeus* (1980) examines the life and the myth of Mozart. It and *Equus* were made into successful movies.

Shaffer's subject is the mystery, the magic, of motivation; and, in their spectacle and their humanity, his plays (as one critic put it) 'take us nearer to God'. Here the disturbed boy, Alan, is watched by his father and a psychoanalyst, Dysart, as he praises his own god-figure, Equus, the horse:

> FRANK As I came along the passage I saw the door of his bedroom was ajar. I'm sure he didn't know it was. From inside I heard the sound of this chanting. . . .
>
> ALAN And Legwus begat Neckwus. And Neckwus begat Fleckwus, the King of Spit. And Fleckwus spoke out of his chinkle-chankle!
>
> [*He bows himself to the ground.*]
>
> DYSART What?
>
> FRANK I'm sure that was the word. I've never forgotten it. Chinkle-chankle.
>
> [ALAN *raises his head and extends his hands up in glory.*]
>
> ALAN And he said, 'Behold – I give you Equus, my only begotten son!'
>
> DYSART Equus?
>
> FRANK Yes. No doubt of that. He repeated that word several times. 'Equus, my only begotten son.'

ALAN [*reverently*] Ek . . . wus!

DYSART [*suddenly understanding; almost 'aside'*] Ek . . . Ek . . .

FRANK [*embarrassed*] And then. . . .

DYSART Yes: what?

FRANK He took a piece of string out of his pocket. Made up into a noose. And put it in his mouth.

[ALAN *bridles himself with invisible string, and pulls it back.*]

And then with his other hand he picked up a coat hanger. A wooden coat hanger, and – and –

DYSART Began to beat himself?

[ALAN, *in mime, begins to thrash himself, increasing the strokes in speed and viciousness. Pause.*]

FRANK You see why I couldn't tell his mother. – Religion. Religion's at the bottom of this.

DYSART What did you do?

FRANK Nothing. I coughed – and went back downstairs.

Peter Shaffer, *Equus*

The 1980s opened with one of the most controversial plays for years, Howard Brenton's *The Romans in Britain* (1980), which, in a scene of homosexual rape, effectively paralleled the Roman occupation of Britain with the contemporary situation in Northern Ireland. Contrasting scenes of the two 'occupations', Brenton draws on epic theatre conventions: this is theatre of war, but with a deeply human concern for history's victims. At the end of the play, we return to the aftermath of the Romans' departure from Britain, as the native characters try to identify something, maybe mythical maybe real, that they can hold on to from the nightmare of their recent past. As so often in British history, the past they evoke reverberates with the name of King Arthur:

CORDA What poem you got then? In your new trade?

FIRST COOK 'Bout a King!

[*A silence*]

CORDA Yes?

FIRST COOK King. Not any King.

CORDA No?

FIRST COOK No.

CORDA Did he have a Queen, this King?

SECOND COOK Yes. [*He hesitates*] Yes, oh very sexy –

FIRST COOK Look let me do the meat, right?

SECOND COOK Oh yeah, I do the vegetables even when it comes to fucking poetry.

FIRST COOK Actually, he was a King who never was. His Government was the people of Britain. His peace was as common as rain or sun. His law was as natural as grass, growing in a meadow. And there never was a Government, or a peace, or a law like that. His sister murdered his father. His wife was unfaithful. He died by the treachery of his best friend. And when he was dead, the King who never was and the Government that never was – were mourned. And remembered. Bitterly. And thought of as a golden age, lost and yet to come.

CORDA Very pretty.

MORGANA What was his name?

FIRST COOK Any old name dear. [*To the* SECOND COOK] What was his name?

SECOND COOK Right. Er – any old name. Arthur? Arthur?

Howard Brenton, *The Romans in Britain*

Howard Brenton's plays have always tackled overtly political themes: from *Brassneck* (co-written with David Hare, 1973) – a panorama of industrial capitalism – and *The Churchill Play* (1974), a dystopian view of the future. Hare and Brenton also collaborated on *Pravda* (1985), one of the most significant plays of the 1980s; it is set in the context of the press, examining the roles of individuals and institutions in a way which anticipates Hare's later trilogy.

COMFORTABLE COMEDY?

Alan Ayckbourn has written more than fifty plays, all of them comedies, from *Relatively Speaking* (1967) to *Comic Potential* (1999). Most of his plays have been very successful in the theatre, both in the provinces (he has his own theatre in Scarborough, in the North of England) and in London's West End. Ayckbourn is an observer of family behaviour, and the conflicts of family life often provide the material for his plays. Over the years his plays have become darker and more serious, and he is now considered by many critics to be one of the most perceptive writers about middle-class Britain in the late twentieth century.

Viewed by some as 'traditional' boulevard comedies, Ayckbourn's plays are seen by others as deeply serious observations on certain social malaises in late twentieth-century Britain. *Season's Greetings*, *Absurd Person Singular* and *Henceforward*, along with the simultaneous-action comedies comprising *The Norman Conquests*, are among his major plays in a prolific output during the 1970s and 1980s. After the three interconnected plays of *The Norman Conquests* (1975), which were played on successive evenings in the theatre, Ayckbourn, with *House* and *Garden* (2000), wrote two plays with interlocking plots and the same characters, which are presented in synchrony, simultaneously in two theatres on the same evening.

Although his plays may be seen as very British middle-class 'boulevard comedy', he touches on serious and painful topics: suicide, mental breakdown, social inadequacy all recur in his plays. *Absent Friends*, for example, is about the discomfort and embarrassment of a group of friends in the company of a bereaved companion, and manages to make pungent comedy out of the characters' inability to face his, and their own, pain. Ayckbourn is probably the one dramatist who, like Graham Greene as a novelist, has enjoyed commercial success while retaining a following among more intellectual or academic communities. Although it is not overtly political, neither is it always 'comfortable' comedy – it can be perceptive and disturbing too, as a reflection of middle-class concerns and of the society it depicts.

CARYL CHURCHILL

Theatre had never been seen as a great vehicle for women's writing, but that began to change in the late 1970s with writers such as Pam Gems, whose play about the French singer *Piaf* (1978) and her play of four women without men, *Dusa, Fish, Stas and Vi* (1977) reached wide audiences and tapped into a new range of theatre-goers' interests. Gems paved the way for the major figure of Caryl Churchill. There have been some accusations that their plays 'only' revisit female historical figures in a contemporary feminist light: this is unjustly to belittle the writers' achievements.

Caryl Churchill's *Cloud Nine* (1979), *Top Girls* (1982) and *Serious Money* (1987) were seen as innovative and topical plays of the 1970s and 1980s. *Cloud Nine* shows up the sexual ambivalences behind the facade of the British Empire, with a fascinating time-shift when a century passes but the characters age only by twenty-five years. Churchill mixes her times again in *Top Girls*, with contrasting types of feminism from Chaucer to a female Pope. With many revivals worldwide this has consolidated its place as major drama of female experience, and has been very widely staged. In *Serious Money* she was among the first to use currency speculators as a paradigm for 1980s Thatcherism. More recently Churchill's *Far Away* (2000) looks through the eyes of a young girl and her aunt at the ongoing inhumanity in world conflicts and the individual's helplessness when confronted with everyday news stories.

In this extract from *Cloud Nine*, performed in 1979 and published in 1985, Churchill plays with stereotyped roles: Betty, the wife of the colonial administrator Clive, in Victorian Africa, is played by a man because she wants to be what men want her to be. Joshua, the black servant, is played by a white man because he wants to be what whites want him to be. Churchill is thus destabilising the dominant discourses of both gender and colonialism and using theatre to make the point (in ways which obviously work less successfully on the page):

> CLIVE I did some good today, I think. Kept up some alliances. There's a lot of affection there.
> HARRY (*an explorer*) They're affectionate people. They can be very cruel of course.
> CLIVE Well they are savages.
> HARRY Very beautiful people many of them.
> CLIVE Joshua! (*To* HARRY) I think we should sleep with guns.
> HARRY I haven't slept in a house for six months. It seems extremely safe.

[JOSHUA *comes.*]

CLIVE Joshua, you will have gathered there's a spot of bother. Rumours of this and that. You should be armed I think.

JOSHUA There are many bad men, sir. I pray about it. Jesus will protect us.

CLIVE He will indeed and I'll also get you a weapon. Betty, come and keep Harry company. Look in the barn, Joshua, every night.

[CLIVE *and* JOSHUA *go.* BETTY *comes.*]

HARRY I wondered where you were.

BETTY (*played by a man*) I was singing lullabies.

HARRY When I think of you I always think of you with Edward in your lap.

BETTY Do you think of me sometimes then?

HARRY You have been thought of where no white woman has ever been thought of before.

BETTY It's one way of having adventures. I suppose I will never go in person.

HARRY That's up to you.

BETTY Of course it's not. I have duties.

HARRY Are you happy, Betty?

BETTY Where have you been?

HARRY Built a raft and went up the river. Stayed with some people. The king is always very good to me. They have a lot of skulls around the place but not white men's I think. I made up a poem one night. If I should die in this forsaken spot. There is a loving heart without a blot, Where I will live – and so on.

BETTY When I'm near you it's like going out into the jungle. It's like going up the river on a raft. It's like going out in the dark.

HARRY And you are safety and light and peace and home.

BETTY But I want to be dangerous.

Caryl Churchill, *Cloud Nine*

A *Number* (2002) marks a departure and has been seen by some critics as Churchill's best play. It is a brief, powerful drama about a father and his son/sons, who are the result of cloning. Like all her work it presents serious and topical issues in very theatrical ways, full of tensions, twists and surprises, and it makes drama both politically engaged and highly entertaining. A *Number* bids fair to be as significant a play for the present decade as *Serious Money* and *Top Girls* were in their own time.

Thatcherism and Blairism

The period from 1979 to 1990, the years during which Margaret Thatcher was Prime Minister and leader of an ultra right-wing Conservative Party, mark a defining moment in British economic, social and cultural history. It was a time when questions of identity were brought clearly to the forefront of national debate, when serious efforts were made to put the 'great' back into Great Britain. These years saw attempts to recover past historical identities: for example, the identity of the still all-powerful, colonial force – momentarily enshrined in the Falklands war of 1982; the identity of the Victorian Age with its clear certainties about the role of *laissez-faire* capitalism and the place of organised labour – which was typified by the repressive stance of the government towards the Miners' Strike of 1984 to 1985; the identity of the independent island race of the 'English' encoded both in the complexities of managing immigration from former British colonies and elsewhere in continuing resistance and opposition to the imperatives of the European Economic Community; and the assertions of the rights of the individual to freedom to buy their own property, choose schools for their children and hospitals in which to be treated within a framework of an ideology of privatisation of public resources, of increased self-help and of independence from the Welfare State.

The power of these policies and their influence on British national life have continued to reverberate since 1990 in the 'Back-to-Basics' campaign of Mrs Thatcher's successor, John Major, and the more balanced but essentially more managerial approach to the same policies in the social democratic politics of the Labour Party leader and Prime Minister Tony Blair, who came to power in 1997 and was re-elected in 2001. Their efforts and differing definitions also have to be seen against an order of global capitalism within which questions of national identity are often compromised by multinational companies and organisations.

The Blair government has, however, espoused the importance of devolution for Scotland and Wales and Northern Ireland, and has taken the question of identity for Ireland seriously by working on a range of policies to establish greater Irish self-determination alongside a gradually increased independence from government in London. These moves have led to greater autonomy for the different parts of the United Kingdom at the same time as they have reinforced the disunited nature of a country which struggles to define exactly what it means to be English or British or European, or, in the continuing strength of the alliance with the United States, Anglo-Saxon. And the questions are being played out against a context of a Europe, especially eastern Europe, in which new nationalities and new nationalisms are established and are on the verge of becoming European.

At the same time the Blair government has worked to establish tests of citizenship for those wishing to make their home in Britain, and has, albeit within a more genial spirit than under recent Conservative governments, none the less refused positively to embrace the multi-cultural, multi-lingual character of modern Britain. Questions of race and nation still continue to haunt the policy makers; and in this regard, too, in the context of post-war literature the ground of questions about and explorations of national identity have been conceded largely to writers from former colonies who are black or brown rather than white British. These writers often raise questions of an ethical nature, in the process reflecting how questions of an ethical nature are only rarely to the fore in British society and are often sidelined by practical, logistical or political imperatives.

In general, most writers reacted to the Thatcher years in a measured, quietistic and – in some cases when looking back in time – in a somewhat nostalgic way. Some would even say that such a reaction was, in keeping with the present time, generally anodyne. British literature is not generally characterised by protest nor by political stridency; however, in the past fifteeen years there has gradually emerged a series of reflective considerations of the questions so forcefully thrust into the public consciousness by Thatcherism and its continuing aftermaths. One novelist, and one novel in particular, however, stands out in reaction to the Thatcher years. Jonathan Coe's *What a Carve Up!* (1994) is an explicit satire on the world of the 1980s, written in a predominant tone of black humour and farce as the only appropriate medium for social outrage and despair at what Coe felt to be the politics of social inequality and division. Other writers who specifically and directly addressed the social fragmentation of these years include Margaret Drabble's *The Radiant Way* (1987) and Martin Amis's *Money* (1984), the latter novel an overt satire on self-indulgence and acquisitive materialism with a central character called Self. In drama the most overt indictment came from Caryl Churchill in *Serious Money* (1987).

Timberlake Wertenbaker is an altogether different kind of playwright. She uses history and myth, art and intertextual references, in a range of plays which are lyrical and poetic while maintaining a strong level of social observation and comment. She uses Greek theatre and Greek myth in *The Love of the Nightingale* (1988), and, in *Our Country's Good* (1987), the eighteenth-century play *The Recruiting Officer* by George Farquhar is woven into the plot about the colonisation of Australia. This is one of the richest and most inventive of all modern plays, encompassing a wide range of themes from the national character to colonisation, from theatre to the nature of representation. *Three Birds Alighting on a Field* (1991) is a critical look at the Britain of the 1980s and 1990s, using the market for works of art as its basis. *Break of Day* (1995) looks at relationships in time, and contains echoes of the Russian dramatist Chekhov's *Three Sisters* in its rich tapestry of themes and allusions. Wertenbaker returns to classical Greek myths in a modern context in her radio play *Dianeira* (1999), using Sophocles's play *Women of Trachis* as her inspiration to look at the timeless but modern theme of women's anger and rebellion. *Credible Witness* (2001) is her latest play.

The Scottish playwright Liz Lochhead also makes use of distant historical reference in several of her works – *Mary Queen of Scots Got Her Head Chopped Off* (1987) uses the historical character to draw parallels with present-day Scotland. *Sweet Nothings* (1984) was written for television, and among the other forms Lochhead has used in her works are poetry, rap, performance pieces, radio plays and monologues. *Dreaming Frankenstein* (1984) was reissued with *Collected Poems* in 1994. Her 'reassembled' version of Euripides's *Medea* was published in 2000.

THE BEAUTY QUEENS OF IRELAND

For most of the twentieth century Irish drama was a rich expression of the land and its struggles, both social and political. The Abbey Theatre in Dublin has been at the heart of this expression, and continues to provide Irish dramatists with a stage for their ideas. In recent years, the works of Frank McGuinness – such as *Observe the Sons of Ulster Marching Towards the Somme* (1985) and *Someone Who'll Watch Over Me* (1992) – and particularly of the prolific Brian Friel, have shown that Irish drama continues to flourish.

Brian Friel has reached audiences worldwide with *Philadelphia! Here I Come!* (1968), *Translations* (1986) and *Dancing at Lughnasa* (1990) – plays which combine an Irish sense of dislocation and chaos with an evocation of the past in lyrical, yet realistic, terms. He is now recognised as one of the major playwrights in English, and *Dancing at Lughnasa* even became a Hollywood movie, without losing its Irish setting and voice. (The title refers to a country festival in August.) Friel writes of the pull of the provincial, and the push towards modern life, a contrast which some critics have seen as depicting Ireland's struggle to find its place as an independent nation in the modern world. Thus his very Irishness is both what attracts the audience's fondness for 'character' and locale, and what, for some Irish people, represents his limitations. But *Translations* shows that he is more than a clever painter of local colour – this is a play about occupation and communication, or the lack of it, between cultures and languages. It tackles what the British usually describe as 'the Irish problem' with power and sympathy – and it has shown British audiences that the problem is at least in part an 'English' problem and a 'British' problem, as well as a universal issue of identity and survival.

Like many modern dramatists, Friel reveres the Russian master Anton Chekhov, and has indeed translated some of his works. *Afterplay* (2002) goes further: it takes two characters from separate Chekhov plays, *Uncle Vanya* and *Three Sisters*, and has them meet many years after the end of their respective plays. It is a play about two losers revisiting their intertextual identities long after their roles are officially played out: a witty and exhilarating game of influences and nuances.

Two other Irish plays by younger writers achieved worldwide success in the 1990s: Martin McDonagh's *The Beauty Queen of Leenane* (1996) and *The Weir* (1997) by Conor McPherson. Both are gentle plays with a lot of talk, but reveal hidden depths in their examination of the tensions under the surface of relationships, and the influence of the past on the present day. McDonagh's first play is a domestic thriller, marvellous in its use of language and theatrical devices to explore the oppression and claustrophobia that are so much a feature of Irish fiction and drama. Two other plays made up a Leenane trilogy: *A Skull in Connemara* (1997) – the title echoes a line in Lucky's speech in Beckett's *Waiting for Godot* – is gruesomely comic in its handling of grave-diggers. And *The Lonesome West*, also staged in 1997, where the West is Ireland, of course, has echoes of the great American play by Sam Shepard, *True West*. McDonagh is an allusive and technically accomplished playwright and *The Beauty Queen of Leenane* seems set fair to be the most widely translated and staged Irish play of the 1990s. His next trilogy is set on the Aran Islands, where almost a century earlier J.M. Synge had set several of his plays and helped to establish the twentieth-century Irish dramatic tradition. McDonagh's black farce *The Lieutenant of Inishmore* (2002) was a considerable success in London.

THE LADS

The 1990s brought a number of strong masculine voices into the theatre. 'Laddish' behaviour and plays representing it suddenly became fashionable – and, at least in part, provoked the feminine response which was to be seen in fiction as 'chick lit' (see pp. 124–127). The television series (originally a novel) *Men Behaving Badly* epitomised this, and in fact television was the medium which most exploited the trend.

Patrick Marber is significant among these voices in theatre and television. His *Dealer's Choice* (1995) is set in the masculine world of card games, and *Closer* (1997) was the first play to bring Internet sexual relations to the stage. This scene shows two characters at their screens, and their online conversation appears on a big screen behind them as they set up a meeting, with Dan pretending to be Anna:

DAN Strangers.

LARRY details . . .

DAN They form a Q and I attend to them like a cum hungry bitch, 1 in each hole and both hands.

LARRY then?

DAN They cum in my mouth arse tits cunt hair.

LARRY [*speaking*] Jesus.

[LARRY's *phone rings. He picks up the receiver and replaces it without answering. Then he takes it off the hook.*]

LARRY [*typing*] then?

DAN I lik it off like the dirty slut I am. Wait,have to type with 1 hand . . . I'm cumming right now . . .

ohohohohohohohohohohohohohohohohohohohoh

ooooooooooooooooooooooooooooooooooooooooooooooooooo

+_)(*&^ %$£"!_*)&%^ &!"!"£$%%^ ^ %&&*&*((*(*)&^ %*((£££

[*Pause.* LARRY, *motionless, stares at his screen.*]

LARRY was it good?

DAN No.

[LARRY *shakes his head.*]

LARRY I'm shocked

DAN PARADISE SHOULD BE SHOCKING

LARRY RU4 real?

[*Beat.*]

DAN MEET ME

[*Pause.*]

LARRY serious?

DAN Y

LARRY when

DAN NOW

LARRY can't. I'm a Dr. Must do rounds.

[DAN *smiles.* LARRY *flicks through his desk diary.*]

DAN Dont b a pussy. Life without riskisdeath. Desire,like the world,is am accident. The bestsex is anon. We liv as we dream,ALONE. I'll make u cum like a train.

LARRY Tomorrow,1pm,where?

[DAN *thinks.*]

DAN The Aquarium, London Zoo & then HOTEL.

LARRY How will U know me?

DAN Bring white coat

LARRY ?

DAN Dr + Coat = Horn 4 me

LARRY !

DAN I send U a rose my love. . . .

LARRY ?

DAN&72;(@)

\ I

\ I

\ I /

\ I

\ I

LARRY Thanks. CU at Aquarium. Bye Anna.

DAN Bye Larry xxxxx

LARRY xxxxxx

[*They look at their screens.*]

Patrick Marber, *Closer*

If Marber's 1990s plays were considered 'laddish' and masculine in their portrayals of male roles and sexuality, *Howard Katz* (2001) takes the theme further, to a mid-life male crisis where the protagonist is near to suicide and is questioning all the values of his life, finally, perhaps weakly, rediscovering the value of his own family.

Mark Ravenhill achieved success and notoriety with *Shopping and Fucking* (1996) which controversially staged explicit sexual and drug activity. This echoed the impact of the political and social concerns of the novel, play and movie of *Trainspotting* (see pp. 140–142). This is a different kind of political theatre from David Hare's: it is direct, flamboyant, outrageous and comically charged, challenging the limits of what can be staged, as so many writers did throughout the twentieth century, from Shaw to Bond and beyond. Ravenhill's second play, *Some Explicit Polaroids* (1999), presents a clash of values between the early 1980s and the late 1990s. The pursuit of individual satisfaction in a society bankrupt of values is explored in terms of sexuality, violence and crime.

Mother Clap's Molly House, staged at the National Theatre and in London's West End in 2001, is a comedy with songs, moving between a gay brothel in the eighteenth century (the original and well-documented 'molly house' run by Mother Clap) and a gay party in the same building in the twenty-first century. Ravenhill explores his favourite themes of sex, commerce, identity and family, with surprisingly sentimental twists to the very politicised argument. Like Tom Stoppard's *Arcadia*, the historical counterpoint serves to underscore unexpected similarities between two societies which may seem distant: the emotional concerns are, of course, paramount, but Ravenhill seems to assert that in terms of the social judgement of sexual diversity the earlier period is less hypocritical, more tolerant even. Coincidentally, the play was first performed the day before gay partnerships were first able to be officially registered in London.

East is East (1996) by Ayub Khan Din was a major achievement – it was the first widely successful play to portray the problems of a Pakistani family who had settled in the North of England. It became a success all over the world, and then an award-winning film, the first popular comedy to handle such delicate subjects as marriage between the races, arranged marriage and homosexuality. Its impact both as a play and a movie was close to the impact of Hanif Kureishi's work in fiction and television with *The Buddha of Suburbia*.

Gregory Burke achieved the same kind of success at the 2001 Edinburgh Festival with his first play, *Gagarin Way*, that Stoppard had achieved more than thirty-five years earlier. Again the play was taken up by the National Theatre and achieved a surprising success in London. The play could not, however, be more different from *Rosencrantz and Guildenstern Are Dead*. *Gagarin Way* is a satire about a factory manager who is taken hostage by three of his own workers after a failed robbery. It is set in Fife, Burke's home county, and the graphic language is post-*Trainspotting* (see pp. 133–134) in its passion and humour. It is an intelligent and hilarious exploration of power, philosophy and locality, bringing serious political subjects back into theatrical entertainment.

Sexuality in 1990s theatre goes beyond sexual roles: after Jonathan Harvey's 'feelgood' gay play *Beautiful Thing* (1993) was unusual in giving a 'feelgood' happy ending to a love story between two teenage boys in a deprived working-class setting. It also became a successful film. The positive vision of gay experience is becoming accepted as a simple fact of life, but the subject holds an eternal fascination for readers and writers. Sexual roles and stereotypes were broken, and sexual violence began to be portrayed as going well beyond questions of sexuality and gender. Harvey later wrote for television, and *Gimme Gimme Gimme* takes sexual openness into the realm of popular sitcom. Kevin Elyot's *My Night with Reg* (1996) was a well-made play about the interlocking lives and loves of a group of gay men, which reached a wide audience. *Mouth to Mouth* (2001), again in the tradition of the well-made play, with clever time-slips, as in the earlier play, examines a disintegrating marriage and the contrasts between youth and middle age.

Theatre has expanded enormously since the 1960s. There are 'alternative' theatres and groups of every kind; and the monolithic presence of the major dramatist has given way to creative enterprise on many levels. Local theatre, community theatre, children's theatre all flourish with little regard for the more traditional West End London theatre scene.

TELEVISION

A great deal of drama is produced on television and radio, and most dramatists have at some time worked in these media, and in the cinema. For example, David Hare has written and directed several films; Harold Pinter has written many screenplays; and Samuel Beckett wrote several of his one-act dramas for radio, as well as the unique *Film* for (and with) Buster Keaton.

In the 1960s the BBC *Wednesday Play* and *Play for Today* brought modern social drama to very wide audiences, often very controversially as in the case of the socially realistic *Cathy Come Home*. There has been constant talk of dumbing down and loss of quality ever since the 1960s, but television continues to provide a range of opportunities for writers, from serious plays to situation comedy.

Alan Bennett, whose successful stage plays include *Forty Years On* (1968) and *The Madness of George III* (1991), has written some of his best work for television, including two series of six monodramas *Talking Heads* (1987 and 1998).

[*Come up on* GRAHAM *sitting on an upright chair. Evening.*]

GRAHAM This morning I went to Community Caring down at the Health Centre. It caters for all sorts. Steve, who runs it, is dead against what he calls 'the ghetto approach'. What he's after is a nice mix of personality difficulties as being the most fruitful exercise in problem-solving and a more realistic model of society generally. There's a constant flow of coffee, 'oiling the wheels' Steve calls it, and we're all encouraged to ventilate our problems and generally let our hair down. I sometimes feel a bit out of it as I've never had any particular problems, so this time when Steve says 'Now chaps and chappesses who's going to set the ball rolling?' I get in quick and tell them about Mother and Mr Turnbull. When I'd finished Steve said, 'Thank you, Graham, for sharing your problem with us. Does anybody want to kick it around?'

First off the mark is Leonard, who wonders whether Graham has sufficiently appreciated that old people can fall in love and have meaningful relationships generally, the same as young people. I suppose this is understandable coming from Leonard because he's sixty-five, only he doesn't have meaningful relationships. He's been had up for exposing himself in Sainsbury's doorway. As Mother said, 'Tesco, you could understand it.'

Alan Bennett, *A Chip in the Sugar* from *Talking Heads*

The Lady in the Van (1999) shows Bennett's relationship with his dying mother and with another old lady who lives in an old van in his garden. The writer appears as two separate but identical characters in this play, discussing the nature of his writing and how he makes creative use of real-life events in his works.

Alan Bleasdale and Dennis Potter wrote more for television than the stage. Potter is widely regarded as the first major television dramatist, such series as *The Singing Detective* (1986) and *Pennies from Heaven* (1978) reaching very much larger audiences than most stage plays. Although Potter achieved fame for his television plays including the series *Karaoke* and *Cold Lazarus*, broadcast in 1996 after his death, a stage revival of *Blue Remembered Hills* (1979, staged in 1996) proved that his work could be very powerful in the traditional medium. In this play adults take the roles of children growing up in the West

Country during the Second World War. Time and memory, adult and child, become telescoped in a daring exploration of the theme of 'the child is father of the man', with the present healing the past and the man forgiving the child who was his father.

Bleasdale is a political dramatist: *Boys from the Blackstuff* (1982) focused on unemployment and social deprivation; *GBH* (1991) on political and social violence; *The Monocled Mutineer* (1986) on class division and hypocrisy, in a First World War setting.

FULL CIRCLE – FROM *SAVED* TO *BLASTED*

If an answer was needed to the masculine voices in theatre in the 1990s, it could not have come more strongly than from Sarah Kane. The physical and verbal violence which would emerge in the mid-1990s finds its most vivid, controversial and powerful expression in her plays. She it was who set the tone for much of what was to become significant in theatre in the decade.

Blasted, first performed early in 1995, starts off in a luxury hotel room in Leeds in the north of England which could easily be a revisiting of the setting for the final scene of David Hare's *Skylight* from the same year. But after a highly charged sexual encounter, possibly involving rape, between the middle-aged protagonist, Ian, a tabloid journalist, and a much younger woman, Cate, there is a stunning image as an armed soldier arrives at the door. The action then moves, almost imperceptibly, into a nameless war-torn city and then fragments into further sexual activity, eye-gouging and the eating of a dead baby, and a coming back to life after death, as the seasons progress. Kane suggests that a domestic assault is never far away from the murder of morality in war.

This graphic scene from *Blasted* recalls the violence of the baby-stoning in Edward Bond's *Saved* and the homosexual rape in *The Romans in Britain* by Howard Brenton, which caused similar shocked reactions when they were staged in the 1960s and 1980s respectively. As an image of man's inhumanity to man, the casual nature of ordinary day-to-day violence, it is no more or less valid than any news item in the daily papers – but somehow, when staged, it brings the subject matter home to an audience with quite a different power and impact.

Ian, a journalist, is about to experience something very similar to what he has written about in the paper:

IAN I write . . . stories. That's all. Stories. This isn't a story anyone wants to hear.
SOLDIER Why not?
IAN (*Takes one of the newspapers from the bed and reads.*)

> 'Kinky car dealer Richard Morris drove two teenage prostitutes into the country, tied them naked to fences and whipped them with a belt before having sex. Morris, from Sheffield, was jailed for three years for unlawful sexual intercourse with one of the girls, aged thirteen.'

(*He tosses the paper away.*)
Stories.
SOLDIER Doing to them what they done to us, what good is that? At home I'm clean. Like it never happened. Tell them you saw me. Tell them . . . you saw me.
IAN It's not my job.
SOLDIER Whose is it?
IAN I'm a home journalist, for Yorkshire. I don't cover foreign affairs.
SOLDIER Foreign affairs, what you doing here?
IAN I do other stuff. Shooting and rapes and kids getting fiddled by queer priests and schoolteachers. Not soldiers screwing each other for patch of land. It has to be . . . personal. Your girlfriend, she's a story. Soft and clean. Not you. Filthy, like the wogs. No joy in a story about blacks who gives a shit? Why bring you to light?
SOLDIER You don't know fuck all about me. I went to school. I made love with Col. Bastards killed her, now I'm here. Now I'm here.
(*He pushes the rifle in Ian's face.*)
Turn over, Ian.
IAN Why?
SOLDIER Going to fuck you.
IAN No.
SOLDIER Kill you then.
IAN Fine.
SOLDIER See. Rather be shot than fucked and shot.

IAN Yes.

SOLDIER And now you agree with anything I say.

(*He kisses Ian very tenderly on the lips.*

They stare at each other.)

SOLDIER You smell like her. Same cigarettes.

(*The Soldier turns Ian over with one hand.*

He holds the revolver to Ian's head with the other. He pulls down Ian's trousers,
undoes his own and rapes him – eyes closed and smelling Ian's hair.

The Soldier is crying his heart out. Ian's face registers pain but he is silent.

When the Soldier has finished he pulls up his trousers and pushes the revolver
up Ian's anus.)

SOLDIER Bastard pulled the trigger on Col. What's it like?

IAN (*Tries to answer. He can't.*)

SOLDIER (*Withdraws his gun and sits next to Ian.*)

You never been fucked by a man before?

Sarah Kane, *Blasted*

The scene continues with the Soldier's description of war, and he then
sucks out one of Ian's eyes and bites it off. In the next scene he blows
his own brain out. Ian survives.

Strange to say, the play is savagely optimistic, like Edward Bond's
Saved or Howard Brenton's *The Romans in Britain*, which were the only
plays similarly to have caused so much controversy in the previous
thirty years. Kane indeed claimed to have used *Saved* as a model and
inspiration for her work. As with so many recent dramatists she also
acknowledged the strong influence of Caryl Churchill, especially of
Top Girls, on her work. The title *Blasted* indicates a society shattered,
violence in the streets, the safe assumptions totally undermined. It is
as harrowing as the worst scenes of *Titus Andronicus*, *King Lear* or the
end of *Timon of Athens*. Comparisons with Shakespeare are not out of
place – Kane's next play, *Phaedra's Love* (1996), was directly based on
the classical tragedy by Seneca, later treated by Jean Racine, and
examines the emotional, personal and political consequences of such
a mythical tragic love between stepmother and stepson. Again there
is vivid stage imagery, both sexually and physically striking, and again
Kane's linguistic acuity and invention are exciting. Where Racine

leaves most of the action and its consequences off-stage, Kane brings them right 'in your face' into the theatre.

Her later plays go deeper into imagery of depression and sexual anxiety. Like Harold Pinter in his later plays, Sarah Kane is overtly political in her examination of the immanent violence just between the surface veneer of society and behaviour. She uses television images of savagery to underscore the on-stage action, with the underlying belief that 'it couldn't happen here' seriously put into doubt. Language itself is questioned, feelings and expression being taken to extremes. Kane said, 'sometimes we have to descend into hell imaginatively in order to avoid going there in reality'.

Skin (1997) is a brief television drama of sex and racial violence, where compassion and hate are inextricably mixed. *Cleansed* (1998) is about love and faith in a time of madness, set in 'a university' or perhaps a madhouse, and it involves all the violence and sexuality of her earlier plays with deliberately non-naturalistic touches, such as a giant sunflower blooming as two of the characters have made love, rats carrying away the amputated feet of one of the male couple of lovers, and the stage filling with daffodils as two of the sibling characters change/exchange genders and identities. There are more Shakespearean echoes, from *Titus Andronicus* again and also from that most gender-bending of the comedies, *Twelfth Night*.

With hindsight Kane's last two plays *Crave* (1998) and the posthumously staged *4.48 Psychosis* (2000) may be read as long theatrical suicide notes. Characters are not named, or, in the latter play, even assigned. There are simply voices, without stage imagery, reminiscent of Beckett's plays but with longer expressions of their psychological anguish, frustration and longings. Without the violence and explicit sexuality of the earlier plays, these are, in fact, much more problematic, challenging and inventive than Kane's earlier work. They recall the novels of Franz Kafka in their bleakness, but are stunningly effective dramatic poems for voices, which have to be choreographed, given a visual context (do they take place in the character's or characters' minds/memories or in a kind of reality?).

After her suicide in 2000 there was a revival of all her works and a re-evaluation of Kane's place in modern drama. She is accomplished in her theatrical craftsmanship, original in her imagery and technical daring, and wonderfully sharp in her use of language. Her plays brought a driving intensity of performance and imagery back to the theatre. She is a very significant figure in late twentieth-century British theatre, and continues to be controversial. Her works enjoy considerable success in Europe. She lacks humour and the traditional finesse that gives plays theatrical longevity, but her imagery and characterisation take theatre in a spectacular and powerful way, which will doubtless have a strong influence. The pain of Sylvia Plath lives on in the drama and the suicide of Sarah Kane.

The plays of Kane and the violent, one might say literally bruising plays of domestic violence by Judy Upton, *Ashes and Sand* (1994) and *Bruises* (1995), gave rise to talk of the angry young men of the 1950s now being challenged by the angry young women of the 1990s. This was a spurious and flashy claim – the political challenges, the domestic roles and the theatrical conventions of the two decades are poles apart. But the theatre as a forum for self-expression, especially the theatre outside London's West End, and in untraditional settings such as prisons and schools, remains vibrant: it only needs courageous writers and directors to keep the flame alive.

Taboos and taboo words

'They fuck you up, your mum and Dad.'
Philip Larkin, 'This Be the Verse' (1971)

The semantic history of taboo words in language and literature serves as an index of the changing social and cultural history of Britain in the post Second World War period. For example, publicly, the word *fuck* has always been a taboo word but it was first – notoriously – uttered in public by the theatre critic Kenneth Tynan on BBC television in 1964. The word still has the same power to shock in public contexts and is often written with missing letters (e.g. f***) but as a taboo word it is now, forty years on, markedly less offensive. In many contexts, especially in informal exchanges, the word has become desemanticised; that is, it is used as a simple intensifier, signalling attitudes expressively and being used, especially in adjectival form, as a kind of hold-all marker of strong feeling about things.

In the writing of James Kelman, for example, the word is never far from the lips of his main protagonists, and the use of the word conveys a sense both of authentic speech and authentic feeling. Here is Sammy, the central character in *How Late It Was, How Late*:

> Now he was chuckling away to himself. How the hell was it happening to him! It's no as if he was earmarked for glory! Even in practical terms, once the nonsense passed, he started thinking about it; this was a new stage in life, a development. A new epoch! He needed to see Helen. He really needed to see her man if he could just see her, talk to her; just tell her the score.
>
> A fucking new beginning, that was what it was! He got out of bed and onto his feet and there was hardly a stumble. The auld life was definitely ower now man it was finished, fucking finished.

James Kelman, *How Late It Was, How Late* (1994)

In a recent study entitled *In-Yer-Face Theatre* Aleks Sierz discusses how in the 1990s the lines between offensive and acceptable words have shifted over the past two decades or so. He says a survey by the Broadcasting Standards Commission found that words such as 'cunt', 'motherfucker' and 'fuck' have remained strongly offensive, but religious words such as 'Christ', 'God', 'bloody' and 'damn' have become weaker. And just as religious insults have generally become less offensive than sexual and Oedipal ones, so now racial slurs have taken the place of both the bawdy and the religious. 'Nigger', 'Paki' and even 'Jew' are now judged to be much stronger insults than 'tart' or 'slut'. Taboos have thus shifted more markedly from the sexual to race so that racist terms are now far more overt and offensive terms than terms describing sexual behaviour, actions or parts of the body. It may also be the case that it is now much more acceptable openly to discuss one's sexuality than it is one's ethnicity. Paradoxically, there is limited scope for discussing religious feelings, though that may have less to do with taboos than with the character of a largely aspiritual age.

CHAPTER 2

The novel – the 1960s and beyond

Old guardians and new guards

The novel has been seen as a major form for over three hundred years since Aphra Behn, Daniel Defoe, Henry Fielding and others began to make it the most widely read literary genre. In the 1960s it was a novel from over thirty years earlier, the late 1920s, which set the tone of the new, more liberated times, D. H. Lawrence's *Lady Chatterley's Lover*: when it was cleared of obscenity after the trial in 1960, the world of things that could be talked about in novels opened up enormously. New voices, new openness about sexual themes, and even new ranges of language, including Englishes, came into the novel and carried it in many exciting new directions over the next four decades.

The novel has moved on from the avant-garde of the 1960s, which reached its peak with B. S. Johnson's 1969 novel in a box, *The Unfortunates*, twenty-seven sections which can be read in any order, narrated by one B. S. Johnson, to the similarly democratic E-novel where the reader clicks on a mouse to follow the text in any direction. Johnson's work made little impact in its own time, and may be seen to be influenced by *Hopscotch* (*Rayuela*) (1966), by the Argentinian writer Julio Cortazar. Such Latin American influences continued with the work of the Colombian novelist Gabriel Garcia Marquez which brought magic realism to fiction – it was Angela Carter, with *The Magic Toyshop* – into British writing in 1967. The avant-garde in modern writing has tended to manifest itself outside Britain: Christine Brooke-Rose, for example, wrote most of her self-consciously 'experimental' novels, such as *Out, Such, Between* and *Thru* in France in the 1960s and 1970s. British fiction has frequently been accused of being parochial and self-referential: as we shall see, influences from far beyond Britain will come to influence all of modern writing.

Among the voices which can be heard more clearly in the novel in recent years are those of the young and the 'lower' classes, the voice of the new educated middle classes, the voices of women, racial minorities, gays, and outsiders of many other types. Traditional romantic novels, by such writers as Barbara Cartland, and the historical novel with a social heart, such as the numerous Tyneside 'clogs and shawls' novels of Catherine Cookson, were a mainstay of every decade. And thrillers of varying quality always make their mark on the best-seller lists. Various sub-genres of novel became popular best-sellers while retaining intellectual acceptability – for example, the working-class novel (it used the be called 'kitchen-sink', but since kitchens have become a status item the term has disappeared), the Hampstead novel, the academic novel, the Scottish novel, and the magic realist novel.

SEX AND VIOLENCE

In the mid-1950s Anthony Burgess had been given only a few months to live; but he survived and went on to produce an enormous range of novels, textbooks, musical works and journalism. The one that will always be remembered is *A Clockwork Orange* (1962), in which he invented a new language, and imagined a whole new society, a violent dystopia, with its own slang and high-tech authoritarianism and making its own rules. It became one of the most talked-about novels and movies of its time, and still causes controversy even today. The movie, made by Stanley Kubrick in 1971, was one of the key image-creators of its decade and caused accusations that it encouraged the violence and amorality depicted on screen. Kubrick eventually withdrew the movie for several years, and its re-release in the late 1990s showed that both the movie and the novel had lost none of their power.

The rest of Burgess's work covers a great range: his Enderby trilogy (1963 to 1974) follows its hero around the world in search of success in literature and love. *The Clockwork Testament*, the last of the series, deliberately reused the adjective in a kind of revisiting of the text of twelve years earlier. *Earthly Powers* (1980) combines real characters and history with the fictional memoirs of a first-person narrator with a massive ego, and rewrites the twentieth century in his image. This kind of biography of the century through a novel's leading character became a popular end-of-the-century mode in the hands of writers from Burgess to William Boyd and Antonia Byatt. *The End of the World News* (1981) was similarly epic in scale.

Something of Burgess's great versatility and range of reference may be seen in *A Dead Man in Deptford* (1993), a historical re-creation of the life and death of Christopher Marlowe. Burgess's final novel, *Byrne* (1995), is a comic epic written in verse, exploring the nature of creativity through the frustrations and successes of a first-person narrator who is not too far removed from Burgess himself.

OUT OF THE BELL JAR

It has been common to talk of 'women writers' as if they were a breed apart. There are still vestiges of an older attitude around: Joanne Rowling was advised to use the name J.K. Rowling in case of some such prejudice in readers. But we are now past the stage of having to discuss a writer by emphasising her or his gender, and soon sexuality or ethnicity will come to be seen as distinctive but not remarkable, as authorship accommodates an ever wider rainbow of voices.

The year 1963 saw a woman called Victoria Lucas's first (and only) appearance in publishers' catalogues. Her first and only novel has become one of the most studied and influential of the 1960s, but her name has been almost totally forgotten. For Victoria Lucas was the pseudonym of Sylvia Plath, and the novel was *The Bell Jar*. Sylvia Plath put her head in a gas oven and committed suicide one month after the novel was published.

Plath's suicide has conditioned her reputation as the epitome of anguish and female suffering, largely because of the reputation and subject matter of her poetry, but *The Bell Jar* is actually very funny in its depiction of the social and sexual environment she grew up in especially in the America of the 1950s. The gases contained in that symbolic bell jar had to be let out: for some liberation was the escape, for the author herself it was suicide. The female narrator's reaction to her first sight of an erect penis is justly famous: 'The only thing I could think of was turkey neck and turkey gizzard and I felt very depressed.' Others may have laughed, and over the next forty years many writers of both genders would indeed laugh at the penis in many of its manifestations.

Plath's husband, the poet Ted Hughes, came in for huge criticism after her death, but can now be seen to have worked tirelessly to secure her reputation as a writer, especially for her poetry. She had published *Ariel* in 1960 (under her own name), and Hughes oversaw the publication of *The Colossus* in 1965, with which her fame was secured. *The Bell Jar* is more than just an adjunct to her poetry, however. It is one of the key texts of the 1960s, in its balance between humour and horror, between the past and the future, between life and death. Nobody else at that time could have written the last line of that much-quoted opening paragraph: 'I couldn't help wondering what it would be like, being burned alive all along your nerves.' That first-person female narrative voice was to be the first of many, and one of the most lastingly vivid, over the next forty years.

MAGIC AND MYSTERY

Lawrence Durrell's quartet of novels set in Alexandria had been precursors of the 1960s relish for all things sexual: published between 1957 and 1960, its lush ornate style and exoticism was out of sympathy with the dashing and very British realism of many novels by younger writers, but with *Tunc* (1968) and *Nunquam* (1970) Durrell consolidated his success, and his fairly pornographic novel *The Black Book*, dating originally from 1938, achieved notoriety when it was first published in Britain in 1973. Durrell was perceived as the master of a kind of risqué exotic with which an older generation could still titillate the young.

Part of the nostalgic recall of 'golden' or mythical days of some decades earlier had led to the success of Laurie Lee's autobiographical account of his country childhood in *Cider With Rosie* (1959). This was one of the consistently biggest-selling books of the last decades of the century, largely because of its Arcadian ideal of golden summers and happy innocence, long since lost. A further volume of memories – *As I Walked Out One Midsummer Morning* (1969) – takes the author off to the Spanish Civil War of the late 1930s; and the golden days are gone for ever, except in written memoirs.

The 1960s also saw the flourishing of the reputation of Flann O'Brien (Brian O'Nolan), whose first major novel *At Swim-Two-Birds* had been published as far back as 1939. *The Third Policeman*, written in 1940, but published posthumously only in 1967, has become one of the most widely read and influential texts of postmodernism.

The impact of the novels of John Fowles when they were first published in the 1960s was enormous: they use magic, artifice, and the very self-conscious fictionality of writing to carry fiction forward. His first was a psychological thriller of imprisonment and obsession, *The Collector* (1963), which established a paradigm for such thrillers for the next twenty years: the male who imprisons the captured female like a butterfly collector, contrasting with her own diary of imprisonment. It was successfully filmed, as many of Fowles's novels were. *The Magus* (1966, revised 1977) plays with reality and myth on a Greek island, and is one of the most evocative novels of its kind, developing the lush style associated with Lawrence Durrell, but making the first inroads in the English novel into what would become known as 'magic realism'. Fowles is not associated with any one trend in the novel, moving with ease from the psychological thriller, through short stories, to the Arcadian Laurie Lee-like evocation of growing up in *Daniel Martin* (1977). As with the plays of Tom Stoppard there is an enjoyment of intelligence, imagination and creativity, a sense of the unexpected in the novels of John Fowles.

They had great academic and commercial success in Europe and the USA: they are intellectual, self-conscious experiments with theme and form, and carry warnings for the reader about the nature of the reading experience. In the most widely known and studied of his works, *The French Lieutenant's Woman* (1969), for example, the Victorian novel form is used and then questioned while the reader is left with a choice between two possible endings. For many readers and critics this is the postmodern novel *par excellence*; innovative while using the traditional form, subversive while telling a good tale, authoritative but questioning. It was also a very successful movie, with a screenplay by Harold Pinter. It remains a major achievement in fiction, although its playing with time is not wholly original, as some critics claimed: the 'alternative ending' idea had been tried out as early as Thackeray's *The Newcomes* in the 1850s.

Always a writer to keep the reader from falling into preconceptions, Fowles has his narrator in *A Maggot* (1985) assert this, on the nature of history and what is called 'genius':

> the retrospective we have of remembering and asserting a past age by its Popes, its Addisons and Steeles, its Johnsons, conveniently forgets how completely untypical artistic genius is of most human beings in any age, however much we force it to be the reverse.

In keeping with many major writers of the century, Fowles uses time to great effect, clashing past with present across centuries or across a character's memories. His novels play with the imagination of the *reader*, just as much as they revel in the creative imagination of the writer. *The Magus* is an exercise in the multiple uses and meanings of imagination and creativity, where the reader can never be sure who is in charge, and indeed, it may be the reader's imagination that, by the end, has to take charge of both the reading and the interpretation. What remains, therefore, can divide critical opinion more than almost any other writer. Fowles can be fascinating and irritating at the same time – a treasure trove for academics, an enjoyable story-teller for those who simply want to read for pleasure.

WILLIAM GOLDING

In some ways William Golding had been the Fowles of the 1950s: *Lord of the Flies* (1954) was a popular yet intellectual novel, and his subsequent novels continued to explore unusual areas of experience, from Neanderthal to modern times. Golding explores related themes of 'decline and fall' and human capacity for choice in several later novels including *The Spire* (1964), and *Rites of Passage* (1980), the first of a trilogy which takes the narrative of an early sea journey to the Antipodes as a metaphor for the progress of the soul. The trilogy was completed with *Close Quarters* (1987) and *Fire Down Below* (1989).

In 1983 William Golding was awarded the Nobel Prize for Literature. He is in the great tradition of the story-teller, and is not afraid to point up a moral truth while keeping the reader entertained.

His final work, the posthumously published, nearly complete *The Double Tongue* (1995), opens up new territory (a female narrator as central character, an ancient Greek setting) and confirms Golding as one of the great explorers of myth, and of how truth and myth interrelate. All his works contrast human potential and the reality of human achievement. As the 'goddess' of his final novel wonders, watching herself being presented to the world *as* a goddess, by Ionides, a cynic and atheist:

> I suppose we all change. I had believed in the Olympians, all twelve of them. How much did I believe now, after years of hearing Ionides inventing speeches for me? How much after years of inventing them myself? How much after years of remembering that the god had raped me, years of part-belief, of searching for a proof that all I had believed in was a living fact and if twelve gods did not live on that mountain, they did in fact, in real fact, live somewhere, in some other mode, on a far greater mountain? It was too much for me. I did not speak out but kept silent, veiling my head completely.
>
> **William Golding, *The Double Tongue***

Golding's fictional search for a truth of humanity ties in with many writers' post-Darwinian attempt in fiction to replace or substitute the faith that has been put in question. He is one of the most widely studied of modern British novelists.

Mapping past into present

Writers have always explored the relationship between the past and the present, but in the post-Second World War period a significant number of writers have excavated the past in order to try to explain a present which in modern Britain paradoxically lacks a sense of history and appears to be caught permanently in an almost timeless and empty vacuum. The certainties associated with grand narrative histories have been displaced and replaced by an age in which history is a commodity rather than a connected memory, a kind of historical theme park offered for entertainment rather than for understanding and enrichment and represented with satirical vividness in Julian Barnes's *England, England*. The more distant past is used to explore the collapse of values and beliefs which once provided order and coherence; and the more recent past of the pre-Second World War period is used to explore the disappearance of political certainties which accompanied the collapse of Cold War ideologies. And in parallel there is also a sense that the Second World War is defined as almost the last time when everything about Britishness and British identity was clear-cut.

The past is thus explored in different layers. For example, Golding's *The Inheritors* examines the move from one stage of Neolithic human consciousness and action into a more 'advanced' stage which is also accompanied by violence and by the crude exercise of power. There are narratives of colonial history such as Paul Scott's *Staying On*, Timothy Mo's *The Monkey King* and *An Insular Possession*, J.G. Farrell's *Singapore Grip* and John Lanchester's *Fragrant Harbour*, which chart the fading of maps that once recorded the cultural geography of the British Empire and in which former values and ideologies are displaced. There are histories which ironically 'celebrate' a now rapidly disappearing national English identity such as Geoffrey Hill's *Mercian Hymns* and personal histories in which the threads between generations and the continuities of social class are sewn and resewn as in Tony Harrison's *v.* (see p. 171)

And there are the many narratives of the past such as those constructed by Pat Barker and Sebastian Faulks in which time and again there is a return to the First World War as the main locus for the shifts in perception of the world, a world which for these and other writers marks a once-and-for-all departure from Victorian confidence in a future. And other texts set in different points in history use the past to contrast with and help to explain the present, exploring, revising and redefining the meanings of the past in the light of the present: for example, Barry Unsworth, *Morality Play* and *The Songs of the Kings*, Tracy Chevalier, *The Girl With a Pearl Earring*, Andrew Miller, *Ingenious Pain*, Jane Rogers, *Mr Wroe's Virgins*, Hilary Mantel, *The Giant O'Brien*. What cannot be denied is the range, extent and seriousness of excavations of the past to be found in the literature of this period. But what cannot be imagined is what a map of the emergent future might look like.

MURIEL SPARK

Muriel Spark began her career in the 1950s and reached huge audiences with a novel which was turned into a play and then a movie, and later a television series. This is the enormously successful and popular story of the Edinburgh schoolmistress, *The Prime of Miss Jean Brodie* (1961). The novel is more complex and problematic than the adaptations, focusing on Catholicism and guilt, with time-shifts from the 1930s to the present day. But the character of Miss Jean Brodie, especially as played by Maggie Smith in the Oscar-winning movie, has become something of a classic and an icon of the opinionated schoolteacher. Here is her philosophy of education:

> Their walk had brought them into broad Chambers Street. The group had changed its order, and was now walking three abreast, with Miss Brodie in front between Sandy and Rose. 'I am summoned to see the headmistress at morning break on Monday,' said Miss Brodie. 'I have no doubt Miss Mackay wishes to question my methods of instruction. It has happened before. It will happen again. Meanwhile, I follow my principles of education and give of my best in my prime. The word "education" comes from the root e from *ex*, out, and *duco*, I lead. It means a leading out. To me education is a leading out of what is already there in the pupil's soul. To Miss Mackay it is a putting in of something that is not there, and that is not what I call education, I call it intrusion, from the Latin root prefix *in* meaning in and the stem *trudo*, I thrust. Miss Mackay's method is to thrust a lot of information into the pupil's head; mine is a leading out of knowledge, and that is true education as is proved by the root meaning. Now Miss Mackay has accused me of putting ideas into my girls' heads, but in fact that is *her* practice and mine is quite the opposite. Never let it be said that I put ideas into your heads. What is the meaning of education, Sandy?'
>
> **Muriel Spark, *The Prime of Miss Jean Brodie***

What Spark does in all her works is to look at how behaviour and character are shaped, by environment, by roles and by upbringing. Religion and belief often play a big part in this, from the controversial *The Abbess of Crewe* (1974), a satirical fantasy on religious and political themes, and *The Girls of Slender Means* (1963), a tragi-comedy set in 1945, to the more recent *A Far Cry from Kensington* (1988).

Many of Spark's works observe landscapes of desolation and solitude even in crowded cities. The lonely inhabitants of London's bed-sitters, solitude and attempts at self-sufficiency are recurring themes. Frequently she looks back at how the past has shaped the present, as here in bed-sitter-land:

> 'Good morning, Mrs Hawkins.' This was the Cypriot next door cleaning his bicycle as I left for the office. 'Good morning, Marky.' That was the name he demanded to go by; he was decidedly embarrassed when any of us made to call him Mr something. It was to be a while before I found myself being addressed by my first name. This certainly coincided with the time when I was moved to lose my great weight. Then, I invited people to call me Nancy, instead of Mrs Hawkins as I was to everyone in that summer of 1954, when I went to my office in the morning partly by bus and partly across Green Park, whether it rained or whether it didn't.
>
> Suicide is something we know too little about, simply because the chief witness is dead, frequently with his secret that no suicide-note seems adequate to square with the proportions of the event. But what we call suicidal action, an impetuous career towards disaster that does not necessarily end in the death of the wild runner, was going on at the Ullswater Press. That spring I had reason to reflect on Martin York's precipitous course towards a heavy reckoning when I heard on the wireless – it was May 6th – that the runner, Roger Bannister, had beaten the world record: a mile in under four minutes. Martin York, I reflected, was going faster than that, he was going at something like a mile a minute, even when he sat hemmed-in, drinking whisky.

Muriel Spark, *A Far Cry from Kensington*

Spark observes her characters with wit and empathy, taking in all ages and classes – *Memento Mori* (1959) is unusual in being a comedy about old age. Her pastiche thriller *The Driver's Seat* (1970) is written in the simple present tense and is a particularly adventurous experiment in form: her middle-aged, unmarried heroine leaves her job, her flat, her normal life, and goes on a journey. On this simple framework, Muriel Spark hangs a comic, threatening, intriguing tale, which asks as many questions as it answers, and takes the reader as close to the edge as any of the fictions of Beckett. She continues to write prolifically. Her recent work includes *Loitering with Intent* (1995), *Reality and Dreams* (1996) and *Aiding and Abetting* (2000).

Spark is Scottish, Edna O'Brien Irish. Both use the idea of young girls seeking their independence in the big city as an image of the search for identity and a role in life. O'Brien's *Country Girls* trilogy (1960 to 1963) combines modern female sensuality with the difficulty of escaping from an Irish Catholic tradition. O'Brien became popular in the 1960s, being seen as sexy and earthy: her Irishness became a selling point. That background is well evoked in the later novel *A Pagan Place* (1971). She has not maintained that level of popularity, but *Johnny I Hardly Knew You* (1977) showed she could still work her old magic.

IRIS MURDOCH

Iris Murdoch is one of the most significant figures in modern English writing from the 1950s through to the 1980s, and the movie of her life and death, *Iris*, was a worldwide success, bringing her name to millions who had never read her novels. In the 1960s two of her novels became successful when adapted for the West End stage (*The Italian Girl* and *A Severed Head*), which brought her serious fiction to a wider readership, culminating in a couple of Booker Prize nominations, and finally victory for *The Sea, The Sea* in 1978, which became her biggest best-seller. *The Bell* and *An Unofficial Rose* also became successful television series, so Murdoch's works reached a much wider audience than serious literary writing might be expected to, and this was reflected in strong paperback sales from the mid-1960s onward.

Many of her earlier works are love stories, with strong literary resonances: *The Black Prince* (1973), for example, owes a lot to *Hamlet*. The high point of this rather self-conscious awareness of the language and literature comes in *A Word Child* (1975), which is a love story where the love object is not only another human being, it is also words themselves. This extract shows the first-person male narrator in a moment where words cannot be enough, and with a delicately evoked background to the conversation with Biscuit:

> 'One day I shall go away.'
> 'How will that be?'

'I will meet a man who will take me away.'

'Poor Biscuit. Have you been waiting for him all these years, your prince, poor disinherited princess?' The words were cruel, as I knew when I uttered them. And yet her enigmatic dignity did not evoke pity. Suddenly I thought and uttered my thought. 'Not me – darling Biscuit – I can't be him.'

'I know.' She got up. 'You see, you love her. They always do.' She began to walk away towards the bridge.

I went after her and caught the sleeve of her coat. 'Biscuit, don't spoil things.'

'What things?'

'Don't – Don't – It's such a lovely day.'

A quartet of Canada geese whizzed under the bridge and took the water with a noisy checked flurry.

'Biscuit, has Lady Kitty talked to you about me? Has she told you why she wants to talk to me? It's not perhaps – what you think at all. Has she told you anything?'

'No.' We watched the geese fussily settling their wings. 'I think nothing. She has told me nothing. Why should she? I am a servant.'

'A plaything. A toy. Come! Biscuit, I may not be the prince but I do love you. I do. Is that any good?'

She smiled, first at the geese and then at me. 'No.'

Iris Murdoch, *A Word Child*

A philosopher by training, her later novels have been accused of being rambling philosophical treatises rather than fiction, but they are a clear extension of her prolific output, which always showed a more philosophical tendency than is usually found in English literature. From the comedy of *Under the Net* (1954), through the novels of relationships from *The Bell* (1958) to *A Fairly Honourable Defeat* (1970), she was extending her range in terms of character, dialogue and setting. *The Nice and the Good* (1967) was one of her earliest novels to deal with questions of philosophy and intertextuality. Her novels always involved a search, complications within a set of relationships, and, very often, a powerful mysterious influence, usually a dominant character, who influences all the others.

This is the final scene, the dawning of happiness at the end of a complex drama; Simon and Axel, a gay couple, are the main survivors of a complex drama of relationships and frustrations:

Axel came out, removing his jacket and rolling up his white shirt sleeves. The sun made gold in his dark hair. 'I've asked the *patron* to bring us a carafe of wine out here straight away. I'm just going up to look at the room. You stay here.'

Simon sat down at the table. The *patron* bustled over wearing purple braces, with a carafe and two glasses. '*Merci.*' Simon poured out some wine and tasted it. It was excellent. The serrated green leaves extended above him, before him, their motionless pattern of angelic hands. The air quivered with warmth and a diffusion of light.

Simon thought, it is an instinct, and not a disreputable one, to be consoled by love. Warily he probed the grief which had travelled with him so far, and he felt it as a little vaguer, a little less dense. His thoughts of Rupert now reached back further into the past, to good times which had their own untouchable reality. He drank some more wine and raised his face to the dazzle of the sun among the leaves and felt his youth lift him and make him buoyant. He was young and healthy and he loved and was loved. It was impossible for him, as he sat there in the green southern light and waited for Axel, not to feel in his veins the warm anticipation of a new happiness.

Iris Murdoch, *A Fairly Honourable Defeat*

Born in Ireland, Iris Murdoch took up the theme of the 1916 Easter uprising in *The Red and the Green* (1965). It stands outside the usual run of her work, although the central character does have to search for his own identity between Irish and English loyalties. This novel is significant in that it looks at the Irish problem before it became the major political and historical issue from the early 1970s. From *The Black Prince* (1973) and *A Word Child* (1975), through *Henry and Cato* (1976), this search takes on a more self-consciously literary and intertextual tone. *The Sea, The Sea* (1978) took that world of literary and theatrical allusion, sexual complications and social philosophy to its peak.

In her novels of the 1980s, such as *Nuns and Soldiers*, *The Philosopher's Pupil*, *The Good Apprentice*, *The Book and the Brotherhood*, and *The Message to the Planet*, the search is more obviously a philosophical one: questions of good and evil, art and life, power and impotence dominate the discussion in *The Green Knight* (1993). Her final novels included

The Message to the Planet (1989), *The Green Knight* (1993) and *Jackson's Dilemma* (1995).

INTERTEXTUALITY AND THE MADWOMAN IN THE ATTIC

More than many novelists, Iris Murdoch revels in intertextuality, using or alluding to a wide range of other writings in her own works. Her terms of reference are vast, covering literature, philosophy and history, and this gives her works an unusual depth and richness of resonance which few others (A.S. Byatt is one) can match. All Murdoch's writing – she also wrote philosophical works on Sartre and Plato – tends towards the affirmation of good, despite the endemic weakness of humanity, and its temptations to move towards evil. They are novels of the human condition seen in terms of weakness and strength, portrayed in thought rather than action, with a high regard for spiritual values. This emerges in her husband John Bayley's three volumes of memoirs, the first of which was the basis for the movie *Iris*, which chronicles their life together and the long illness which silenced her writing in the last years of her life.

Jean Rhys is one of a much older generation, and she wrote several very significant novels in the 1930s, but it was in the 1960s that she made her memorable contribution to modern writing. She was born in Dominica in the Caribbean, and it is there that her best-known novel, *Wide Sargasso Sea*, is set. It was published in 1966, after a gap of almost thirty years from her early works. *Wide Sargasso Sea* is set in the 1830s and takes as one of its main characters the woman who has come to be known as 'the madwoman in the attic': Mrs Rochester in Charlotte Brontë's *Jane Eyre*. The character has come to be seen by feminist critics as something of a symbol of misunderstood female suffering in marriage, and it is this aspect of the character which Jean Rhys explores, with great psychological penetration and sympathy. This is the most intertextual of novels, going far beyond the kind of reference to other texts that Iris Murdoch excelled in. Here the author actually bases her novel on a previous novel, using the characters, especially the most neglected character, Mr Rochester's first wife Bertha, a Caribbean half-caste. Jean Rhys's novel has come to be one of the most influential and studied works of the

1960s; it is fascinating in the contexts of feminism, postcolonialism and textuality.

Jean Rhys depicts the loneliness and bitterness of unhappy marriage in many of her works, and her uncompleted autobiography, *Smile Please* (1979), reveals how much personal suffering was transmuted into the art of her novels and stories.

THE OLD DEVILS

When Kingsley Amis won the Booker Prize in 1986 for his novel *The Old Devils*, it was very much a triumph for the old school against the spirit of youth which had dominated most of the media since the early 1960s. But Amis too had been a young rebel in the 1950s, and by the mid-1980s he was probably better known to readers as the father of Martin Amis than for his own novels.

Kingsley Amis's *Lucky Jim* (1954) had been one of the most successful and controversial novels of its time, anticipating the later campus novel in having as its central character a university lecturer of lower-middle-class origins. Subsequently Amis tried to create similar shock effects, with greater or lesser success. His best novels tackle difficult themes, usually with comedy. *Ending Up* (1974) and *The Old Devils* (1986) are studies of old age, close in theme, but not in style or sympathy, to Muriel Spark's *Memento Mori* (1959). *Stanley and the Women* (1984) concerns mental disturbance; in *The Riverside Villas Murder* (1973) Kingsley Amis imitates successfully the classic early twentieth-century detective story; in *The Folks That Live on the Hill* (1990) his characters live in Hampstead, that area of London where many writers and media people settled. In many ways this novel shows the progress of the angry young man of the 1950s to the reactionary of the 1980s, with little left to fight for, but with much to complain about! Some critics have accused Amis of misogyny and right-wing attitudes. However, there is little doubt that he was a major figure in continuing the tradition of social and comic realism which is one of the English novel's enduring strengths. *You Can't Do Both* (1994) and *The Biographer's Moustache* (1995) were Amis's final works.

Alan Sillitoe is one of the 1950s angry young men who has not been tempted away from the subject matter he knows best, and he has thus remained the most consistent of the writers of the 1950s – his semi-autobiographical *Raw Material* (1972) is particularly vivid. Sillitoe returned to Arthur Seaton, the hero of *Saturday Night and Sunday Morning*, in *Birthday* (2001), which underlines his move away from the 'angry young man' label he was originally encumbered with. In the intervening years he has written a wide range of novels (more than twenty-five), plays and poetry, proving himself to be one of the most versatile and uncategorisable of modern writers. His trilogy about the war in Algeria, including *The Flame of Life*, deserves to be more widely known. Alan Sillitoe has stayed outside the mainstream of London literary life, which has led to his work frequently being less noticed in his home country than abroad, where his reputation remains very high. The first volume of his autobiography was published in 1995 with the title *Life without Armour*.

THE LONG . . . NOVEL SEQUENCES

Several writers in English have followed the French writer Marcel Proust in writing multi-novel sequences, of which Proust's *A la recherche du temps perdu* (1912 to 1927) – in English, *Remembrance of Things Past* – is the prime example (1922 to 1931, revised 1981 and again in 1992 by the poet D. J. Enright with the title *In Search of Lost Time*). Anthony Powell set his twelve-novel sequence *A Dance to the Music of Time* (1951 to 1975) among the upper and middle classes, following a wide range of characters, including the hero Nicholas Jenkins and the ambitious Kenneth Widmerpool, through the period leading up to the Second World War and its aftermath. It presents a panorama of the period, but preserving its clear-sighted view of the unfolding tragedy despite frequent passages of high comedy. For some readers Powell is the major novelist of the post-war period.

The same vein of tragedy and comedy distinguishes Simon Raven's sequence of ten novels *Alms for Oblivion* and seven novels in *The First Born of Egypt* (both series begun in the 1960s), whose strong narratives touch frequently on homosexual themes and give a more rumbustious view of the times they describe than Powell's sequence. C.P. Snow's sequence *Strangers and Brothers* (1940 to 1970) consisted of eleven novels following the career of Lewis Eliot in his progress from a humble provincial upbringing, like the author's own, through Cambridge University to a law career and politics. Less rich in characterisation and humour than Powell or Raven, Snow gives a documentary rather than a panoramic view of life in the cloisters of academe and the corridors of power. Snow was a scientist, and his famous lecture *Two Cultures and the Scientific Revolution* (1959) was an important attempt to break down barriers between 'the two cultures'. The debate between 'the sciences' and 'the humanities' was very characteristic of the 1960s.

Olivia Manning's *The Balkan Trilogy* and *The Levant Trilogy*, which were published between 1960 and 1980, observe the Second World War, in Romania, in Greece and in the Middle East, through the eyes of newly married Harriet Pringle. They are novels of character, with a wide range of British expatriate characters, and became very successful when adapted for television with Kenneth Branagh and his then wife Emma Thompson. *The Battle Lost and Won* (1978), the second volume of *The Levant Trilogy*, also gives one of the most vivid and harrowing accounts of a battle (Alamein) to be found in any modern novel.

Manning was among the first to set a trend for overviews of war and of the century that had given rise to so many wars. Susan Hill, Pat Barker, Sebastian Faulks, Adam Thorpe and others would continue the trend (see pp. 114–115), although most of the late century war writing was about the First World War rather than the Second. Olivia Manning remains, with Evelyn Waugh, one of the best British novelists to write about the Second World War.

The White Hotel (1981) by D.M. Thomas was one of the most unusual of Second World War novels: it is a complex psycho-sexual handling of memories of Russian extermination camps, and caused controversy when it was published, but made the Booker Prize shortlist. It became a worldwide best-seller. It retains its fascination, although Thomas's later novels in a similar psychological and poetic vein did not reach the same kind of popular acclaim. Five of them came to be known as the *Russian Nights* sequence, again mixing psychoanalytical/sexual revisions of history and experience (1983 to 1990).

. . . AND THE SHORTER STORIES

When he died in 1997 V.S. Pritchett was as old as the century, and Britain's most venerable 'man of letters' – the most highly regarded writer of short stories in the language. The publication of *The Lady from Guatemala* in 1998 confirmed his reputation as a lively and vivid master of the language, which his *Collected Stories* had underlined in 1990. Colm Tóibín reckons 'a Pritchett sentence is unmistakable' and quotes two classic examples; their tone, their voice and their content almost make a story in a single sentence: 'She was a smart girl with a big friendly chin and a second one coming,' and 'What the unconverted could not forgive in us was first that we believed in successful prayer and, secondly, that our revelation came from Toronto.'

Pritchett is generally acknowledged to be the most accomplished English short-story writer of the twentieth century, and also has a notable reputation as a travel writer and essayist. He is that almost extinct phenomenon in late twentieth-century Britain: a 'man of letters', who made a career from writing in a number of forms, including criticism, without ever working in an academic institution.

COMING IN . . .

The spy novel took a great leap forward in 1963 with the publication of John Le Carré's third novel *The Spy Who Came in from the Cold*. The title, the atmosphere and the ethos have come to be seen as characterising the period of the Cold War between the Eastern bloc countries, which lasted until the late 1980s, and was fertile ground for novels of betrayal, intrigue and sometimes romance. The James Bond series, by Ian Fleming, also hit its peak of commercial success in the 1960s, with the first cinema versions of the novels – and the franchise continues forty years on.

John Le Carré has continued to develop the genre, and from Cold War espionage he has moved on to wider arenas examining wider questions of trust, loyalty and betrayal. His novels of the 1960s and 1970s, *The Looking Glass War* (1965), *A Small Town in Germany* (1968) and the trilogy *Tinker Tailor Soldier Spy* (1974), *The Honourable Schoolboy* (1977) and *Smiley's People* (1980) took the genre into a fuller novelistic range of character and action which many critics felt rose above any limitations of genre. *The Little Drummer-Girl* (1983) moved the arena of action to the Middle East. Le Carré has been prolific in his writing, and many of his books achieved wider success on television in the 1980s. More recent novels include *A Perfect Spy*, *The Secret Pilgrim*, *The Night Manager*, *Our Game*, *The Tailor of Panama*, which is almost a parody of the Bond-type of story (it was filmed with the same star who plays Bond), and *Single & Single* (1999).

The senior novelist Graham Greene had acclaimed *The Spy Who Came in from the Cold* as the best spy story he had ever read. This was a genre which Greene had excelled at since the 1930s. His career continued to flourish through the 1960s and 1970s, often with spy novels such as *The Honorary Consul* (1973) and *The Human Factor* (1978), both of which were filmed. Greene's more serious late fables, such as *Doctor Fischer of Geneva or The Bomb Party* (1980), take the anxiety level to a new pitch: greed and total amorality threaten the superficial veneer of civilised behaviour, as they have done in all the threatened landscapes Greene had visited, as traveller, critic or novelist. From West Africa to Indo-China, Brighton to Cuba, wartime London to the Stamboul Train, the threats of betrayal are the same. In *A World of My Own: A Dream Diary* (1992), published after his death, Greene makes a close analysis of how dreams and anxieties are related throughout his long and wide-ranging writing career, leaving us with the thought, 'God is suffering the same evolution as we are, perhaps with more pain'.

Other kinds of genre novel have made rapid strides towards acceptance as mainstream literature, especially the 'mystery'; some of the very best social observation is found in the crime novels of such figures as Ruth Rendell, P.D. James, Reginald Hill and Val McDermid (see pp. 83–86).

. . . AND COMING OUT

The best-known writers who happened to be gay before decriminalisation in 1967, such as Christopher Isherwood, Angus Wilson and Thom Gunn, had been less explicit than they might have been, but Wilson, for instance, had always included gay characters in his works, and it was the novels which became more ambitious in the 1960s and 1970s, rather than the subject matter becoming more explicit. From *Late Call* (1964), through his masterpiece, the great family saga of the century *No Laughing Matter* (1967), to *As If By Magic* (1973) and *Setting the World on Fire* (1980), sexuality is part of character and motivation.

After 1945, Christopher Isherwood (like his former partner, the poet W.H. Auden) had remained an American citizen. Isherwood's huge contribution to modern writing lies in the fact that he persisted with a semi-autobiographical strain in his writings, which might be usefully termed 'auto-fiction': his pre-war novels of Berlin became the theatrical musical and then the movie *Cabaret* in the late 1960s and 1970s, catching the mood of sexual liberation and decadence of the times and bringing the author great fame in the final decades of his life. 'I am a camera' had become something of a slogan to describe his technique, and it reached a kind of perfection in *A Single Man* (1964), a deceptively simple fictional depiction of a day in the life of a gay academic in California. This was followed by the directly auto-biographical *Christopher and His Kind* (1977), the first of a series of ever-more confessional (and self-indulgent) memoirs. These two books have become classics of modern literature and touchstones of gay writing because of their fresh, unabashed directness which in many ways demystified the subject and opened the way for others. Even the very elderly E.M. Forster allowed his gay novel *Maurice*, written in the early years of the century, to be published, but only in 1971, the year after his death.

Few writers would want to lay claim to being known only as gay writers, although many, from E.M. Forster through Christopher Isherwood and Angus Wilson among men, and Radclyffe Hall through to Jeanette Winterson among women, have been openly gay, as have the poets W.H. Auden and Thom Gunn, to mention only two. The sexuality of an author gives less and less cause for comment, and the understanding of an author's sexuality can lead to a deeper understanding and appreciation of his or her achievement. With this development, text which might have been edited out or censored, such as the opening chapter of D.H. Lawrence's *Women In Love*, has been reinstated, and editions published of otherwise censored or suppressed novels such as *Teleny*, associated with the name of Oscar Wilde and finally published in a complete version only in 1986.

Homosexual themes have become more and more evident and explicit in modern novels by writers whether or not they are gay, and several landmarks, such as Robin Maugham's understated 1948 novel *The Servant*, which became a memorable film in 1963, Isherwood's *A Single Man* (1964) and Alan Hollinghurst's *The Swimming Pool Library* (1988) are significant. Robin Maugham was the nephew of Somerset Maugham, who had also been gay, but was secretive about his private life. His uncle had, in fact, advised him not to handle such themes, saying 'it would ruin your reputation', as late as 1961. Robin Maugham had written an explicit homosexual novel, *The Wrong People*, in 1958, but it was not published until 1967, and then pseudonymously in the US; in Britain, with the author's name in 1970 it became a number one best-seller, and did much to change readers' perceptions of the subject matter in the new climate of the 1970s. It is about a schoolmaster's repression and the attractions of Tangier, about using people and trying to mould them. Like E.M. Forster's *Maurice*, this is gay love played out as fantasy, with the requisite punishments and disappointments. It is only recently that happy endings in gay stories have become more frequent.

Isherwood's novels had always been relatively open in their treatment of homosexuality. *A Single Man* is something of a classic in several ways, and not only because of its leading character's sexuality. It is a simple story of a life in a day: a single man, in a single place, in a single day. Where Isherwood described one day in the life of an individual, Hollinghurst takes the name of William Beckford, the eighteenth-century writer and homosexual, for his main character, to examine a whole society from schooldays to club days, from high society to low, in the days before AIDS changed homosexual culture. Hollinghurst's next novel *The Folding Star* (1994) was a love story set in Flanders, and *The Spell* (1998) is a modern comedy of sexual manners.

Neil Bartlett's novels *Ready to Catch Him Should He Fall* (1999) and *Mr Clive & Mr Page* (1996) are important explorations of the gay world, past and present. The earlier novel looks back at a time when gay men had to be discreet, closeted; the second takes a meeting in a bar, and goes on to tell the story of a happy marriage between two men. Pat Barker and Colm Tóibín (see p. 114 and p. 146) are among novelists who have frequently tackled various kinds of homosexual themes in their novels.

The major Irish gay novel of the turn of the century, *At Swim Two Boys* by Jamie O'Neill (2001), set in the lead-up time to the Easter Rebellion of 1916, echoes Flann O'Brien (see p. 47) in its linguistic inventiveness (and its title), and brings new viewpoints to the now familiar story of the uprising which has been the subject of novels by writers as different as Iris Murdoch and Roddy Doyle.

There are many examples of the modern gay novel, and of homosexual themes in mainstream novels, as well as in genres such as thrillers and historical novels. Chris Hunt, for example, has written a series of gay 'bodice-rippers', well-researched historical novels of the kind that Catherine Cookson made popular in the traditional form. They range from *Street Lavender* (1986), with a late Victorian setting, to *The Honey and the Sting* (1999), set at the time and in the court of King James VI and I. In the theatre, Joe Orton was the most significant gay writer of the 1960s. Two 'novels' written with his partner Kenneth Halliwell (who murdered him), *Lord Cucumber* and *The Boy Hairdresser*, were finally published together in 1999.

Colm Tóibín examines the relationship between a writer's sexuality and his work in *Love in a Dark Time* (2002), a collection of essays on eleven gay writers and artists. He handles many questions which are only alluded to in his novels. Being Irish himself, he is good on the way Catholicism, Ireland and homosexuality have affected his own writings, and one of his best essays is on Thom Gunn. He would be the last to assert that a writer is important because he or she is gay, but he does give vital perceptions as to how a 'writing self' is created and expressed, and how readers benefit from the awareness of sexuality, gender, concealment or acceptance.

Paul Bailey's novels usually involve gay experience, handled with passion and sensitivity. He is one of the finest of writers about old age – *At the Jerusalem* (1967) rivals Muriel Spark, for instance. His later novels, such as the grief-laden *Gabriel's Lament* (1986) and *Sugar Cane* (1993), belie their sad subject matter with delightful comic observation and sardonic wit.

The novels of Patrick Gale are enjoyable and elegant explorations of social and moral values. *Rough Music* (2000) is his most accomplished, containing two of the things he handles best – a family with a gay component, and Cornwall. *The Facts of Life* (1995/6) is a serious story with a profoundly gay theme, and *Tree Surgery for Beginners* (1998) an ambitious comedy of identity and sexuality which travels the world. His earlier novels tend to be lighter in tone, but presage the deeper handling of themes in his current work. His first novel, *The Aerodynamics of Pork* (1986), has a character called Seth, a violin prodigy, who recurs in *Rough Music*, after he has died. Other novels include *Little Bits of Baby* (1989) and *The Cat Sanctuary* (1990). Gale is no follower of fashion, but has stayed true to his compassionate, humanist view of life without having to be labelled or categorised.

WRITING FOR YOUNGER READERS – SO-CALLED CHILDREN'S LITERATURE

There has been a considerable boom in writing for younger readers since Victorian writers first wrote for that specific readership. Originally these tales were often moral, instructional books, but the move recently has been more towards fantasy and adventure. The best 'children's' literature also reaches huge numbers of adult readers.

It was Roald Dahl who brought children's writing into the late twentieth century with a punch. His stories often feature how cruel and nasty children can be, antagonising their parents and making fun of vulnerable characters. *The Twits* (1980) is about an ugly and unpleasant husband and wife, and *George's Marvellous Medicine* (1981) and *Revolting Rhymes* (1982) epitomise this kind of gruesome grotesquerie. Dahl's ability to combine the unspeakable with the everyday has ensured his enduring popularity with young and adult readers, and movies of stories such as *Matilda* and *James and the Giant Peach* have expanded his audience enormously.

Watership Down was one of the major worldwide publishing phenomena of the 1970s. An epic story of rabbits, it not only became a very successful movie, but it set a new trend for cross-over between so-called children's writing and adult publication when it was published in two editions, each with different covers. This trend was revived when the Harry Potter phenomenon happened in the late 1990s. The author of *Watership Down*, Richard Adams, continued to write about the rabbits in *Tales from Watership Down*, and also made a successful career of writing (often on animal themes) with the novels *Shardik*, *The Plague Dogs*, *The Girl on the Swing* and *Maia*.

Many writers known for other kinds of writing have also written for children, including Ted Hughes whose novel *The Iron Man* (1968) complements many of his poetical writings also directed to younger readers, and became a successful movie in the late 1990s.

Possibly the biggest event in terms of reading in the 1990s was the advent of Harry Potter, and his totally unforeseen and unprecedented success. What J. K. Rowling has done is, in effect, to combine elements of Dahl, Tolkien, the fairy-tale genre, the mystery and the school novel into a very enjoyable mixture which brings a love for story-telling to readers from the age of 8 to over 80. The series began with *Harry Potter and the Philosopher's Stone* (1997) (*the Sorcerer's Stone* in the American edition), and continues with *Harry Potter and the Chamber of Secrets* (1998), *Harry Potter and the Prisoner of Azkaban* (1999), *Harry Potter and the Goblet of Fire* (2000) and *Harry Potter and the Order of the Phoenix* (2003). There will be a total of seven novels in the series, taking Harry from the age of 11 to 17. Of course Hollywood has taken Harry Potter and made him a movie franchise, but the films under the author's watchful eye do maintain the narrative quality and atmosphere of the novels.

Philip Pullman finally achieved what so many authors had deserved before him when a novel originally categorised as children's literature won the Whitbread Novel of the Year Award in 2001. This was *The Amber Spyglass*, (2000), the final novel in the trilogy *His Dark Materials*. These three novels (*Northern Lights* (1995) and *The Subtle Knife* (1997) are the others) create a magical fantasy world where a young girl, Lyra, is the heroine and saves the universe. Hollywood has already started work on the movie franchise.

Anne Fine was nominated Children's Laureate in 2001. She is author of more than forty books for both younger and more mature readers. One of the main aims of her writing is avowedly to encourage the discovery of the pleasures of reading. She manages to combine humour, character and sometimes rather dark plots (school bullying, for instance) into entertaining and readable stories which have reached a wide audience. The Hollywood movie *Mrs Doubtfire* was based on her novel *Madame Doubtfire*.

The poet Benjamin Zephaniah, like Anne Fine, has targeted much of his fiction at teenage readers. His concerns are realistic and social, more than the fantasy worlds of Rowling and Pullman, as can be seen in this scene of a car chase, from *Face*:

> Mark ranted frantically. 'You won't get away with it, you'll get caught. I'll tell them everything. You didn't tell us that the car was bloody nicked when we got in it.' Taking a deep breath, Mark let out a scream at the top of his voice. 'STOP THE BLOODY CAR, WILL YA.'
>
> Apache and Pete only looked at each other and laughed.
>
> As they approached the junction with Green Street, the could hear more police cars in the distance. The lights were on red and cars were crossing on their right of way.
>
> Mark and Martin shouted, 'STOP! STOP!'
>
> Pete shouted, 'Go for it, man.' As they accelerated across the junction, they were hit. The car rolled over once, throwing Pete out of the front window and sending glass flying. It landed on the opposite side of the road, upside down and was immediately smashed into by a post office van. The car rolled over once more and landed on its wheels.
>
> There was a moment of silence as other drivers looked on in shock. The police car in chase arrived. The two officers from the chase car left their vehicle and approached the wreck in the centre of he cross-roads. Apache climbed out of the front window and tried to run, straight into the arms of a police officer.
>
> Mark climbed out of his side window and screamed, 'Help, Martin's in there. My mate's in there.'
>
> **Benjamin Zephaniah, *Face***

Refugee Boy (2001) handles the vibrant issue of asylum-seekers, the leading character being Alem, a teenage boy fleeing from the war between Ethiopia and Eritrea. Zephaniah's novels, like his poetry, face up to very serious issues in clear and unpretentious language: they are bold, powerfully emotional, simple and eminently readable, by younger readers – and by any readers. (See pp. 183–184.)

JOIN THE CULT

Douglas Adams, with what was originally a late night radio series in 1978, *The Hitch-Hiker's Guide to the Galaxy*, created a cult, and he went on to write an ongoing 'trilogy' of five books which took the imaginative leaps further. The book with the same title as the series (not to be confused with the later book of the scripts of the series) was a best-seller for some two full years after its publication in 1979. His wondrously subversive titles such as *The Restaurant at the End of the Universe* (1980), *Life, the Universe and Everything* (1983), *So Long, and Thanks for All the Fish* (1984) brought in a whole new style of comic science-fiction which in its turn paved the way for the new style comic detective genre novels *Dirk Gently's Holistic Detective Agency* (1987) and *The Long Dark Tea-time of the Soul* (1988). Adams went beyond the Galaxy in every way: satire and parody, the postmodern and the comic-book, science-fiction and realism are all combined in Adams's work. Only he could begin a novel with the sentence 'It can hardly be a coincidence that no language on earth has ever produced the expression "as pretty as an airport."' After Adams that kind of perception became almost commonplace.

What Adams brought to fiction, to radio and television, and to the wider sensibility of the 1970s and 1980s was an attitude: intelligent, subversive, wildly imaginative. He was a changer of perceptions, a joyous free spirit. In many ways Douglas Adams was as big an influence on humour and perceptions, as was the seminal television series which he claimed as one of his main influences, *Monty Python's Flying Circus* in the early 1970s.

Terry Pratchett has long been one of the most popular of writers. His are books of fantasy ('with witches and dragons' as he wryly puts it), and so have not been considered as serious literature until he recently won a major prize. His first book, *The Carpet People*, dates back to 1971. The Discworld series, now well over twenty novels and innumerable related computer games, brings together slapstick and philosophy, the linguistic zest of Roald Dahl and the imaginative world of all the best fantasy fiction. The first novel in the series was *The Colour of Magic* in 1983. Terry Pratchett is a worldwide best-seller and one of the most widely read of all authors currently writing. *Night Watch* (2002) continues his prolific output.

So, what was self-consciously 'avant-garde' in the early 1960s has morphed into cult classics and fantasy, sex and violence have settled in as permanent residents in the literary landscape, and the range of experience of gender, sexuality and genre has expanded in the writing of the past four decades.

In the next chapter we will look at how the cultural and intellectual terms of reference have changed, as well as at how the maps of the English language and the world geography of writing in English have been redrawn.

CHAPTER 3

The novel – the 1970s and beyond

Old empires and new Englishes

CAMPUS NOVELS

In Britain, the academic as novelist tends towards comedy. After Angus Wilson, Malcolm Bradbury (in the same university – University of East Anglia) and David Lodge continued to explore society in novels which introduce a new element of reader awareness and intellectual subject matter to literature. Readers of upmarket fiction had now been largely university educated and would catch the literary and social nuances of the academic context. The setting is often a university or college, the characters often academics or writers; for example, in Bradbury's *The History Man* (1977) and *Cuts* (1987).

The problems, however, remain the standard concerns of love and money, religion (especially in Lodge, who arguably is the most significant English Catholic novelist of his generation), and success or failure. Where, in earlier writing, success was seen in social terms, here the scope is often reduced to academic success, with the result that there is a profoundly comic questioning of the whole ethos of success, failure, career and private life, extending well beyond the English university system. Both writers use their experience of travel and other cultures to examine the ambivalence of the attitudes of the newly educated mass readership which has benefited from the worldwide expansion in education and social awareness. Both are also perceptive literary critics, particularly strong on modernism and modern critical theory.

David Lodge's earlier novels reflect his own experience, in the army (*Ginger, You're Barmy*, 1962), in marriage and starting a career (*The British Museum Is Falling Down*, 1965), and a wartime childhood (*Out of the Shelter*, 1970), which brings in Anglo-American relationships for the first time, a field which would become rich source material for later novels. His own experience as a young Catholic worried about contraception is material for *How Far Can You Go?* (1980), which is one of the few major texts to handle Catholicism seriously in the modern English novel. Lodge's campus novels set in Rummidge (and in universities all over the world), *Changing Places* (1975), and its sequels *Small World* (1984) and *Nice Work* (1988), not only established definitively the popularity of the genre, but they opened up a whole new range of intertextual possibilities for a readership who could catch many of the literary references and university jokes. This was a new kind of writing for a new kind of reader: the post-*Lucky Jim* generation of university-educated readers. Characters recur as the campus expands to encompass the universe, and Lodge even has himself and Malcolm Bradbury commenting briefly from the sidelines in a moment of *Small World*. Self-referentiality has become one of the modes of modern writing. *Paradise News* (1991) moved on to Hawaii for its setting and *Therapy* (1995) looked at 1990s angst and the power of the media in settings ranging from Kierkegaard's Copenhagen to the pilgrim's road to Santiago de Compostela. *Home Truths* (1999) is a novella based on an earlier playscript.

Lodge develops the campus novel further in *Thinks . . .* (2001), on a greenfield campus in Gloucestershire, bringing together – in a kind of cross-cultural comedy – a successful female novelist, an abrasive and self-regarding cognitive scientist and the subject area of human consciousness. As always, the novel is plotted and constructed very carefully, taking familiar Lodge themes such as Catholicism, intellectual debates both scientific and literary, sexuality and love, British Council visits, an appearance by a recurring character from earlier novels, Dr Robyn Penrose, and bringing them all together at a final academic conference. It is an examination of 'how the mind works still to be sure', as Samuel Beckett put it, and of how 'literature is a written record of consciousness, arguably the richest we have'. The humanities and the sciences are here brought together, personal and professional lives interact, and small personal triumphs and tragedies are played out. The novel also plays imitation games with the styles of several modern writers from Henry James and Gertrude Stein to Martin Amis, Fay Weldon and Irvine Welsh. In a self-parodying postmodernist world, imitation is perhaps the sincerest form of flattery.

Tom Sharpe brought a vein of farce to his campus novels, featuring Henry Wilt, Assistant Lecturer (Grade Two), who has to teach texts such as *Sons and Lovers* and *Lord of the Flies* to gasfitters, plasterers, bricklayers and plumbers. *Wilt* dates from 1976, and *Wilt on High* from 1984. Sharpe had lived for ten years in South Africa before being deported. His first novels, similarly farcical in tone but with serious elements of political satire, were *Riotous Assembly* (1971) and *Indecent Exposure* (1972) which brought this satirical viewpoint to bear on the apartheid regime. *Porterhouse Blue* (1974) was a huge success on television, the adaptation being done by the senior academic novelist of his time, Malcolm Bradbury.

Bradbury, in *Stepping Westward* (1965), and Lodge, in *Changing Places* (1975), its sequel *Small World* (1984), and *Paradise News* (1991), were attracted to the United States as a vehicle to examine contrasts between British and American cultures. Bradbury, notably in *Rates of Exchange* (1983) and *Doctor Criminale* (1992), also examined changing relationships within Europe, an indication, as with many other writers, that the English novel's horizons are not as England-centred as they were a century before. A new internationalism is very much a keynote of their and much modern fiction. Bradbury's *Dangerous Pilgrimages* (1996) is a fascinating critical and autobiographical account of writers writing between the USA and Europe. Bradbury continued this international theme in his 2000 novel *To the Hermitage*, and expanded the range of the academic or campus novel considerably. The novel consists of dual narratives, one set in the time of the Age of Reason at the court of Catherine the Great and featuring the philosopher Denis Diderot, the other a modern academic narrative centring on a conference in Sweden in the 1990s.

One of the most vital of all examinations of British/American academic and social contrasts is found in *The Battle of Pollock's Crossing* (1985) by J.L. Carr. Carr cannot be classified easily – he has written about the end of the First World War (*A Month in the Country*, 1980), about frustration and helplessness (*A Day in Summer*, 1963), and about the Second World War (*A Season in Sinji*, 1967), moving from localised concerns and settings, to personal drama against a wider background.

The Battle of Pollock's Crossing is very close to the concerns of Bradbury and Lodge in its portrayal of the clash of cultures, and reveals Carr as one of the less widely recognised but consistently rewarding writers of his time:

> George's foreignness rated close attention for, in those far-off days, Europe was many days distant and only veterans of the 1917 Expeditionary Force had set eyes upon an Englishman. So he was examined with unusual interest, his weight and height calculated, the unsuitability of his clothing marvelled at, his love-quotient assessed, the unjustly high salary with which the School Board had lured him from his green and pleasant island bitterly censured.
>
> 'I shall depart from custom and call upon George G. Gidner to say something,' the Superintendent announced – doubtless to reassure his subordinates that they were not to be burdened with a language problem. No public institution ever before had invited George to address it, but he managed to mutter his delight at finding himself in Palisades and that he was enjoying the unusually settled weather. This drew mild applause and a man in the next seat shook his hand warmly, saying, 'Hadlestadt (Speech and Debate) – say, that was some declam. My old Grandpa was an Englishman from the city of Norfolk and, because of this, I could follow every word you uttered. Am not so aged as you may be supposing. Thirty-two in fact, no more than. My hair I lost being required unjustly to sponsor the Junior Prom four years in a row. Have much hope it will come again: my wife don't like me this way.'
>
> **J.L. Carr, *The Battle of Pollock's Crossing***

Carr is a writer who usually works on the kind of small scale that Jane Austen cultivated to perfection.

Michael Frayn was never an academic, nor did he use a campus setting for any of his novels. But his intellectual range of enquiry, his terms of reference as novelist, playwright, translator and philosopher, and his high-powered wit and humour bring him close to the academic novelists. He is more engaged in questioning than in social comedy. He can bring humour and philosophy together in such novels as *The Trick of It* (1989), *A Landing on the Sun* (1991) and *Now You Know* (1992). He is one of the most wide-ranging intellectual writers of his time, tempering the intellectual challenge of his ideas (on the nature of artistic creation and love, for instance, in *The Trick of It*) with some of the brightest comedy in the modern novel. *Headlong* (1999) continued to bring together themes of art and reality in a comic context, and achieved considerable critical and popular success. It is the story of the discovery of a lost painting and the resulting problems of authenticity and greed. *Spies* (2002, the Whitbread Novel of the Year) is an exploration of what might have happened if the mother of a boyhood friend had been a wartime German spy.

This is indicative of Frayn's writing: he is not spurred on just by the urge to tell a story. Rather he is engaged in all his work in the investigation of 'what if . . .', of how things might have been and how things happen. His subjects are the nature of trust, inspiration and creativity, and what motivates human achievement. Among Frayn's many plays, his best known is the farce *Noises Off* (1982), which has enjoyed huge and continuing worldwide success in the theatre, and was later filmed. *Copenhagen* (1998), a completely different kind of philosophical discussion play, was also a success worldwide. All of Frayn's works, novels, plays and translations are intellectual entertainment, a field where he has few equals.

Howard Jacobson's novels are both comic and deeply sad. *Coming from Behind* (1983) fitted with the 1980s campus novel, but very deliberately challenged and subverted the Bradbury/Lodge handling of the subject from inside, as may be seen in the punning possibilities of the title.

His latest, *Who's Sorry Now* (2002), is his darkest, although many readers will take the very raunchy sex as the main theme, and enjoy it at that level. Again the pitch is insider/outsider – the 'hero', Kreitman, is one of modern fiction's more objectionable leading characters, a rapacious, arrogant sexual predator. Some readers will view his hero's posturing against homosexuals, his view of women as sex objects and his affirmation of everything as a sexual opportunity with disgust; others will see him as a comic portrayal of the worst of 1990s masculine attitudes. For some critics Jacobson is a finer comic writer than Martin Amis or David Lodge (who are very different from each other), and comparisons are made between Jacobson and American writers such as Philip Roth and John Updike. What he is striving towards is a role as a moral observer, but if he is satirical there may sometimes be a lingering doubt in the reader's mind about where the author's heart lies in relation to his ghastly heroes.

MEMOIRS OF SURVIVORS

Doris Lessing's stature as one of the major writers of her time has been assured for many years. Her early stories and novels move between Africa and England, and her five-volume *Children of Violence* series, beginning with *Martha Quest* (1952), is perhaps the richest of the novels of self-discovery of a young woman in post-war years. *The Golden Notebook* (1962), a long novel which combines the political, the social and the psychological to narrate the disintegration of a personality, is one of the most highly regarded novels of the 1960s. Since then Lessing has moved on to examine middle age, in *The Summer Before the Dark* (1973), other worlds in the *Canopus in Argos: Archives* series (five novels, 1979 to 1983), and 'inner space', continuing the exploration of the disintegration of a character, in *Briefing for a Descent into Hell* (1971) and *The Memoirs of a Survivor* (1974). *Love, Again* (1996) is a story of love and passion set at the end of the nineteenth century. *Mara and Dann: An Adventure* (1999) goes into the realms of dystopia. Political and committed, Lessing is sometimes not as accessible as some of her contemporaries, but she has expanded the boundaries of fiction, especially of fictional and psychological realism, in ways which will continue to be important.

An interest in sexuality and gender, poor backgrounds, and black humour distinguishes the novels of Beryl Bainbridge, whose style is spare, allusive and wry. *The Bottle Factory Outing* (1974) shows her empathy with the deprived, and such novels as *Injury Time* (1977) and *An Awfully Big Adventure* (1990) confirm her insight into characters who react against the frustrations of their backgrounds, but who never in fact progress very far. Beryl Bainbridge's novels on historical themes, *Every Man for Himself* (1997) about the sinking of the *Titanic* in 1912, and *Master Georgie* (1998) about the Crimean War, almost won her the Booker Prize. She has won every other major award since her first novels appeared in the 1970s. By transferring her observation to historical contexts Bainbridge brings a new approach to the novel

– exploring forgotten aspects of character and motivation in the backwaters and on the sidelines of history. *According to Queenie* (2000) goes even further back in time, to look at the life of Doctor Samuel Johnson and his companion Mrs Thrale through the eyes of a servant-girl, Queenie.

Susan Hill is not classified easily as a novelist. In the 1970s her novels and short stories of isolation and torment brought her considerable critical acclaim, as she tackled unusually risky themes for a young woman novelist: the relationship between two soldiers in the First World War in *Strange Meeting* (1971), which presages J.L. Carr's *A Month in the Country*; a young widow's desolation in *In the Springtime of the Year* (1974); schoolboy violence in *I'm the King of the Castle* (1970); and a wide range of themes in short stories, such as *A Bit of Singing and Dancing*, a vivid picture of the loneliness of old age. When she married, Susan Hill stopped writing fiction for some time, but *Air and Angels* (1991) and *The Service of Clouds* (1998) marked a return to the novel. Using fragmented time and multiple points of view, the former is a moving and original love story, while the latter explores death, love and memory.

In the novels of Margaret Drabble, unlike those of Beryl Bainbridge with contemporary settings, the characters do make progress, as indeed did their author. The achievements and failures of the characters mirror the progress of England in a series of novels which reflects the 'state of the nation' more deliberately than almost any other recent fiction. Drabble's earlier novels, from *A Summer Bird-Cage* (1963) to *The Ice Age* (1977), go further than Edna O'Brien in examining how character and society are interdependent, with female concerns emerging as central. They are always very much novels of their time, and Drabble may come to be seen as the writer who represents and narrates the decades with most acuity, especially the 1960s and the 1980s. From a provincial background, the characters of her 1980s trilogy – *The Radiant Way* (1987), *A Natural Curiosity* (1989) and *The Gates of Ivory* (1991) – achieve success in the new liberated society of London.

The Witch of Exmoor (1996) takes a different direction, looking at family, madness, and the themes of distance and closeness in a tragi-comedy of the end of the century. *The Peppered Moth* (2001) fictionalises her own mother's struggle in a Yorkshire mining community. Some of Drabble's writing has been classed unfairly as 'the Hampstead novel', but her settings have ranged from Yorkshire to Cambodia, from Southern Italy to Stratford, and her social and political terms of reference are among the widest of her generation. Drabble's work displays a sense of the social concerns which has been a strong characteristic of the English novel since the eighteenth century, but which is found in only a few writers' works today. Angus Wilson shared it too, and it is no coincidence that Margaret Drabble is his biographer. This is the opening of the 1980s trilogy:

> When Liz Headeland woke on the first day of 1980 and found herself in bed with her husband, she remembered instantly the scene of the night before, and wondered how she could ever have been so upset by it. Lying there at seven o'clock in the morning, suddenly wide awake, as was her manner, it seemed to her quite obvious that she and Charles should get divorced: it had surely long been inevitable, and if Charles really wanted to marry that woman (or had he perhaps been *joking*? – no, perhaps not), well then, let him. She had plenty to get on with meanwhile. Why ever had she taken it so badly? She had an embarrassed recollection of having burst into tears, of demanding to know how long the affair with Henrietta had been going on. I must have been tired, she said to herself reasonably. Tired and a little drunk. All those people in the house. That's what it was.
>
> **Margaret Drabble, *The Radiant Way***

A.S. Byatt is a former academic whose novels are rich in historical, literary and mythical allusion. *The Virgin in the Garden* (1978) is the first of an ambitious four-part series chronicling England from the 1950s to the early 1970s. It portrays Yorkshire at the beginning of the new Elizabethan age in 1952, and is an ambitious contrast of the sixteenth-century Elizabethan age with the present. Its sequel *Still Life* (1985) continues the rich observation of England in the 1950s. *Possession* (1990) brought Antonia Byatt wide acclaim, winning several major prizes and becoming a Hollywood movie. Once more it contrasts past and present, with the search for a Victorian poet's past illuminating a contemporary university researcher's life and times.

Somewhere in the locked-away letters, Ash had referred to the plot or fate which seemed to hold or drive the dead lovers. Roland thought, partly with precise post-modernist pleasure, and partly with a real element of superstitious dread, that he and Maud were being driven by a plot or fate that seemed, at least possibly, to be not their plot or fate but that of those others. And it is probable that there is an element of superstitious dread in any self-referring, self-reflexive, inturned post-modernist mirror-game or plot-coil that recognises that it has got out of hand, that connections proliferate apparently at random, that is to say, with equal verisimilitude, apparently in response to some ferocious ordering principle, not controlled by conscious intention, which would of course, being a good post-modernist intention, *require* the aleatory or the multivalent or the 'free', but structuring, but controlling, but driving, to some – to what? – end. Coherence and closure are deep human desires that are presently unfashionable. But they are always both frightening and enchantingly desirable. 'Falling in love', characteristically, combs the appearances of the world, and of the particular lover's history, out of a random tangle and into a coherent plot.

A.S. Byatt, *Possession*

Byatt's *Angel and Insects* (1992) explores the background to Tennyson's *In Memoriam* in the context of travel, scientific discovery and inherited wealth. It became a successful film. *Babel Tower* (1996) follows on from *The Virgin in the Garden* and *Still Life*. It is an ambitious, long, rather sprawling novel about the 1960s. The period is seen as a time of social and intellectual revolution, but in particularly English terms. It is a novel about words and ideas, and contains within it a novel called 'Babbletower' which is prosecuted for obscenity in an echo of the *Lady Chatterley's Lover* trial. Byatt takes postmodern pastiche, intertextuality and contemporary history to new heights in this extended romp through recent fashions, preoccupations and intellectual concerns. *A Whistling Woman* (2002) concludes the quartet, bringing it up to the 1970s. Byatt does not like to be mentioned in the same breath as her sister Margaret Drabble, but their novels are often remarkably complementary in theme and direction – Drabble chronicles the 1980s much as Byatt chronicled the 1950s and 1960s.

Anita Brookner and Barbara Pym have both been compared to Jane Austen, but could hardly be more different from each other. One of the major literary events of the late 1970s was the rediscovery of Barbara Pym. In January 1977 the *Times Literary Supplement* published a survey in which two major writers, Lord David Cecil and the poet Philip Larkin, named her as the most underrated living writer of the century. This launched a wonderful late flourish of interest in her work, her earlier novels were all successfully reissued, and *Quartet in Autumn* became a best-seller all over the world and made the Booker Prize shortlist.

Barbara Pym's novels explore the note of sadness in spinster life in small parishes, often in cities, and touch upon emotional depths in what always seems to be a rather comic setting. From *Excellent Women* in 1952 to the tragic *Quartet in Autumn* in 1977, Pym explores a world that is small in scale, but profound in its emotional impact. *The Sweet Dove Died*, published in 1978, consolidated her reputation. Pym's novels work on a knife-edge of comic fragility, ironic social observation, and the sadness of solitude and dashed hopes. The following scene is the essence of her understatement in its depiction of age and changes in society. What is most remarkable, and characteristic of the author, is how much drama is contained in the very understated narrative:

> 'It never rains but it pours,' said Norman the next morning when Letty told them in the office about the new development in her retirement plans. 'First your friend getting married and now this – whatever next? There'll be a third thing, just you wait.'
>
> 'Yes, troubles do tend to come in threes, or so people say,' Edwin remarked. There was of course an undeniable interest and even unadmitted pleasure in the contemplation of other people's misfortunes, and for a moment Edwin basked in this, shaking his head and speculating on what the third disaster might be.
>
> 'Don't tell us you're getting married too,' said Norman jauntily. 'That might be the third thing.'
>
> Letty had to smile, as she was meant to, at such a fantastic suggestion. 'No chance of that,' she said. 'But I can still go and live in the country if I want to. There's a nice house in the village where I could get a room.'
>
> 'An old people's home?' Norman asked, quick as a flash.
>
> 'Not exactly – you can have your own furniture there.'

'An old people's home where you can have your own furniture – your bits and pieces and treasures,' Norman went on.

'Of course you won't necessarily have to leave your room in London,' said Edwin. 'The new landlord may be a very good man. A lot of splendid West Africans come to our church and they do very well in the sanctuary. They have a great love of ritual and pageantry.'

This was cold comfort to Letty, for it was these very qualities that she feared, the noise and exuberance, all those characteristics exemplified by the black girl in the office which were so different from her own.

'Oh, she'll find their way of life so different,' said Norman, 'the cooking smell and that. I know about bed-sitters, believe me.'

Barbara Pym, *Quartet in Autumn*

Pym's handling of homosexuality and of female solitude in all its non-liberated senses was far ahead of her time, and her depiction of small-time London offices takes the irony of Muriel Spark a step further. Her final novel, *A Few Green Leaves* (1980), concludes in elegiac mode, and several unpublished novels achieved considerable posthumous success, among them *An Unsuitable Attachment* (1983) and *An Academic Question* (1986)

After her death Barbara Pym's work continued its success, perhaps surprisingly considering her image as a middle-class spinster: but that belies her dashing wit, her affectionate handling of not particularly likeable characters, and her gift for the telling put-down. In America John Updike is a great admirer, and the novelist Anne Tyler offers the highest of praise, accounting for her continuing appeal: 'Whom do people turn to when they've finished Barbara Pym? The answer is easy: they turn back to Barbara Pym.' As with Muriel Spark, she reminds us that displacement happens to everybody.

Penelope Lively won the Booker Prize in 1987 for *Moon Tiger*, a novel set largely in Egypt in wartime, echoing many of her own experiences while growing up. *Cleopatra's Sister* (1993) is also set in North Africa, in an imaginary nation. She is a novelist of a wide range, from children's fiction (*The Ghost of Thomas Kempe* is a wonderful story) to gentle social and sexual comedy in such books as *The Road to Lichfield* (1977) and *Next to Nature, Art* (1982). *According to Mark* (1984) tackles the subject of writing a biography, rather in the way that Julian Barnes would later make popular. Ways of remembering are a large part of her writing: her memoir *A House Unlocked* (2001) becomes almost a social history of the century in its documentation of her grandparents' home in the West Country. It illuminates the concerns of her fiction which has tended to bring present and past together: the title of her 1989 novel *Passing On* encompasses neatly the two senses of ending and continuity which all her works embody.

Like Barbara Pym, Anita Brookner writes beautifully about the solitude of women, the consolations for her characters frequently being found in literature and art. Her novels have remained steadily popular, despite their characteristic sadness, and she has created for herself a place in modern literature as one of the great chroniclers of modern urban solitude.

> There was within Sally a kind of readiness for friendship, but for a friendship based essentially on amusement. She was not inclined to, or stimulated by, acts of altruism. Blanche could see that her feeling for Elinor was based on a certain spasmodic camaraderie; and that was why the child, to a limited extent, trusted her. What the child resisted was precisely her pleasure-loving insubstantiality, her desire to be diverted, her readiness to accept the next invitation, her availability. Blanche saw that as a mother, or as a putative mother, Sally was indeed nymph-like; she would provide a temporary shelter for the little girl and educate her to a sort of viability, but it would be senseless to demand of her further guidance. At the age of seven Elinor would be expected to be self-reliant; at the age of ten she would be given her sexual education; at the age of fifteen or sixteen she would be expected to have left home for good. Her refusal to speak was based on her foreknowledge of this fate.
>
> **Anita Brookner, *A Misalliance***

Brookner's characters are also frequently spinsters, and her novels of loneliness and pain are among the most classically refined treatments of the theme of solitude in the twentieth century. They continue in some ways from the 1920s novels of May Sinclair, but with more of a sense of submission than challenge. Hers is not a world of comedy, nor of the consolation of religion, but of solitary struggle and renunciation. Her characters are usually single women of intelligence but restricted

means, and her examination of solitude and the rejection of depen-
dence is a marked contrast to traditional feminine 'love-story' fiction.
Her Booker Prize winner *Hotel du Lac* (1984) is her best-known novel,
but *A Friend from England* (1987), *Lewis Percy* (1989) with its male
protagonist, *Fraud* (1992), and *Incidents in the Rue Laugier* (1995) show
her constantly refining and deepening her art as an observer of the
darker sides of human isolation.

Incidents in the Rue Laugier moves between France and England, and
contains deliberate echoes of Proust in its construction of the lives of
a mother in the mind of her daughter. Its opening line 'My mother
read a lot, sighed a lot, and went to bed early' opens up an exploration
of past and present, character and motivation that expands Brookner's
range, creating echoes of novelists such as Henry James and especially
Edith Wharton in a modern time-frame which moves from the 1970s
to even beyond the time of the actual writing of the novel. Its final lines
are a clear indication of many novelists' preoccupation with the distant
and not so distant past, and why it is such a significant part of modern
fiction from Brookner herself to Beryl Bainbridge and Salman Rushdie:
'The dead, perhaps even more than the living, have a right to their
mysteries. And who knows? We, the survivors, may be called upon
to explain them, if only to ourselves.' This need to 'explain . . . if
only to ourselves' the significance of events both significant and
insignificant in the past has led many novelists to move their concerns
back from the present to the past, despite having perhaps established
a clear fictional space of their own in modern settings.

Falling Slowly (1998) is perhaps her bleakest work, an elegiac
novel of love, loss, loneliness and resignation. In some ways she, or
her character, questions the roles expected of women: 'How had she,
a not unintelligent woman in the late twentieth century, when women
were supposed to know everything, come to this?'.

This is a neat sideways observation on and reaction to the growth
of feminist attitudes. Her nineteenth novel *Undue Influence* (1999)
gave readers her youngest heroine, and is a story of the perhaps
unexpected loneliness of a generation of women Brookner has not
examined until now. *The Bay of Angels* (2000) takes this further,
contrasting loneliness and freedom: many characters (and readers)
would still like a happy ending. *The Next Best Thing* (2002) is her most

acclaimed novel in years, this time with a male central character; it is a kind of masculine *Falling Slowly*. She is clearly writing now at the height of her considerable powers, a feeling confirmed by the complementary, echoing novel *The Rules of Engagement* (2003).

Restoration (1989), by Rose Tremain, examines a crucial period in English social and intellectual history to reinterpret it in the light of contemporary concerns and attitudes. The novel's central character, Robert Merivel, is a Falstaffian figure whose progress towards a deeper understanding of himself and others is charted with wit and profundity. *Restoration* has established Rose Tremain as an important writer who would continue to make a significant contribution to the English novel. She expanded her range in *The Way I Found Her* (1997) which uses a 13-year-old boy as its narrator. Her return to the historical novel in *Music and Silence* (1999) was more successful. This is an ambitious novel, set in Denmark in 1630 at the royal court, where an English lutenist is the central character, an outsider observing the action.

STEEPED IN BLOOD

Since the 1920s it is remarkable that the most significant crime writers have been women. Since Dorothy L. Sayers and Agatha Christie, P.D. James, Ruth Rendell, Margaret Yorke and Val McDermid have taken the crime novel to new heights of psychological and social observation. What was considered by some to be an inferior genre now stands with equal importance beside mainstream writing – such novels as *Innocent Blood* (1980) and *Devices and Desires* (1989) by P.D. James, *A Small Deceit* (1991) and *Evidence to Destroy* (1987) by Margaret Yorke, *A Dark-Adapted Eye* (1986, under the pseudonym Barbara Vine), *Live Flesh* (1986) and *Talking to Strange Men* (1987) by Ruth Rendell clearly rise above the constraints of the genre and can take their place as major novels of their time.

P.D. James is a serious moralist, and her detective stories are pictures of the moral climate and ethical dilemmas of society just as much as, say, the novels of George Eliot were in their day. She was the first crime writer to become a peer of the realm, an honour which has now also been conferred on Ruth Rendell. *A Certain Justice* (1997) and *Death in Holy Orders* (2001) use settings in the legal profession and religion to set up profound moral examinations of character and motive, woven in the classic pattern of the mystery story. *The Murder Room* (2003), set around a museum in Hampstead, is a fine novel of morals and murder, with the slightest of touches of romance.

Ruth Rendell has become one of the major novelists of London with such books as *King Solomon's Carpet* and *The House of Keys*, and uses her novels to explore the social conditions and psychological pressures of the times in ways which many more 'serious' novelists must envy. Her 2002 novel, *The Babes in the Wood*, has a title which has serious resonances in the context of real-life crimes of the year 2002. Her Barbara Vine novels are among the best psychological presentations of character in modern fiction, both atmospheric and disturbing. *The Blood Doctor* (2002) pits the present against the past in a psychological investigation in the present into crime (medical misdeeds in this case) in the Victorian era, a genre variation Ruth Rendell had worked on successfully in *Asta's Book* in 1993, also as Barbara Vine. Rendell, whether writing under her own name or as Barbara Vine, is one of the most consistently reliable, innovative and socially perceptive of all modern writers.

Minette Walters and Val McDermid have established themselves as leading figures in the genre. *The Sculptress* reached a very wide television audience, and many others of Minette Walters's titles have become television dramas (as opposed to series, which has been the fate of many crime novels – Walters does not have an ongoing series hero). Her earlier novels worked on isolated locations and the psychology of the criminal who was distanced from society, as in her first novel, *The Ice House* (1992) and *The Dark Room*. More recently she has worked on social situations where there is more of a shared responsibility: a troubled city estate in *Acid Row* (2001) and a village of country retreats in *Fox Evil* (2002).

Val McDermid has explored the world of psychological profiling of criminals in her long, atmospheric novels *The Mermaids Singing* (1995), *The Wire in the Blood* (1997), *A Place of Execution* (1999) and *Killing the Shadows* (2000). She also has one of the sassiest female private eyes in her Kate Brannigan novels. She has taken the serious crime novel and its context as a mirror of the social history of the present day to new heights in *The Last Temptation* (2002) and *The Distant Echo* (2003). Male counterparts, such as Ian Rankin, Colin Dexter and Reginald Hill, are similarly adept in their use of crime plots to explore questions of human good and evil, although often with less publicity, unless and until their novels are televised.

Colin Dexter's novels featuring Inspector Morse are set in Oxford, and the grateful city now does Morse tours for his fans. These novels continue the tradition of the cultured, intelligent detective novel, often in an academic setting, as in *The Secret of Annexe 3*. Dexter emulates Ruth Rendell's experiment of bringing together Victorian mystery and modern detective work in *The Wench Is Dead* (1989).

A strong local setting is becoming an important feature in detective novels. Barbara Vine uses London very knowledgeably, and Ian Rankin sets most of his stories in and around Edinburgh. Rankin has written more than a dozen detective thrillers under his own name and the name of Jack Harvey, from *Knots and Crosses* (1987) to *Set in Darkness* (2000), *The Falls* and *Blood Hunt* (2001), mostly featuring the hard-bitten, cynical and world-weary detective Jack Rebus, and set in present-day Edinburgh. *Beggar's Banquet* (2002) is a collection of stories, many of them also featuring Rebus.

Reginald Hill is one of the most accomplished writers in the genre, setting many of his stories in the North of England. His novels tackle social issues and perspectives with sympathy and wit. His characters include a sympathetic if unprepossessing gay police officer, and a feminist novelist, handled with sympathy and humour, just like the bullying, loud-mouthed Yorkshire hero Andy Dalziel, 'the fat man'. Hill is an acute social observer, and his novels are usually neatly intertextual, full of literary allusions and topical social references. In his 2001 Dalziel and Pascoe novel this passage might be read as a sideways reflection on his own work:

> They are not great works of art, but they make very good, not unintelligent recreational reading. Their televisation, as so often happens, manages to disguise, dilute or simply dissipate most of those elements which make the novels special and give them their unique flavour.
>
> **Reginald Hill,** *Dialogues of the Dead*

This is probably more true of Hill's novels than of other successful television adaptations such as Colin Dexter's Morse series. Hill's other series, with a black private investigator Joe Sixsmith, has not yet been subjected to the televisation process. From *A Clubbable Woman* (the title is a very neat pun), through *Exit Lines* to *Death's Jest Book*, which continues the story set up and carefully resolved in *Dialogues of the Dead*, Reginald Hill has written several major novels which the Booker Prize judges have assiduously and shamefully ignored, but which reach ever-increasing numbers of devoted readers.

Christopher Brookmyre uses a Glasgow detective, Jack Parlabane, in some of his thrillers, such as *Quite Ugly One Morning* (1996) and *Country of the Blind* (1997). His *Not the End of the World* (1998) is a comedy thriller about religious fanaticism and the millennium, set in California. In *Boiling a Frog* (2000) Parlabane ends up in prison, and meets again some of the characters he had earlier helped to convict. The new Scottish Parliament, and the topical subject of paedophilia, provide the background to this comic but serious thriller. No one is better than Brookmyre at the angry, hysterical rant against anything institutional. *A Big Boy Did It and Ran Away* is longer than it needs to be, but is remarkable in its handling of international terrorism, seeing that its publication coincided with the events of 11 September 2001. *A Big Boy Did It and Ran Away* anticipated these events by literally two days, as his latest novel reminds us. *The Secret Art of Stealing* (2002) goes back to his comic but seditious mode. It is an altogether lighter cops-and-robbers story with several postmodern twists. (Iain Banks, in *Dead Air*, goes further with 9/11, and uses the World Trade Center attacks as part of the universal background for his new novel.)

WELDON'S WICKED WOMEN

Fay Weldon is probably the closest of present-day writers to the tradition of May Sinclair, and the other female writers of the 1920s and 1930s whose novels were reissued by feminist publishers such as Virago in the 1960s and 1970s. Her novels, which she refuses to describe as feminist, are concerned with every aspect of female experience, including the (apparently) humdrum experience of being a wife and mother. In making this kind of 'normal' life the material for her numerous novels, Weldon has widened the focus of the modern novel with considerable humour and insight. But her concerns are not limited to explorations of downtrodden women; she is particularly acute on the difficulty of women's relationships with other women, and on the insecurities of the settled life. From *The Fat Woman's Joke* (1967), through *Down Among the Women* (1971) and *Female Friends* (1975), she expands her range, achieving considerable acclaim with *Praxis* (1978), *Puffball* (1980), and *The Life and Loves of a She-Devil* (1983), the latter being perhaps her best-known work, having been both televised and filmed. *Big Women* (1997) is about a female publishing house, *A Hard Time to be a Father* (1998) is a collection of stories which looks at male and female issues from different points of view, and *The Godless of Eden* (1999) is a collection of articles and opinions on the same subjects. *The Bulgari Connection* (2001) is an interesting development in fiction: it is a sponsored novel, commissioned as a corporate gift for guests of the Bulgari company. Despite this, or perhaps even because of it, the novel is one of Weldon's sharpest and wittiest satires, full of turn-of-the-century characters and crimes, taking the brand-name novel of excess to new heights.

Letters to Alice on First Reading Jane Austen (1984) is an enthusiastic defence of the novel and its traditions in the television age, in the form of letters to a student who is beginning to study English literature: 'I speak as one studied by Literature Departments (a few) and in Women's Studies courses (more).' Weldon goes on to affirm the vitality of reading and writing throughout history, whether it is studied or not. 'Fiction', she asserts, 'on the whole, if it is good, tends to be a subversive element in society', and this is just as true of the fiction of Jane Austen as it is of Fay Weldon herself, or of the addressee of the letters, Alice, who by the end of the book is not only a reader, but a writer too.

A similar exploration of a young female character has continued with Jeanette Winterson's novels since the late 1980s. She is one of the most outspoken of lesbian writers. In *Oranges Are Not the Only Fruit* (1987) she treats female homosexuality and religious oppression; in *Written on the Body* (1992) the gender of the narrator is not clear, opening up the question of sexual identity. *Art and Lies* (1994) and the essays in *Art Objects* (1995) take such questions on to a wider level of discussion, centring on the role and position of the artist as the new century beckons. *The World and Other Places* (1998) is a powerful collection of stories, daring in its themes and styles. Her *The.Powerbook* (2000) is based on the conventions of e-mail, but is a story with many traditional elements (tales of witches and knights) mixed with twenty-first-century settings and gender concerns. This is a highly innovative novel, using tradition and canonical writers (for example, Malory, Spenser, Donne) as well as a new medium for the narration. *The.Powerbook* confirms Winterson as a very original novelist, not afraid to risk using ephemeral trends in her pursuit of new ways of handling the oldest themes of literature: love, possession and passion.

Helen Dunmore is a story-teller in the tradition of Susan Hill, with a lot of the spirit of Fay Weldon. She has written several prize-winning novels, from *Zennor in Darkness* (1993), which fictionalises the time spent in Cornwall by D.H. Lawrence and his German wife Frieda during the First World War, *Burning Bright* (1995) and *A Spell of Winter* (1995) to *Talking to the Dead* (1996), which is a novel of high summer, and the short-story collection *Love of Fat Men* (1997). *Your Blue-Eyed Boy* (1998) is about the past catching up with the present. It was followed by *With Your Crooked Heart* (1999) and *Ice Cream* (2000). Her novels tend to be psychological examinations of family and relationships, atmospheric in setting and carefully plotted. *The Siege* (2001) takes Dunmore's fiction on to a new level. It is an ambitious and realistic historical novel of the siege of Leningrad during the Second World War, focusing, as does all her writing, on the roles of women, in what is usually portrayed as a man's war. Dunmore's familiar poetic observation is blended carefully with documentary realism, and the novel works as a powerful domestic tragedy set in the midst of the wider human tragedy.

Helen Dunmore is also an accomplished poet: the collection *Secrets* won the 1995 Signal Poetry Award. Her poetry is collected in *Out of the Blue: Poems 1975–2001* (2002). She also writes for children, and a recent volume of stories gives us one of the best titles in this book, *Aliens Don't Eat Bacon Sandwiches* (2000).

OUT OF SCHOOL: THE EAST ANGLIA ANGELS

In the mid-1970s and 1980s a distinctive group of younger writers emerged who had been associated with Malcolm Bradbury at the University of East Anglia. Andrew Motion took over Bradbury's role in the mid-1990s, and Rose Tremain has been associated with it for many years. Many of the writers who have emerged from the programme share a concern with non-English experience. Kazuo Ishiguro was born in Japan, and Ian McEwan spent part of his childhood outside Britain. Other writers who do not belong to this group, such as William Boyd and Salman Rushdie, were also raised outside the United Kingdom, and Julian Barnes has set his novels in countries as diverse as France and Bulgaria. This echoes the sense of an enlarging world, an ever-growing internationalism, which emerged in writing at the end of the nineteenth century, when 'outsiders' such as Shaw and Conrad began to make their mark on English literature.

Ian McEwan came to prominence with two volumes of vivid stories – First Love, Last Rites (1975) and In Between the Sheets (1978) – involving the kind of graphic revulsion that Martin Amis was also using in the mid-1970s, though McEwan's prose is more detached than Amis's. When he moved on to the full-length novel he mined a vein which explores Europe's post-war heritage, and in The Innocent (1990) and Black Dogs (1992) he has related the nightmare of the Cold War to present-day realities, bringing past and present together in an attempt to examine and assuage guilt while exploring a new post-Cold War identity. His The Child in Time (1987) is also a novel of discovery after loss – about the kidnapping of a child, and the ensuing re-establishment of a life and marriage.

McEwan finally won the Booker Prize for his short novel Amsterdam (1998), a slight piece about love and death. Many people consider Enduring Love, published the year before, to be his masterpiece. It is a painful novel about love and obsession, much more powerful than Amsterdam, but perhaps less immediately appealing. Its opening chapter, considered by some to be one of the most striking in any modern novel, describes an accident to a hot-air balloon. Here the narrator reflects on what is happening, as he and others try to stop the balloon escaping:

Mostly we are good when it makes sense. A good society is one that makes sense of being good. Suddenly, hanging there below the basket, we were a bad society; we were disintegrating. Suddenly the sensible choice was to look out for yourself. The child was not my child, and I was not going to die for it. The moment I glimpsed a body fall away – but whose? – and I felt the balloon lurch upwards, the matter was settled; altruism had no place. Being good made no sense. I let go and fell, I reckon, about twelve feet. I landed heavily on my side and got away with a bruised thigh. Around me – before or after, I'm not so sure – bodies were thumping to the ground. Jed Parry was unhurt. Toby Greene broke his ankle. Joseph Lacey, the oldest, who had done his National Service with a paratroop regiment, did no more than wind himself.

By the time I got to my feet the balloon was fifty yards away, and one man was still dangling by his rope. In John Logan, husband, father, doctor and mountain rescue worker, the flame of altruism must have burned a little stronger. It didn't need much. When four of us let go, the balloon, with six hundred pounds shed, must have surged upwards. A delay of one second would have been enough to close his options. When I stood up and saw him, he was a hundred feet up, and rising, just where the ground itself was falling. He wasn't struggling, he wasn't kicking or trying to claw his way up. He hung perfectly still along the line of the rope, all his energies concentrated in his weakening grip. He was already a tiny figure, almost black against the sky. There was no sight of the boy. The balloon and its basket lifted away and westwards, and the smaller Logan became, the more terrible it was, so terrible it was funny, it was a stunt, a joke, a cartoon, and a frightened laugh heaved out of my chest. For this was preposterous, the kind of thing that happened to Bugs Bunny, or Tom, or Jerry, and for an instant, I thought it wasn't true, and that only I could see right through the joke, and that my utter disbelief would set reality straight and see Dr Logan safely to the ground.

Ian McEwan, *Enduring Love*

McEwan has cast his net across Europe for the settings of his novels. *The Innocent* is set in Berlin and exploits echoes of the genre. *Black Dogs* is powerfully set in the grim and mysterious Larzac region of Southern France where the atmosphere matches the dark emotional mood of the story. This is an area to which he returns again and again, even if very briefly – a minor character in *Atonement* comes from Millau, in the same area, and his pain is among the greatest in that novel. The climax of *Amsterdam* has to be in that city, both for the politics and the historical associations of the story.

Despite that, most of McEwan's novels are very English in their setting. The emotions, such as the loss of a child in *The Child in Time*, obsessive love in *Enduring Love* and the lasting regret in *Atonement*, are universal. In *Atonement*, his most widely acclaimed novel as well as his most popular, the very Englishness of the atmosphere, especially in the long, slow evocation of the 1930s country house where the significant action happens, makes an effective contrast with the violence of the emotions involved. McEwan has always employed this kind of delicate balance between superficial calm and underlying violence – this is the basic tension of his works from the raunchy earliest stories to the mature, more elegiac explorations of adult pain. McEwan is particularly good at pinpointing in detail the turning-point moments which transform a life, and, by extension, a whole society.

In the opening chapters of *Atonement* there are echoes of similar settings and class-ridden cast lists in novels by Elizabeth Bowen, E.M. Forster, Virginia Woolf and, in the exploration of innocence lost, of L.P. Hartley's *The Go-Between* (1953). Indeed the novel is rich in reference to other novels and is itself, in part, a novel about writing a novel and the dangers of the literary imagination. The 'crime' committed by a young girl, Briony (who is a budding writer), is a crime of exaggerated perception, an act committed frequently by writers. The epigraph to the novel comes from *Northanger Abbey*, another novel of misplaced accusation that leads to final shame and loss. Throughout sixty subsequent years Briony tries to rectify things as the action moves from local emotional violence to a wider panorama of the devastation of the Second World War – sequences which present McEwan at his most raw and harrowing. One main theme is the extent to which errors, including the errors of war, can ever be corrected; and the question, whether atonement or redemption are ever possible in a modern world without any framework of Christian forgiveness, is left deliberately ambiguous. Such ambiguity is reinforced further by the reader being offered, in the manner of Fowles's *The French Lieutenant's*

Woman, alternative endings so that the action is resolved from different points rather than any one single point of reference.

LATE EMPIRE

The decline of the British Empire had been a subject for fiction since Kipling: E.M. Forster's *A Passage to India* is arguably the major novel on the theme in the first half of the twentieth century. The novels of Paul Scott, from *Johnnie Sahib* (1952) to *The Raj Quartet* (*The Jewel in the Crown*, 1966; *The Day of the Scorpion*, 1968; *The Towers of Silence*, 1971, and *A Division of the Spoils*, 1975), take the concern with India up to and beyond independence: *Staying On* (1977) is almost a requiem for the colonial era, seen through the eyes of survivors of its modern decline.

The Siege of Krishnapur, by J.G. Farrell, which won the Booker Prize in 1973, was, like *Staying On*, both a prize-winner and a huge best-seller. It is a detailed historical reconstruction of the events of the Indian Mutiny, and it was followed by *The Singapore Grip* (1978) which analysed another of the fatal blows to the British Empire: the fall of Singapore to the Japanese in the Second World War. J.G. Ballard, one of the widest ranging of modern novelists, exploring science-fiction, urban nightmare (the novel and movie *Crash*) and memories of childhood in his many novels, similarly handles the fall of Shanghai to the Japanese, as witnessed by a young boy in *The Empire of the Sun* (1984), which was also filmed, with a screenplay by Tom Stoppard. This takes Farrell's historical documentation further, making the boy's experience almost a rite of passage of the twentieth century: history becomes personal, as it has continued to do in the writing of the new generation.

CLEANSING THE LANGUAGE?

V.S. Naipaul is the grand old man of British literature – yet he was not even born in Britain; born in Trinidad, he settled in England in 1955, but is a constant traveller. Naipaul is perhaps the clearest example of the changing cultural identity of Britain, of English, and of literature in English. From *The Mystic Masseur* (1957) to *A Way in the World* (1994), he has written about the processes of history, power and culture. He moves with ease from high social comedy, such as the glorious Caribbean novel *A House for Mr Biswas* (1961), to deeply serious examinations of colonialism and Third World problems, such as *A Bend in the River* (1979), set in Africa and redolent with echoes of Joseph Conrad. Naipaul won the Booker Prize for *In a Free State* (1971) and was awarded the first David Cohen British Literature Prize, in 1983, and finally the Nobel Prize for Literature in 2001. His *The Enigma of Arrival* (1987) was described as 'the best novel of Englishness of the past fifteen years'. Naipaul's *Half A Life* (2001) explores a world of displacement in which expatriates and locals live in a borderland between two uncertain worlds.

V.S. Naipaul acknowledged that one of the great masters of English prose from India was R.K. Narayan. In a long career he invented an entire world in the small town of Malgudi, the setting for his timeless social comedies. He began in autobiographical vein in the 1930s and 1940s with the trilogy *Swami and Friends*. With *Mr Sampath* (1949, also known as *The Printer of Malgudi*) he began a new vein.

Narayan was never involved in independence campaigns or politics or in what came to be known as postcolonialism, but in his creation of Malgudi and in such works as *The Man-Eater of Malgudi* (1961) and *The Painter of Signs* (1976) he created a fully realised world *à la* Jane Austen. As Naipaul said, 'Narayan cleansed his English . . . of everything but irony, and applied it to his own little India.' He never provided a glossary, letting the language speak for itself. Naipaul adds to his praise: 'He explains little or nothing; he takes everything for granted; there is no distance between the writer and his material. It is what distinguishes him from most Indian writers.'

ROTTEN ENGLISHES

In the 1950s Sam Selvon was the first writer of West Indian origin to write novels and stories about immigrants to England. As such his voice is a very important one, and has been ignored all too often. But his social observation, his humour and his linguistic inventiveness deserve to be widely recognised. He practically invented the literary use of a new variety of English, London Caribbean English, in such novels as *The Lonely Londoners* (1956) and its sequels *Moses Ascending*

(1975) and *Moses Migrating* (1983), in which the main character finally returns to Trinidad. This extract from the story 'Brackley and the Bed' (1957) shows the richness of this particular brand of new English, with its own music, its own grammar, its creation of a complete world:

Well, a pattern begin to form as the weeks go by, but the main thing that have Brackley worried is the bed. Every night he curl up in the corner, shivering, and by the time he doze off: 'Six o'clock, get up, you have to go to work.'

Brackley ain't sleep on bed for weeks. The thing like an obsession with him. He window-shopping on the way home and looking at them bed and soft mattress on show and closing his eyes and sighing. Single divan, double divan, put-you-up, put-you-down – all makes and sizes he looking at.

One night when frost was forming on the window pane Brackley wake up and find he couldn't move.

'Teena.'

'What?';

'You sleeping?'

'Yes.'

'Teena, you want to get married?'

'Married? To who?'

'To me.'

'What for?'

'So-I-could-sleep-in-the-bed – I mean, well, we uses to know one another good in Tobago, and now that you are here in London, what do you think?'

'Well, all right, but you have to change your ways.'

'Yes, Teena.'

'And no foolishness when we married. You come home straight from work. And I don't want you looking at no white girls.'

'Yes, Teena.'

No sooner said than done. Brackley hustle Teena off to the registry office as soon as things was fixed, thinking only how nice the bed would be after the hard floor and the cold, with Teena to help keep him warm.

'What about honeymoon?' Teena say after the ceremony.

'In the summer,' Brackley say. 'Let we go home. I am tired and I feel I could sleep for weeks.'

'Bracks,' Teena say as they was coming away. 'I have a nice surprise for you. Guess who coming to London this evening?'

'Father Christmas,' Brackley says yawning.

'No. Aunty. I write telling her to come up, as the room not so small and we could manage until we get another place. And then she and me could get a work too, and that will help.'

'You putting hell 'pon jackass back,' Brackley moan. But it was only when they reach home that a great fear come to Brackley. He had was to sit down in a chair before he could talk.

'But Teena,' he say quietly, 'we ain't have no place for Aunty to sleep?'

'Don't worry,' Teena say. 'She can sleep with me until we find another place.'

Sam Selvon, 'Brackley and the Bed', from *Ways of Sunlight*

Selvon uses a multiplicity of linguistic resources – not only does he create a London Tobagan English; his character Moses can be as formal as any Victorian, but can bring in American movie slang, his 'correct' English, and references that range from garbled Greek mythology to present-day pop music. As Selvon said himself, 'When I wrote *The Lonely Londoners*, my intention was not primarily to be realistic and to differentiate between the several West Indian groups . . . I only tried to produce what I believed *was thought of* as a Caribbean dialect. The modified version in which I write my dialect may be a manner of extending the language. It may be called artificial and fabricated' (emphasis added). By the time of the continuation in the Moses novels Selvon's narrative technique had changed considerably, becoming more versatile in the presentation of point of view through a first-person narration rather than the original novel's third-person narrative. Selvon also co-wrote (with the director Horace Ové) one of the first black British movies, *Pressure* (1978), where the theme is how a British-born 'West Indian' outsider remains on the margins of his 'own' society. It is a subject which would be taken up in movies again by Hanif Kureishi. The language of several poets moves on from Selvon's pioneering experiments (see pp. 184–185).

Victor Headley's *Yardie* (1992) created a whole new readership and a whole new way of writing about sex and drugs and rock'n'roll. It is a gangster rap, street novel of coke-dealing in modern urban Britain. Headley followed it with *Here Comes the Bride* in 1996 and *Seven Seals*,

Seven Days in 2002. The language moves on from Sam Selvon into the code and rap of Caribbean gangs: it is to West Indian English what *Trainspotting* is to Scottish English. It was rave reviewed in the *Caribbean Times* as 'the ruffest, tuffest and the boo-yacka of all modern gangster novels'. The truth, man.

This new kind of local English was defined subversively by the Nigerian writer Ken Saro-Wiwa in the subtitle to his novel of the Nigerian civil war, *Sozaboy, a Novel in Rotten English* (1985). It emerges from local patois, and contains influences of standard English, sometimes pidgin and Creole, and grammatical forms from local languages. It can come from anywhere in the world, and indeed writers in the British Isles from Scotland and Ireland and English dialect writers have exploited non-standard forms in literature for centuries.

What is standard, who is standard, what is English?

Do we speak the same language? Are we from the same place? Are we the same?

Zadie Smith, *White Teeth* (2000)

And their judges spoke with one dialect
But the condemned spoke with many voices,
But never the dialect of the judges.

And the judges said:
'No-one is above the Law.'

Tom Leonard, 'Reports from the Present'

Language is not only the medium of literature but has itself become a theme in much recent writing. It is a theme through which questions of identity and relationships to the world may be explored. At the same time the development of new voices through English and the alignment of these new voices with new Englishes result in the frontiers and boundaries of the English language being questioned and new territory felt out. Non-standard English has always been part of literature in English. Can standard English provide the expressive means for writers who feel that the English language is not owned by any one nation but, as a world language, is a property owned by everyone? The following extract is from a poem by Grace Nichols in 'The Fat Black Woman Goes Shopping':

> Shopping in London winter
> is a real drag for the fat black woman
> going from store to store
> in search of accommodating clothes
> and de weather so cold
>
> Look at the frozen thin mannequins
> fixing her with grin
> and de pretty face sales gals
> exchanging slimming glances
> thinking she don't notice
>
> Lord is aggravating . . .

The playful contrast of standard and 'new' Englishes here reflects the two worlds which the woman occupies. There are contrasts on many different levels from temperature to skin colour to cultural expectation of size (slimness is a western European preference), and the contrasts are patterned into the grammar and lexis of the poem, providing indirect comment on often taken-for-granted value systems and modes of expression through English.

Modern Scots writing offers similar challenges (see also pp. 139–143). The poetry of Tom Leonard is a good example of an attempt to give a voice to the perceptions, attitudes and feelings of working-class people using a language which is close to people's own speaking voices and which is markedly distant from the use of standard English with its connotations of a culturally unified British nation. Leonard does more than give literary status to demotic speech; there is also resistance to the cultural and political

imperialism of English and the English and, more generally, to the power
of an 'educated' middle class:

> sumdy wia digree
> in fuck knows what
> getun peyd fur no known
> whut thi fuck ti day way it.
>
> **Tom Leonard, 'Intimate Voices'**

However, Scots and English have always collided and colluded in writing
and speaking and, as in the poetry of Grace Nichols, it is not simply
opposition to the 'standard' which is being expressed. It is also an assertion
of different value systems which, although easily dismissed as marginal,
can serve as a reminder to the 'centre' (often a metropolitan administrative,
political centre) that greater health, vigour, creative difference and authority
may be found in other voices. One main aim of Leonard and others such
as James Kelman and Irvine Welsh is to ensure that the people they
stand for are read and above all heard. In the context of modern Britain,
with its multiple ethnic groups and polyglot languages, many contemporary
writers continue to push hard against linguistic boundaries as a way of
asking awkward and unsettling questions about Englishness and English
identity.

ARTISTS OF THE FLOATING WORLD

Kazuo Ishiguro is of Japanese and British descent. His best-known and
most commercially successful novel, *The Remains of the Day* (1989),
examines loyalties, personal and political, mistaken or otherwise,
between the upper classes and a butler and in the butler's own personal
relationships in England in the 1930s. The butler's stiff and opaquely
dignified style of communication acts as a kind of a mask for what
he refuses to see and acknowledge, and his dutiful position parallels
that of his master who is involved in secret high-level negotiations to
appease and to some extent collude in the growth of Nazi Germany.
The novel is narrated from the year 1956, a year which saw British

surrender of the Suez Canal to Egypt and the beginning of the most intense period of collapse of the British Empire. *The Remains of the Day* was also made into a very successful film.

Ishiguro used his Japanese background in his first two novels, *A Pale View of the Hills* (1982) and *An Artist of the Floating World* (1986), to bring into English literature a different point of view in examining post-Second World War consciousness of guilt in a time of rebuilding. His later novels continue, in a characteristically understated narrative style, to explore the nature of memory and what reality might be. *The Unconsoled* (1996) is a long, mysterious novel about a piano player, which was generally not well received. Moving between the London and Shanghai of the inter-war years, *When We Were Orphans* (2000) uses the classic English detective story form to explore questions of identity and the need to return. In the process, the limitations of a Lord Peter Wimsey character who tries to unravel mysteries and impose order against the background of a rapidly changing world immediately prior to the Japanese invasion of China are exposed. Ishiguro's presentation throughout his novels remains, however, one of fleeting impressions and unresolved problems rather than one of clear-cut plots and solutions. In this respect he is an artist of the floating world.

From an Anglo-Chinese background, Timothy Mo examines cross-cultural and post-colonial stresses, both in England – with the black comedy *Sour Sweet* (1982) – and in the Far East, with the huge, historical *An Insular Possession* (1986) and with contemporary politics and war in *The Redundancy of Courage* (1991). Mo had to publish *Brownout on Breadfruit Boulevard* (1995) himself: it was seen by publishers and most critics as badly written, scatological and ill-conceived. It could alternatively be seen as a graphic, satirical critique of Third World corruption. Its inventive representation of local Englishes, especially in the Philippines, is an exciting contribution to the awareness of new Englishes in modern writing.

> There seemed even more giggling among the girl students than usual, if this was possible. (Carla hadn't thought it was.) She still found it very charming. They were so much more accessible than American teenagers. 'Hey, what's with you guys?'

More giggling. 'You're not jealous, Mrs Giolitti?'

'Jealous? I don't understand. You mean of youth and beauty?'

Further tittering. 'Maybe you're a fan of Roel Escarcinas? You know him?'

'Never heard of him, honey. He's a Philippine heart throb?'

'Maribeth going to bed with him every night, mum. She hugs his photo when she goes to sleep.' Screams of protest.

Carla entered into the spirit of things, light-hearted banter though her guts felt like lead. 'So what's the problem. Is Maribeth accusing me of seducing her picture?'

'No, mum. Maribeth can kiss Roel when he's coming here, day before yesterday.'

Timothy Mo, *Brownout on Breadfruit Boulevard*

In 1999 *Renegade or Halo*[2] won the James Tait Black Memorial Prize, which did a lot to restore Mo's reputation. Again the story originates in the Philippines, but this time it goes around the world in its exploration of globalisation, tribalism, the hybridity of cultural identity and migration.

Hanif Kureishi caused a considerable stir with the novel *The Buddha of Suburbia* (1990), later televised, and the movie *My Beautiful Laundrette* (1985). He examined cross-cultural conflicts, social inhibitions and taboos, such as gay relationships and interracial marriage. His later writings have been less controversial. *The Black Album* (1995) and *Intimacy* (1998) combine personal stories of family breakup and social concerns of racial difference. *Midnight All Day* (1999) is a bright collection of stories about the lost generation of the 1960s, 'disorientated by the eighties and bereft of a personal and political map in the nineties', as one reviewer put it. In *Gabriel's Gift* (2001) Hanif Kureishi handles a family crumbling under the weight of its own disappointments. The hero, Gabriel, is 15 years of age, and emerges as possibly the sanest and most level-headed of the characters, keeping his head while all about him are losing theirs. It is his artistic talent, his imagination, that saves him: his ambition is to move from writing and sketching to become a film-maker. Echoes of Kureishi's own career are, it is to be presumed, purely coincidental. Like Rushdie and indeed some others, Hanif Kureishi is turning life into art. He maintains his narrative drive and his splendid characterisation, but does not quite recapture the sparkle of his first novel and movie.

IMAGINARY HOMELANDS

Salman Rushdie's novels move from realism to what has become known as magic realism. Rushdie was born in India, and the subcontinent is the setting of what many regard as his best works – *Midnight's Children* (1981), about the children born as India passed to self-rule in 1947, and *Shame* (1983) – which are deeply concerned with the culture, politics and religion of that vast land and its neighbours. Rushdie recalls an oral tradition of story-telling applied in a modern context, evoking sights, sounds and smells of the world in realistic terms, side by side with the spinning of wild fantasies and improbable tales.

Rushdie is at the same time the most controversial novelist of his time and among the most critically acclaimed. *The Satanic Verses* (1988) gave rise to charges of blasphemy, and the Iranian government issued a *fatwa* (death sentence for religious reasons) against the author. The controversy over this – possibly his least exciting novel – has often overshadowed the very real achievements of his major novels. In *Midnight's Children* Rushdie uses the image of chutney, one jar per year, to indicate the glorious rich mixture that is India. Towards the end of the novel, the narrator reflects:

> The process of revision should be constant and endless; don't think I'm satisfied with what I've done! Among my unhappinesses: an overly-harsh taste from those jars containing memories of my father; a certain ambiguity in the love-flavour of 'Jamila Singer' (Special Formula No. 22), which might lead the unperceptive to conclude that I've invented the whole story of the baby-swap to justify an incestuous love; vague implausibilities in the jar labelled 'Accident in a Washing-chest' – the pickle raises questions which are not fully answered, such as: Why did Saleem need an accident to acquire his powers? Most of the other children didn't. . . . Or again, in 'All-India Radio' and others, a discordant note in the orchestrated flavours: would Mary's confession have come as a shock to a true telepath? Sometimes, in the

pickles' version of history, Saleem appears to have known too little; at other times, too much . . . yes, I should revise and revise, improve and improve; but there is neither the time nor the energy. I am obliged to offer no more than this stubborn sentence: It happened that way because that's how it happened.

There is also the matter of the spice bases. The intricacies of turmeric and cumin, the subtlety of fenugreek, when to use large (and when small) cardamoms; the myriad possible effects of garlic, garam masala, stick cinnamon, coriander, ginger . . . not to mention the flavourful contributions of the occasional speck of dirt. (Saleem is no longer obsessed with purity.) In the spice bases, I reconcile myself to the inevitable distortions of the pickling process. To pickle is to give immortality, after all: fish, vegetables, fruit hang embalmed in spice-and-vinegar; a certain alteration, a slight intensification of taste, is a small matter, surely? The art is to change the flavour in degree, but not in kind; and above all (in my thirty jars and a jar) to give it shape and form – that is to say, meaning. (I have mentioned my fear of absurdity.)

One day, perhaps, the world may taste the pickles of history. They may be too strong for some palates, their smell may be overpowering, tears may rise to eyes; I hope nevertheless that it will be possible to say of them that they possess the authentic taste of truth . . . that they are, despite everything, acts of love.

Salman Rushdie, *Midnight's Children*

Rushdie's reputation was fully restored with the publication of *Haroun and the Sea of Stories*, one of his very best works, *East West* (1994) and *The Moor's Last Sigh* (1995). Where *Midnight's Children* took the historical moment of Indian independence, *The Moor's Last Sigh* takes the departure of the Moors from Spain in the fifteenth century as its starting point: what is lost and what is gained are explored in a panoply of fantasies, tales, realism and magic, which reaffirm Rushdie's place in modern fiction, and show him returning to the height of his creative powers, although *The Ground Beneath Her Feet* (1999) was a not altogether successful attempt to bring music and popular culture into a socio-historical novel. It uses fictional and real pop music to trace a personal, quasi-autobiographical history of western culture of the late twentieth century. Rushdie, as always, uses reflections on time and slippages of time to weave together myth (here very modern myth and myth-making) and reality.

Fury (2001) is more clearly a semi-autobiographical tour around an author and his concerns, echoing in its main character Rushdie's own move from England to the United States, his frustrations and moods. These two novels show a new Rushdie, one who is engaged perhaps more in constructing an *oeuvre*, a body of work, rather than the kind of stand-out novels which much of his earlier work represents. His individual voice is distinctive in modern fiction, his authority and scope unquestioned, although some readers may feel that the greatest myth at the heart of his work is now the myth of Rushdie himself. Few authors have been the subject of such attention for their work: the case of *The Satanic Verses* was unprecedented in its worldwide impact, and it would have been impossible for Rushdie not to have become a different person as a result. If his novels are now more solipsistic than universal, they are no less ambitious, readable and resonant of the times they document. It is not accidental that when he collected his essays of the 1980s in volume form Rushdie gave it the title *Imaginary Homelands* (1991): displacement is the only constant.

Vikram Seth is also of Indian origin, but he spends much of his time in Europe. He is an adventurous and wide-ranging writer, producing travel books, poetry and a stunning range of novels. *The Golden Gate* (1986) is a California novel written entirely in sonnets. It is a comedy, a soap opera and a mystery story as well as one of the most sustained and entertaining technical *tours de force* in modern fiction. With *A Suitable Boy* (1993) Vikram Seth attempted the huge Indian epic. At nearly 1400 pages this family saga of the century is sometimes tiresome, sometimes gripping: Seth's musical range of styles makes him a very varied writer, but for some readers this story of the search for the boy of the title as a marriage object was a boy too many. *An Equal Music* (1999) is a quarter of the length, and allows Seth's musical talents their full scope. He says, 'Music is dearer to me even than speech. When I realised I would be writing about it I was gripped with anxiety. Only slowly did I reconcile myself to the thought of it.' The novel is a paean to love and music and beauty, an immensely enjoyable love story set in London, Venice and Vienna. Some of the music of love and loss emerges here:

Susurrus, sussurus, the wind in the poplars, electric-pitched. The swans hiss at me. They swim between the ice-floes on the Round Pond, and the sky is as blue as in summer.

Panes of ice, frosted and clear: the wind pushes them onto the southern shore. They slide upon each other, give gently and break clean. Seven layers thick, half-beached, they lie as clear as glass and creak and shift as the water moves with the wind.

No, not like an un-oiled door; more like a tired boat. But no, it's not that, it isn't quite that. If I were not reading these surfaces, could I interpret their noises? Creaking, rippling, shifting, easing, crackling, sighing: this is not something I have heard before. It is a soft sound, easy, intimate.

This is the spot where I learned she could not hear. I break a sliver off; it melts in my palm. I met her in winter, and lost her before winter came.

Vikram Seth, *An Equal Music*

The most successful novel of the Indian subcontinent in the 1990s was Arundhati Roy's *The God of Small Things*, which won the Booker Prize in 1997. It is verbally inventive, sexy and funny, and deeply involving in its story of family tragedy. Roy said she only ever wanted to write the one novel, and spent many years doing so. Since its success she has devoted herself to environmental causes.

Anita Desai has reached the Booker Prize shortlist several times with her elegantly understated novels of India and cross-cultural relations, such as *In Custody* (1984). Where Roy is seen as wholly Indian, but writing for a world readership, Desai has been accused of pandering to western tastes: she spends most of her time in Europe, and her novels' subject matter almost always has to do with some kind of cultural coming to terms, acceptance, if not resignation. Her best known is the teenage story *The Village by the Sea* (1982), a classic growing-up tale, set in India, contrasting country and city, small ambitions and larger discontents. *Baumgartner's Bombay* (1988) contains the essence of the conflicts between India and Europe that she is so good at describing, but her later, more elegiac novels such as *Fasting, Feasting* (1999) show a maturing of her art and a widening of her range which take the European novel of the subcontinent and the theme of displacement to new heights. This novel ends up being a stunning contrast between Indian society and its civilisation, with the civilisation and standards of middle-America. Desai is one of the finest short-story writers around: from *Gales at Twilight* (1978) to *Diamond Dust* (2000) her miniatures present complete, fully realised worlds.

Salman Rushdie was one of the first to celebrate what became a huge success as a first novel, Zadie Smith's *White Teeth* (2000). It is about multi-cultural life in London, where the mix is both Asian and Caribbean and profoundly British too. Like Kureishi's *The Buddha of Suburbia*, it transferred successfully to television. Its themes of unhappiness and displacement, lack of communication between races and between generations, its humour and its secrets, all are universal. In this extract we can see something of that range in the conversation between the older man, Samad, and the younger woman, Irie:

'I sometimes wonder why I bother,' said Samad bitterly, betraying the English inflections of twenty years in the country, 'I really do. These days it feels to me like you make a devil's pact when you walk into this country. You hand over your passport at the check-in, you get stamped, you want to make a little money, you get yourself started . . . but you mean to go back! Who would want to stay? Cold, wet, miserable; terrible food, dreadful newspapers – who would want to stay? In a place where you are never welcomed, only tolerated. Just tolerated. Like you are an animal finally house-trained. Who would want to stay? But you have made a devil's pact . . . it drags you in and suddenly you are unsuitable to return, your children are unrecognisable, you belong nowhere.'

'Oh, that's not true, surely.'

'And then you begin to give up the *very idea* of belonging. Suddenly this thing, this *belonging*, it seems like some long, dirty lie . . . And I begin to believe that birthplaces are accidents, that everything is an *accident*. But if you believe that, where do you go? What do you do? What does anything matter?'

As Samad described this dystopia with a look of horror, Irie was ashamed to find that the land of accidents sounded like a *paradise* to her. Sounded like freedom.

'Do you understand, child? I know you understand.'

And what he really meant was: do we speak the same language? Are we from the same place? Are we the same?

Irie squeezed his hand and nodded vigorously, trying to ward off his tears. What else could she tell him but what he wanted to hear?

'Yes,' she said. 'Yes, yes, yes.'

Zadie Smith, *White Teeth*

Zadie Smith's second novel, *The Autograph Man* (2002), was widely acclaimed, but *White Teeth* remains something of a one-off, and is the book she is more likely to be remembered for.

Many writers from the Indian subcontinent have settled in Europe (Canada is another popular destination and many writers such as Michael Ondaatje, Rohinton Mistry and Shyam Selvadurai work from there). Amit Chaudhuri, originally from Calcutta, is now based in England. He has used the kind of Indian musical resonance that is found in Vikram Seth in his novels, particularly the slow, gentle *Afternoon Raag* (1993). His more recent novels have achieved great success, especially *A New World* (2000), which brings together the American Midwest and Calcutta in an involving story of marriage, family and roots. *Real Time* (2002) follows Vikram Seth: it is a memoir in verse, without the spirit and sense of fun of Seth's *Golden Gate*, but a more elegiac vision of India.

Many writers who have achieved fame for their writing in English have *not* actually been based in Britain: for example, the Nigerian Chinua Achebe. Buchi Emecheta settled in England in the early 1960s, but she has never left her native Nigeria as the setting for her novels and plays for radio and television. Much of her writing is autobiographical. She is both feminist and postcolonial, and her works have attracted admirers and detractors in almost equal measure. She dares to be a questioner, challenging African preconceptions in novels such as *The Slave Girl* (1974) and *The Bride Price* (1976), both of which are novels of women's escape from traditional bounds. *The Joys of Motherhood* (1979) is considered a high point of her more traditional mode. Her civil war novel *Destination Biafra* (1982) may be read as a companion piece to Ken Saro-Wiwa's masterpiece *Sozaboy* for a related but different perspective. *Kehinde* (1994) is probably the best of her more recent work. This moment from *Second Class Citizen* (1974), a description of an older man, Pa Noble, shows neatly the mix of cultures that is characteristic of all her writing:

A face that had been battered by gallons of African rain, burned almost to scorching point by years and years of direct wintry winds of England, a face criss-crossed like a jute mat by bottled-up sorrows, disappointments and maybe occasional joy.

Buchi Emecheta, *Second Class Citizen*

Wilson Harris is originally from what is now Guyana and settled in Britain in 1959. He is a genuine magic realist, a writer who celebrates the carnivalesque, and delves deep into the 'unfinished genesis of the imagination' through myth, legend and history. His *Guyana Quartet* in the early 1960s was followed by a prolific outpouring of novels leading to the trilogy *Carnival* (1985), *The Infinite Rehearsal* (1987) and *The Four Banks of the River of Space* (1990), which are a frequently dense, postmodern and postcolonial interplay of individual and shared history, coming together to make a kind of spiritual autobiography, questioning the nature of fiction, representation and historical experience. Harris has been more influential academically than popular as a novelist: he makes no concessions, and has been seen as one of the great innovators in his 'uncompromising imagination'. He is a thought-provoking and original writer, stimulating in his use of language and symbolism, the poetic density of his narration, and rich in the range of intertextual allusions. The following is a characteristic Wilson Harris scene:

'You are on trial,' said the noble judge matter-of-factly, 'because Rose set you free even as you let Canaima escape. Is the gift of life but a pattern of escape from death, a pattern of escapism? How guilty are you, how guilty is Rose, how guilty is Canaima in leading an escapist dance?'

I was bowled over by the question – its configuration took me completely by surprise – it managed to reply. – 'Rose was my mother, Canaima my brother.' I spoke softly, automatically. No one heard me except the judge. I was glad no one did, I was ashamed to advance such a plea or revelation of bias. Indeed – even if I had known how related I was to Canaima and Rose – I had never really welcomed it, I had suppressed the knowledge in childhood, suppressed it over the long years until it flared into the obituary notice or film of Proteus's death, flared into scorched sanctuary and blackened courtroom.

Perhaps I had advanced the plea not simply out of the biased flare of instinct but in the light of the carnival crown, carnival heirloom or kingship conferred upon me. But Canaima and I were twins. . . . Were we not both equally entitled to the crown? What did such entitlement and equality imply? Was carnival a legacy of escapism, licence and abandonment, suppressed criminality, or was it a profound universal theme and a reinterpretation of the great masks of legend and history, the progressions, digressions, reversals of great myth?

Wilson Harris, *The Four Banks of the River of Space*

Caryl Phillips is seen by some critics as a young Naipaul. His subject matter is often identity and settlement, questioning state, culture, and even the flow of time, in historical and geographical terms. Phillips is West Indian by birth (from St Kitts), British by upbringing, but universal in his concerns. Among his novels are *Crossing the River* (1993) and *A State of Independence* (1986). *Cambridge* (1991) is the story of a slave who ironically bears the name of the English city of Cambridge. In *The Nature of Blood* (1997) Phillips links stories of persecution, race and memory in an epic tale.

David Dabydeen, originally from Guyana, has written two novels bringing together themes of art and slavery: *The Counting House* (1996) and *A Harlot's Progress* (1999), which starts from an eighteenth-century painting by William Hogarth to examine the role of black people in England. *Disappearance* (1998) uses an image of the cliffs of the South of England crumbling and falling apart as a metaphor for the state of England. Dabydeen is better known as a poet, and used the paintings of Turner as a title for a long poem in 1994.

Romesh Gunesekera's landscape is usually Sri Lanka, where he grew up, and he handles the pull of history and nation and the sense of displacement in three different but complementary works. The first, *Monkfish Moon* (1993), was an evocative collection of stories which celebrated the island. The second, the Booker shortlisted novel *Reef* (1994), is more of a historical treatment, where the main perception is through the eyes of a chef who observes his masters cynically; a historical and geographical movement makes the novel rich and profound in its handling of time and place. The third, *Heaven's Edge* (2002), is a novel of love and memory, of uncharted territories in a futuristic (but unnamed) island, a dystopia with elements of something of a lost paradise. It continues the search for an elusive safety, security of place and relationships even where the security of geography and place is not an option. As Marc, the hero, reflects on the alternatives (England, the island, elsewhere) towards the end of the story, 'Would we be safer with rosemary and thyme? Rosebuds? Swallows from Africa? Or are we, like the birds, what we are, no matter, where we happen to be?'

So the landscape, space and voices of fiction have leapt far beyond their traditional boundaries. A little over a century from the introduction in Britain of universal schooling in the three Rs the dialogues between writers, readers and texts have become intertextual, multivocal, some genres offering solutions, others opening up questions.

It is the imagination that takes us inside these imaginary homelands, and make us trust the tellers and the tales. But sometimes, as we will see, the teller is unreliable, and the tale has to be retold.

CHAPTER 4

The novel – the 1980s and beyond

Old forms and new genres

YOU DON'T WANT TO BELIEVE A WORD HE SAYS

William Boyd made his name as a comic novelist with *A Good Man in Africa* (1981) and followed this by examining a marginal wartime episode in *An Ice-Cream War* (1982), American and British cultural differences in *Stars and Bars* (1984), the history of the twentieth century seen through the eyes of a self-absorbed maniacal film director – *The New Confessions* (1987), which is reminiscent of Burgess's *Earthly Powers* – and anthropology and truth in *Brazzaville Beach* (1990). More recently his novels have been set in other distant locations such as the Philippines (*The Blue Afternoon*, 1993) and in London (*Armadillo*, 1998). Boyd's concerns are huge, and his novels consequently run the risk of failure, but their narrative drive and humour carry them forward with great readability.

William Boyd went for length again in *Any Human Heart* (2002). Again he attempts to cover the history of the century, this time through the journals of an ambitious literary character, Logan Mountstuart, born in South America and brought up in England. Real figures such as James Joyce, Virginia Woolf and Ernest Hemingway appear and give the story the same kind of spurious credibility that Boyd played with in the hoax biography of the artist 'Nat Tate' that Boyd published in 1998. Although he can become rambling and disconnected, it is in the nature of this kind of novel to take off in different directions: the narrator is almost by definition unreliable. Boyd has always been interested in attempting the overview, and in this novel he frequently reflects on what 'the true journal' might be – echoing the kind of fictional dilemma in which the very first novelists found themselves three centuries ago: Is the story true or is it a story? How are readers to take it? Like *The New Confessions* this is fiction as life and/or life as fiction. In this moment from his classic story 'Long Story Short' (in the 1981 volume *On the Yankee Station*), the narrator, William (how close to the author?), tells his story, but also gives some indication of how he can manipulate the telling, fictionalise the fiction:

> Frank. Frank was the sort of older brother nobody needs. Tall, socially at ease, rich, good job (journalist on an up-market Sunday). Very attractive too. He had a polished superficial charm which, to my surprise, managed to take in one hell of a lot of people. But he was a smug self-satisfied bastard and we never really liked each other. He always needed to feel superior to me.
>
> 'Pleased to meet you, 'Frank said to Louella, holding on to her hand far longer than William thought necessary.
>
> 'Hi,' said Louella. William's told me so much about you.'
>
> Frank laughed. 'Listen,' he said. 'You don't want to believe anything he says.'
>
> He didn't say that, in fact. But it's typical of the sort of thing I can imagine him saying. Anyway I only did that just to show how easy it is – and how different. I can make Frank bald, add four inches to Louella's bust, supply William with a flat in Belgravia. But it's not going to solve anything. Because – to cut a long story short (quite a good title, yes?) – I really did love Louella (we'll still call her that, if you don't mind – saves possible embarrassment). I wanted to marry her. And that bastard Frank steadily and deliberately took her away from me.
>
> **William Boyd, 'Long Story Short'**

Barry Unsworth has been writing novels of very high quality for many years, since *The Hide* in 1970, and he won the Booker Prize jointly in 1992 with his slave-trade story *Sacred Hunger*. His 1980 title *Pascali's Island* was the first to make the shortlist. It was later filmed (and rather tamely called *The Idol* in the USA). It is a tale of intrigue and spying on a Greek island in 1908. From that setting Unsworth moved on to Venice in 1432 in *Stone Virgin*, anticipating A.S. Byatt in his mixing of modern investigation and old mystery. *Losing Nelson* (1999) again mixes the telling of history with modern settings. *Morality Play* (1995) again mixes history and mystery, genres and styles: it is a murder story with a fourteenth-century setting, a group of strolling players and knights: Umberto Eco gives a sly nod in the direction of Terry Pratchett, but in Unsworth's own uniquely gripping style.

His *The Songs of the Kings* (2002) was described by Ruth Rendell as 'close to perfect in an imperfect literary world', but failed to make the Booker Prize shortlist. It is a rewriting of the story of the Trojan War, finding echoes and resonances of today's conflicts in that oldest of literary subjects. Unsworth's novels tend to look into the present through the prism of the past, with individual obsession sparking off a well-told tale. He is one of the most widely travelled and richly international of modern British novelists. Here we see how the past and present come together, 'as these our times have wonderfully shown'.

> As we sat there round the fire, with the decision made, I thought again of the knight, how he came riding slowly up the hill through the falling snow with the red breath of the Beast above him. I took that front rider for Death, but I know now that it was his own death that he bore about him. I remembered his pale face, the calm, reckless glance, the long scar down his cheek, that effeminate square of silk to guard his finery against the touch of the snow. The knights are a killing class, they are trained from childhood in the use of weapons and the doling out of grievous hurt. But if we believe our fathers, or their fathers before, this training had a purpose once, just as the practice of players has a purpose. As it is the purpose of the Devil's Fool to console the Devil, and that gives him licence for buffoonery, so it was a knight's purpose to protect the weak against the oppression of power and to fight for Christ in the Holy Land, and this it was that gave him licence to deal in death and the right to hold estates. But perhaps our fathers' fathers say only what they heard from their fathers before them and it was never true that the knights had this role, it was the Church that said it in hope to soften their ways or the king that said it to explain the grants of land he made to them. They were necessary and so some role had to be assigned to them. However it maybe, if they had a part to play once they have lost it now, even in battle – it is the common people that win battles, the archers and the pikemen, as these our times have abundantly shown, while the knights and their

war-horses flounder in blood and are butchered together. And so they turn to sport. They deck themselves out to kill in play, as this one was decked out.

Barry Unsworth, *Morality Play*

TALKING IT OVER

Rewriting and reinterpreting the past have been a major concern of recent novelists. Julian Barnes mockingly rewrites the history of the world in *The History of the World in 10½ Chapters* (1989) and reinterprets the life of the French novelist Flaubert in *Flaubert's Parrot* (1984). *Porcupine* (1992), published in Bulgaria a few weeks before it was published in Britain, traces the fall of communism in a fictional country not too far from Bulgaria. Barnes has also written effective love stories – *Before She Met Me* (1982) and *Talking It Over* (1991) – which play with time and point of view in the search for elusive truths of the heart. *Cross Channel* (1996) returns to France; it is a collection of stories which show Barnes extending his range with humour, simplicity, and gentle cross-cultural perception. *England, England* (1998) is a satire about England becoming a theme park, a kind of state within a state. *Love, Etc* (2000) continues the story of the characters in *Talking It Over*.

Graham Swift and Nigel Williams are more concerned than Boyd, Barnes and others with English settings, but their subjects are no less wide-ranging. Swift's *Waterland* (1983) is set in the Fens of East Anglia and is a saga of family and growing up which involves history, and even the life cycle of the eel, in a rich and complex novel that is at the same time regional and universal. His *Last Orders* (1996), which won the Booker Prize, is similarly complex and rewarding. It is again a study of a family, this time in London and Kent, preparing for a funeral. Swift plays with time, class, success and failure in an ambitious novel which, like much of Peter Ackroyd's writing, uses careful local description to give a solid basis to his examination of changing values. His latest is *The Light of Day* (2003).

Nigel Williams is a prolific comic novelist, and his visions of suburban London life are satirical manipulations of genre with social comedy and high farce, combining to give a pointed view of twentieth-century life, equalled only by the similarly irreverent Fay Weldon. *East of Wimbledon* (1993) is a neatly comic mystery, and *Star Turn* (1985) a comic view of Britain before and during the Second World War, seen through the eyes of two boys from the East End of London.

THE PITY OF WAR

Sebastian Faulks's fourth novel *Birdsong* (1993) achieved great acclaim, being called 'quite simply one of the best novels written about war, and about the First World War in particular'. He recalls the poetry of Edward Thomas in his evocation of the local suffering caused by wide-scale events. Where *Birdsong* brought a new perspective to the First World War, *The Girl at the Lion D'Or* (1988) looked at small-town France in the 1930s in a new way. *Charlotte Gray* (1998) is set in the Second World War. The heroine is a Scottish woman who goes to France to search for her missing lover, and becomes a witness of the French collusion with the Nazis and the sending of Jews to concentration camps. It is a love story as well as an examination of how civilisation can descend easily, almost imperceptibly, into barbarism. It was made into a movie, but did not reach a wide audience. Like many end-of-the-century writers, Faulks looks back, not in anger, but in a sympathetic re-examination of some of the concepts, such as duty and honour, which guided and shaped the century, looking at some of the greatest events of the century from the perspective of an individual caught up in the historic events.

Some eighty years after the First World War, and more than fifty years after the Second World War, both wars remain favoured subjects and settings for contemporary writers. Pat Barker's trilogy – *Regeneration* (1991), *The Eye in the Door* (1993) and *The Ghost Road* (1995) – uses the First World War to explore the disrupting effects of the conflict on the individual soldier: class, identity, sexuality and personal responsibility are key questions. The third novel in the trilogy won the Booker Prize in 1995 and *Regeneration* was made into an excellent movie.

Pat Barker began her career with *Union Street* (1982), a novel of working-class women. *Blow Your House Down* (1984) is about a city threatened by a serial killer, and the reactions, especially of women, to the crisis. *Another World* (1998) is set in the city of Newcastle, and is a powerful examination of the role of memory, echoing many of the themes of the *Regeneration* trilogy in a family context. Pat Barker writes novels of deep moral concern: from a wide range of settings such as the First World War to local areas such as the city of Newcastle, she examines individuals and their moral responsibilities. *Border Crossing* (2001) is the story of a very handsome 23-year-old who now has a new identity on his release from a long prison sentence for a particularly brutal murder he committed when he was 10. An intricately plotted novel with Barker's mix of psychology, social observation and vivid dialogue, *Border Crossing* is both very topical and timely and full of lasting resonances and concerns.

Adam Thorpe, already known as a poet, made a huge impact with *Ulverton* (1992), a long pastoral overview of the English countryside covering three centuries, innumerable stories, and an extremely wide range of linguistic and technical resources. He followed that with *Still* in 1995 and then went on to explore Pat Barker territory in his novel set in the battlefields of France immediately after the First World War, *Nineteen Twenty One* (2000). This is a powerful late re-examination of the Great War, graphic and horrible in detail, astonishing in its discovery of new areas to explore and very emotional, as all Thorpe's writing is, in its impact.

Captain Corelli's Mandolin (1994) by Louis de Bernières is a novel about the German occupation of a Greek island. It became a big Hollywood movie, but lost much in the transformation. As with de Bernières's other novels, *Captain Corelli's Mandolin* combines 'magic realism' – both fantastic and eerily comic – with a deep concern for the pain inflicted by politics and politicians on innocent victims. Louis de Bernières is one of the few British writers to use South America as a setting. Writers such as Gabriel Garcia Marquez, from Colombia, gave 'magic realism' great popularity, and de Bernières develops that technique in such novels as *The War of Don Emmanuel's Nether Parts* (1990), *Senor Vivo and the Coca Lord* (1991) and *The Troublesome Offspring of Cardinal Guzman* (1992). He writes long, well-told novels, to match his (usually) long titles, and he is one of the great story-tellers among contemporary novelists.

Nicholas Shakespeare established a considerable reputation in the early 1990s for his novels of passion and politics in unusual settings. *The Vision of Elena Selves* (1989) took him to South America, and *The Dancer Upstairs* (1995) continued to explore that continent in a complex thriller/love story about the policeman charged with capturing a Peruvian guerrilla leader. Shakespeare creates a vivid atmosphere and locale, and raises major themes of family, love, passion and ideals. *The High Flyer* (1993) moves to an enclave in North Africa opposite Gibraltar, as a projected tunnel threatens to change its historical and geographical roles, and mingles this theme with a love story involving a British diplomat, once the promising careerist of the title. Nicholas Shakespeare went on to write the biography of another literary traveller, Bruce Chatwin.

LONDON NOVELISTS

The novels of Peter Ackroyd explore the worlds of literature, art and culture: *The Last Testament of Oscar Wilde* (1983) purported to be by the great aesthete himself; *The Great Fire of London* (1982) was a cross-referential story based on a fictional film of Dickens's *Little Dorrit*. Ackroyd is also the biographer of William Blake, Charles Dickens and T.S. Eliot, occasionally incorporating fictional moments into his biographies. His *Chatterton* (1987) is based on the 'marvellous boy' poet of the eighteenth century, and *Hawksmoor* (1985) moves between present and past as it explores the London of the great church architect and his buildings. Ackroyd is the most London-centred of modern novelists, using history, culture and intertextuality in a constant redefining and rediscovery of the city, of Englishness and identity. *The House of Doctor Dee* (1993) goes back to Elizabethan times; *Dan Leno and the Limehouse Golem* (1994) to late Victorian popular culture, taking the story of Jack the Ripper and placing it in the context of the theatre of the time. *The Clerkenwell Tales* (2003) is a London-based historical set of Chaucer-inspired tales. His great 'biography' *London*, published in 1999, is in many ways a culmination of all his interests in the city, its many places, representations and characters through time. *Albion* (2002) expands outward from the city to encompass the whole of British society in a great cultural history from Anglo-Saxon times to the present. Ackroyd's journalism is collected in the appropriately entitled *The Collection* (2002).

Like Ackroyd, Iain Sinclair is considered a novelist of London. He is currently engaged on a twenty-year London Project, which already has a dozen published titles. The best known of these is *Downriver* (1991), a massive and complex novel exploring layers of history, society, characters and stories of London through the ages. Sinclair's novels have been described as similar to hyper-links, shooting off in many directions while being united, in this case, by the river that runs through the city. *Landor's Power* (2001) goes back to Sinclair's origins in Wales and uses the poet Walter Savage Landor as its conduit to history, society and identity. Sinclair is the British writer who comes closest to the American Thomas Pynchon in the wide postmodern range of his novels: for some readers he is one of the more exciting modern novelists, for others he remains baffling. He himself describes his fiction as 'versions of my own history'.

Michael Moorcock is another major documenter of the city of London: *Mother London* (1988) is one of the very best novels of the city and its subcultures. Moorcroft has also probably done more than any other writer to establish science-fiction and fantasy writing as popular and accessible genres. He is very prolific and wide-ranging in his fiction. His inspiration can range from the literary, such as the poetry of Edmund Spenser in *Gloriana* (1978), to Arthurian legends (*The Dragon in the Sword*, 1986), to the city of London and its inhabitants.

Charles Palliser, although American by birth, uses English Victorian settings and fictional conventions in his novels. *The Quincunx* (1989) is a huge inheritance-plot novel largely set in early nineteenth-century London, and full of echoes of Dickens, his settings, characters and plot devices. Since then, Palliser has continued to experiment in various ways with the vein of historical re-creation, but his second novel, *The Sensationist* (1991), seems as far as it is possible to be from that setting: it is a short novel set in modern-day Glasgow. To the aware reader it could be as one of Dickens's short stories is to his novels: allusive, mysterious and cinematic. Palliser returns to explicit earlier models in *Betrayals* (1995), which reads like a psychological version of a Victorian suspense thriller, with touches of Wilkie Collins and Conan

Doyle, elements of intertextuality which put it on a high level of postmodern achievement. For Palliser manages to pull off parody without descending to the level of pastiche: he subverts the story while maintaining a strong and engrossing plot. *The Unburied* (1999) mixes a setting worthy of Anthony Trollope (a cathedral close) and a murder story worthy of Wilkie Collins, in what is both an old-fashioned ghost story and a modern tale of sexuality and solitude. In 2002 Sarah Waters achieved considerable success when *Tipping the Velvet* was televised, and her Dickensian *Fingersmith* was shortlisted for the Booker Prize.

'PARROT AND COCKATOO WERE CALLING'

The reconsideration of historical processes and the re-examination of conventions is a significant feature of modern fiction. While the fashion has been for ever shorter novels for readers with brief attention spans, Lawrence Norfolk has worked on immense tomes, novels of huge scope, great intelligence, wide-ranging scholarship and research. His first novel, *Lemprière's Dictionary* (1991), ranges historically from the East India Company to the French Revolution. It is impossible to summarise, taking in as it does history, romance, intellectual highjinks, high comedy and adventure fantasy. It was followed by the even more ambitious *The Pope's Rhinoceros* (1996) which tells the story of a shipwreck off Gujarat, India in 1516 – the ship was taking a rhinoceros to the Pope. This is a rich investigation of the Renaissance and the Reformation, moving from continent to continent through Asia, Africa and Europe, from papal intrigue to the art of Albrecht Dürer. As with all Norfolk's writing, it plays with language and ideas with great verve and enjoyment. *In the Shape of a Boar* (2000) is, if anything, even more wide-ranging. It moves from prehistory right through to the twentieth century: the emblem of the boar as the object of hunt and pursuit (in animal and human form) allows for an exploration of man's humanity and inhumanity throughout history – even with the appropriate historical footnotes, which some readers may find daunting in the opening pages.

Matthew Kneale won the Whitbread Novel of the Year Award for his *English Passengers* in 2000. This is a multi-voiced historical novel linking the Isle of Man and Tasmania, and one of its most striking and effective aspects is that Kneale invents a new English for Peevay, the representative of the Tasmanian aboriginals, whom the English will eradicate, or ethnically cleanse in modern parlance. Here is a sample of Peevay's thoughts on the events on his island in 1829:

> Weather stayed woeful, all strong wind and noisy rain, so we never met any white men to kill us as we went looking for war. Thus we went hither and thither, day after day, hunting and walking, till my feet were sore and even dog animals got tired. By and by we were gone right through Roingin's world and into Tommeginer's, though this was just empty now, as Tommeginer were all with us or killed.
>
> Then one morning we walked out from mountains, and parrot and cockatoo were calling, wombat dirt was there on that track, telling us we were near good land. Just after we found one puzzle to confound. Stuck on wattle tree was a tiny spear made from shining stuff like Mother's gun, very beautiful, and hanging from it was some strangest thing. This was like some dried skin, but thin and easy to tear like leaf, and when wind came it moved, like dead bird's wing. Black lines were on it, like pictures of nothing, plenty of them, so they covered that whole thing.
>
> 'That's just some white man's shit,' said Mother, as if we were foolish fellows to be so curious. We all wanted to burn this new thing but Mother said no. 'It means white men are near. If we make fire then they'll know we're coming.'
>
> Nobody answered her. Nobody ever did. We were Mother's mob now, and Mother knew more about white men than anyone.
>
> **Matthew Kneale, English Passengers**

'NOT A CONVENTIONAL COOKBOOK'

Jim Crace is wide-ranging in his exploration of history, from an invented new world in *Continent* (1986) and the earliest stages of human development in *The Gift of Stones* (1988), to a future cityscape in *Arcadia* (1992), the 1830s in *Signals of Distress* (1994), and the time of Jesus Christ in *Quarantine* (1997). *Being Dead* (1999) is, however, bang up to date in its examination of what is still one of the greatest taboos: death. In a series of flashbacks and time-warps, *Being Dead* traces the death of a couple, two zoologists, who both willingly and unwillingly re-enact their first moment of passion against the backdrop of an uncaring Darwinian landscape. Crace is innovative and exciting, challenging the reader and the form in his handling of major themes, and writing with power, passion and invention. *The Devil's Larder* (2001) goes slightly further in the foodie realm than the novels of John Lanchester and Joanne Harris (p. 123). This is a wondrously enjoyable literary feast in sixty-four episodes averaging only two or three pages (but as long as ten pages and as short as two words!), covering appetites for food and drink in all possible forms. In a market where cookery books are among the strongest perennial best-sellers food has taken some time to get there, but has now become a major theme in fiction.

John Lanchester, in three completely different and quite unique novels, has defined his times in a way that is rare. *The Debt to Pleasure* (1996) is a recipe book and a mystery story about the art of murder, recalling Thomas De Quincey's essay *On Murder Considered as One of the Fine Arts*. Given that food and cookery books are among the biggest sellers of the past twenty or so years, the fictionalising of food has been a long time coming. Towards the climax of the story the narrator asserts:

> the artist's desire to leave a memento of himself is as directly comprehensible as a dog's action in urinating on a tree. The murderer, though, is better adapted to the reality and the aesthetics of the modern world because instead of leaving a presence behind him – the achieved work, whether in the form of a painting or a book or a daubed signature – he leaves behind him something just as final and just as achieved: an absence. Where somebody used to be, now nobody is. What more irrefutable proof of one's having lived can there be . . . ?
>
> **John Lanchester, *The Debt to Pleasure***

Among the unique achievements of this novel was that it not only won several prizes for fiction, but it also won a major award for 'literary food writing'.

Mr Phillips (2000) does not attempt to emulate that, but is quite distinctive in its own way. It is simply a day in the life of a very ordinary man in London, who goes to work although he no longer has a job to go to. As a description of present-day anxiety and 'normal' behaviour, its resonances and reverberations go to the very heart of modern existence in ways that English writers do not normally face – comparisons might be made with European novels of the early twentieth century such as Robert Musil's *The Man Without Qualities* (in German, 1930 to 1943; in English, 1953 to 1960), or the novels of Franz Kafka. For Mr Phillips, in the novel that bears his name, is undoubtedly an English example of the man without qualities, but, however, with a life, a soul, a mind. His is the kind of life that novelists usually turn into some kind of patronising comedy. Lanchester has given us an end of the century 'hero' who is not so much the typical anti-hero of twentieth-century literature, but consciously and affirmatively a *non*-hero.

Fragrant Harbour (2002) is a historical novel about Hong Kong since the 1930s, close in some ways to Timothy Mo's *An Insular Possession* and Mo's first novel *The Monkey King* (1980), but with very humane narrators' voices that make it more of a personal epic than a postcolonial narrative. The novel explores the dubious moral legacy of colonialism in the tradition of Kipling, Conrad, Maugham and, more recently, Burgess, J.G. Farrell and J.G. Ballard. The novel is based in Hong Kong (the words Hong Kong (Heung Gong) in Chinese mean 'fragrant harbour'). The novel tells, through the eyes of four Anglo and Chinese characters, how a distinctive British identity, an identity based on the certainties which attempted to create Hong Kong in its own image, is no longer available – a fact symbolised by the handback of the colony to China in 1997. In its place there is a world of changing cultural assumptions and radically mutating identities which change before the eyes of the characters as they try to give stability and order to their lives and relationships.

SOMETHING TO LAUGH ABOUT

Jonathan Coe's *The Rotters' Club* (2001) combines nostalgia for the 1970s as a good time to be adolescent and full of optimism together with the feeling that the decade was 'the fag-end of the 1960s' and was also a time of clearly drawn battle-lines, anticipating the materialism of the 1980s. It was the time when the trade unions were beginning effectively to be quashed, and Coe's comic novel is almost a historical novel of the decade. It is set in Birmingham, which was a centre of the car industry, and also the scene of one of the worst acts of urban terrorism in mainland Britain. This is the first of a pair of novels, with a promised sequel examining new attitudes to race in today's world. Coe is that rare thing: a comic novelist who is also seriously political. *What a Carve Up!* (1994) was the novel that made his name. It is a social and political satire covering Britain from the 1940s to the 1990s.

Magnus Mills came to wide public notice when his first novel *The Restraint of Beasts* (1998) was nominated for the Booker Prize. Mills was then working as a London bus driver. His novels have a unique, deceptively simple ironic style, and examine how men work, and how they balance day-to-day life with dreams and ideals. *The Restraint of Beasts* is about a working team of fence builders. *All Quiet on the Orient Express* (1999) again examines the world of work, but this time with an individual rather than a team at its heart. It is a fascinating account of how work can fill a life, and contains one of the best reversals of fortune jokes in all modern fiction as it builds to its cleverly foreshadowed climax. *Three to See the King* (2001) moves further into the world of wishful thinking and is a very neatly balanced novel of ambition and irony. The unnamed narrator is in search of a simpler life: he wants to live in a canyon, but instead ends up in a tin shack on a windswept plain. Again the whole novel builds to a stunning reversal, which changes the reader's perception of the tale and its purpose.

Magnus Mills is a distinctive voice making acute observations in a readable and entertaining series of novels which, as they progress, show him creating an ironic world that is coming to be recognisably his own.

FRENCH CONNECTIONS

Michéle Roberts is one of the most consistent and prolific novelists currently writing. *Daughters of the House* (1992), her sixth novel, was shortlisted for the Booker Prize and won the W.H. Smith Literary Award. It reflects the author's French and English background, as do many of her novels, and, again like many of her works, reflects the influence of the past, guilt and secrets on the present. Her more recent novels expand her range: *Fair Exchange* (1999) is a historical novel set between England in the 1780s and France in the early 1800s and featuring the characters of Mary Wollstonecraft and the poet Wordsworth. *The Looking Glass* (2000) also uses literary inspiration: suggested by events in the lives of the French authors Flaubert and Mallarmé, it takes female first-person narration into the mind of an orphan servant girl who lives for stories, and tries to tell herself stories for her life. Here she is at the beginning of what she hopes will be a new story, immediately after making love:

> Afterwards we lay collapsed. We talked in low voices, addressing each other's pillows as though, big and solemn in their frilled white cases, they were bewigged judges able impartially to decide our fate.
>
> 'Men don't marry their housekeepers,' I objected: 'it isn't done.'
>
> I had given myself a promotion. Housekeeper sounded a lot better, more possible, than servant. And I had constituted myself counsel for the prosecution so that I could enjoy hearing Gérard speak up for the defence.
>
> 'The poet Mallarmé married a governess,' Gérard returned: 'a working woman; it's not so unusual.'
>
> 'If we were married,' I pointed out: 'you wouldn't have to pay me. You'd save on my wages.'
>
> The verdict was given. It was decided. We fell asleep.
>
> But it didn't happen like that. No, it didn't happen like that at all. I had told myself the false story, which annoyed the true one, and so the true one burst out and took over, a torrent which could not be stopped.
>
> **Michéle Roberts, *The Looking Glass***

Joanne Harris has also achieved great success with the literary use of her French/English background. Her subject tends to be the liberation of provincial limitations through the discovery of natural sensual pleasures. Food with a touch of magic is her recipe. *Chocolat*, for instance, which became a successful movie, contrasts the narrow-minded religiosity of a small French village with the sensual pleasures offered by the heroine's chocolate shop, and the contrasting lifestyle of a band of gypsies. *Blackberry Wine* affords a not dissimilar contrast between growing up poor in England in the 1970s and coming to life again in the French countryside today, with a hint of wine and a few touches of magic. *Four Quarters of the Orange* became an even bigger best-seller, but *Coastliners*, set on an offshore island, was over-long and less magical in its evocation of the contrasts between traditional life and modern sensual and artistic aspirations.

DEAR DIARY

Since the 1980s fictional diaries have become a fashionable mode of documenting the trials and tribulations of modern life. The two most successful have been the diaries of Adrian Mole and Bridget Jones. Adrian Mole grows from a schoolboy of 13¾ in the 1982 *The Secret Diary of Adrian Mole aged 13¾* through several instalments to the age of thirty-something on the eve of Tony Blair's 1997 election victory in the 1999 *Adrian Mole: The Cappuccino Years*. The author, Sue Townsend, uses the ingenuous but sympathetic character and his diary to make many political and social points about British society in the 1980s and 1990s, from the government of Margaret Thatcher to the new mood of Blair's Labour government. New Labour is also the subject of her pungent and clever satire in *Number Ten* (2002). Sue Townsend has written several plays, a comic anti-monarchist novel and play, *The Queen and I* (1991), and two darker and more serious novels, *Rebuilding Coventry* (1988) and *Ghost Children* (1997), which show her deeper social political concerns.

CHICK LIT

Helen Fielding's diarist, Bridget Jones, is single, preoccupied with her weight and her lack of a love life. Her fictional diaries became very popular, and like Adrian Mole's became successful in other forms: newspaper and cinema in this case, theatre and television in the case of Adrian Mole. *Bridget Jones's Diary* (1996) and *Bridget Jones: The Edge of Reason* (1999) created a figure who came to represent the fears and anxieties of a generation. Helen Fielding's first novel *Cause Celeb* (1994) was a comic account of celebrity charity media work, contrasting Third World hunger with western media obsessions, a reflection of the contemporary fascination with image, celebrity and the power of the mass media.

Bridget Jones is the clearest heroine of chick lit. This was the burgeoning of novels in the mid- to late 1990s which featured thirty-something single females and their preoccupation with men, weight, sex and fashion. *Does My Bum Look Big in This?* by Arabella Weir hit the big time in 1997, the year after *Bridget Jones's Diary* was published, and other successful chick lit titles include Jenny Colgan's *Talking to Addison*, and *Sushi for Beginners* by Marian Keys. For some, chick lit is postmodern feminism, and for 'serious' writers such as Doris Lessing and Beryl Bainbridge it is 'froth'. It is strange that they should be so dismissive of the phenomenon, because in many ways it is as old as the novel form itself. *Bridget Jones's Diary* is intertextually related to Jane Austen, especially *Pride and Prejudice*, and the actor who played the role of Mr Darcy in a 1990s television adaptation is one of Bridget's fantasy figures: the height of something postmodern is reached in the movie where the actor, Colin Firth, appears. Here is Bridget's diary on the morning of Valentine's Day, when she 'cannot believe' she is spending the day alone 'again', and other problems intrude:

8.45 a.m. Oh my God. Am £200 overdrawn. How? How? How?

8.50 a.m. You see. Something good comes out of everything. Have found weird cheque on statement for £149, which do not recognize. Convinced it is cheque that wrote out to dry-cleaner's for £14.90 or similar.

9 a.m. Rang up bank to see who it was to, and it was a 'Monsieur S. F. S.' Dry-cleaners are fraudsters. Will ring Jude, Shazzer, Rebecca, Tom and Simon telling them not to go to Duraclean any more.

9.30 a.m. Hah. Just went into Duraclean to check out 'Monsieur S.F.S.' under guise of taking little black silk nightie to be cleaned. Could not help remarking that staff of dry-cleaner's seemed to be not so much French but Indian. Maybe Indo-French, though.

'Could you tell me your name, please?' I said to the man as I handed in my nightie.

'Salwani,' he said smiling suspiciously nicely.

S. Hah!

'And your name?' he asked.

'Bridget.'

'Bridget. You write your address here, please, Bridget.'

You see that was very suspicious. Decided to put Mark Darcy's address as he has staff and burglar alarms.

'Do you know a Monsieur S.F.S.?' I said, at which the man became almost playful.

'No, but I think I am knowing you from somewhere,' he said.

'Don't think I don't know what's going on, 'I said, then shot out of the shop. You see. Am taking things into my own hands.

10 p.m. Cannot believe what has happened. At half past eleven, youth came into office bearing enormous bunch of red roses and brought them to my desk. Me! You should have seen the faces of Patchouli and Horrible Harold. Even Richard Finch was stunned into silence, only managing a pathetic, 'Sent them to ourself, did we?'

Helen Fielding, *Bridget Jones: The Edge of Reason*

'Froth' it is in some ways, and its moment may be a transitory one which will be forgotten in ten years – but that has always been true of popular novels with a feminine appeal: witness Dale Spender's recovery of more than a hundred female novelists, 'the mothers of the novel' who were writing before Jane Austen, but whose female-oriented works had been forgotten. In the Victorian Age George Eliot wrote a wonderful subversive and still very relevant essay called 'Silly Novels by Lady Novelists'. Women have always written for women – it is the outspokenness of the subject matter that is indicative of recent trends from the 1960s through the 1990s. Just as significant as this flourishing of chick lit is the fact that Sarah Kane's violent and controversial plays were being staged at exactly the same time.

'Chick lit' has been neatly and conveniently seen as a fashion statement in response to the kind of 'lad lit' of Nick Hornby, but is in fact much more than that. Affirmation and fun, sex and sushi, it takes Sylvia Plath's anxieties and makes them as comic as that other Fielding, Henry, made Tom Jones's sexual exploits 350 years before.

Meera Syal is slightly different: *Life Isn't All Ha Ha Hee Hee* (1999) looks at life through the eyes of North London Indian young women and is comic, social and sassy – a different perspective and range from the more serious (but enormously popular) novel on similar ethnic themes, Zadie Smith's *White Teeth*. Here a character who has in some ways 'escaped' reflects on 'her people' at an Indian wedding where she is trapped between two gossiping matrons:

> Tania leaned forward pointedly, hoping to obscure their view of each other and save herself another half-hour of homely wedding quips in stereo. But the women merely adjusted themselves around her, heaving bosoms into the crevices of her elbows. She suddenly remembered why she had stopped attending community events, cultural evenings, bring-a-Tupperware parties, all the engagements, weddings and funerals that marked out their borrowed time here. She could not take the proximity of everything any more. The endless questions of who what why she was, to whom she belonged (father/husband/Workplace), why her life wasn't following the ordained patterns for a woman of her age, religion, height and income bracket. The sheer physical effrontery of her people, wanting to be inside her head, to own her, claim her, preserve her. Her people.
>
> Tania checked her watch, angry at herself for hoping that the wedding might be running to schedule. Indian time. Look at the appointed hour and add another two for good measure.
>
> **Meera Syal, *Life Isn't All Ha Ha Hee Hee***

Again, television has played an important role in shaping perceptions and introducing new subject areas to a wide audience. Meera Syal herself has been closely involved with two comedy series which brought the English Indian family into the cultural mainstream: *Goodness Gracious Me* and *The Kumars at No. 42*.

Kathy Lette's novels are a kind of chick-Tom Sharpe: they are farcical, well observed, chick lit with a plot. *Girls' Night Out* (1988) may be said to have kick-started the subgenre. Her novels tend to have punning titles such as *Foetal Attraction* (1991) and *Altar Ego* (1998).

Mad Cows (1996) is full of funny one-liners and outrageous situations, from Harrods to Holloway Prison in one easy leap. It was filmed, but, unlike Helen Fielding's work, Kathy Lette's books have not yet transferred well to the screen.

AMIS TOO

The publication of Kingsley Amis's letters in 2000 coincided with the publication of the autobiographical work *Experience* by his son Martin, also a very successful novelist – the different attitudes of father and son illuminate many of the differences in their novels and in society towards the end of the twentieth century. Martin Amis is a quite different writer from his father, and the differences are more than simply generational: Martin Amis's language and subject matter are violent, reflecting the collapse of the established class system which the 'angry young men' of the 1950s could rail against. A parallel moral and spiritual violence in his novels has caused some shock – when his second novel *Dead Babies* (1975) was published in paperback, the publishers preferred to retitle it *Dark Secrets* in order not to cause offence. *London Fields* (1989) – its very title is paradoxically ironic – is an exploration of morality and murder in the television age: its central character Keith Talent may be seen as a symbol of the 1980s in the way Jim Dixon in *Lucky Jim* was of the 1950s: he is amoral, fascinated by television ('TV!' is his favourite adjective of praise), and prepared to do anything to achieve fame and fortune by appearing on television as a darts player.

> I sidled up, placed my coin on the glass (this is the pinball etiquette), and said, 'Let's play pairs.' In his face: a routine thrill of dread, then openness; then pleasure. I impressed him with my pinball lore: silent five, two-flip, shoulder-check, and so on. We were practically pals anyway, having both basked in the sun of Keith's patronage. And, besides, he was completely desperate, as many of us are these days. In a modern city, if you have nothing to do (and if you're not broke, and on the street), it's tough to find people to do nothing with.
>
> **Martin Amis, *London Fields***

City slang

Perhaps more than any other English-born novelist, Martin Amis has forged a 'new' language: going beyond 'old' language, using new rhythms, incorporating American English, street English and minority dialect Englishes, to give a representation of some of the range of Englishes spoken in England at the end of the twentieth century.

Different styles of language can reveal different facets of personality, and the various speaking styles of narrators, in particular, can reveal much about their attitudes and their ways of seeing. A distinctive speech style can also mark off a narrator or character from the position of the author, allowing a viewpoint to emerge which can be critical of the character, satirising the lifestyle which the character represents or allowing more ironic perceptions to emerge.

In the following extract from Martin Amis's novel *Money* (1984) the main character, John Self, is revealed through a distinctive use of contemporary slang, in this case a specifically urban speech style cultivated by the character who inhabits a world of decaying social and cultural fabrics:

> In LA, you can't do anything unless you drive. Now I can't do anything unless I drink. And the drink-drive combination, it really isn't possible out there. If you as much as loosen your seatbelt or drop your ash or pick your nose, then it's an Alcatraz autopsy with the questions asked later. Any indiscipline, you feel, any variation, and there's a bullhorn, a set of scope sights, and a coptered pig drawing a bead on your rug.

Slang words and phrases abound. 'Pig' is a term used for a policeman; 'rug' is American slang for a toupee; 'coptered' is a word derived from helicopter; 'drawing a bead' means to take aim and, in addition, we need to know that Alcatraz is a famous prison in San Francisco Bay in California.

The city slang in *Money* is used to create a sense of place which is both every metropolitan city and nowhere. John Self's speech is fast-paced, slick, witty, often obscene, and at the same time constitutes a kind of linguistic litter of easy joking phrases which matches the empty character of Self and the urban wasteland he inhabits. The urban decay is matched by a verbal decay in which communication beyond a small, knowing in-group is not seen to matter. Language becomes here an index of and mirror to the changing social and cultural contexts of modern metropolitan Britain.

Time's Arrow (1991) is an experiment in the backward narration of time, returning from the present to the Holocaust of the Second World War. Martin Amis is a daring experimenter in form, style and content, capable of shock and of clear-sighted social observation. *Money* (1984) and *Success* (1978) may now be seen as very revealing novels about the preoccupations of the me-generation 'yuppie' 1980s. Amis has said that one of his favourite themes is 'men doing each other down', and this reaches its high point in *The Information* (1995), where two novelists – one a popular success, the other an ambitious failure – are pitted against each other in their careers, relationships and destinies. He again broke new ground with *Night Train* (1997), which uses the police procedural novel as a framework for a serious examination of innocence and guilt, power and responsibility. *Heavy Water* (1998) is a collection of stories which shows the range of Amis's experimentation with language and themes. His memoir, *Experience*, published in 2000, is a fascinating document, often more revealing in what it does not say (for example, about his father and his marriages), than what it does. It discusses at length the trauma of the disappearance of his cousin in 1973. Twenty years later she was found to have been the victim of one of England's most famous mass murderers. As always, Amis uses his own experience to write very perceptively about his times, how experience has formed him, and by extension how society itself is changing: what Hamlet described as 'the form and pressure of the time'. In *Koba the Dread* (2002) Amis brings together the personal and the political in a way that few writers of the comfortable kind of literature Britain now produces and consumes dare to do. Subtitled 'Laughter and the Twenty Million', this is both a history of Stalinism in Russia and a personal memoir (of his father and of his sister's death, and of the fall of communism), as well as an indictment of the kind of intellectual complacency that has distinguished western attitudes to communism.

Like several other major writers Amis tackles the political issues of the day head on. Christopher Brookmyre and Iain Banks were among the first to use the events of September 11 2001 in their fiction. Amis uses the transforming nature of the attacks to fashion a transforming, surreal, almost comic novel – although being Amis, of course even the definition of what is comic is questioned. *Yellow Dog* (2003) contains a lot of recognisable Amis themes – masculinity, violence and aggrandisement, and the power of language, but expands the international scope of the work, and extends his range significantly, and of course, controversially.

Martin Amis's collected critical writings between 1971 and 2000 were published in 2002 under the perhaps surprising title *The War Against Cliché*. It gives us nearly thirty years' worth of posturing but elegant and stylish prose, full of wit and insight showing Amis's reactions to many of his contemporaries, such as Iris Murdoch and Angus Wilson, as well as many of the American writers he reveres, some of whom he also talked about in *Experience*. He admits that he has become kinder as he has matured: 'Enjoying being insulting is a youthful corruption of power.' He is an insightful critic, using language creatively and inventively, and selecting his evidence carefully: 'Quotation is the reviewer's only hard evidence' he says. In his dynamic critical attitudes Amis puts reading and writing into a vital symbiosis as part of modern cultural practice and life.

ONE OF THE LADS

The novels of Nick Hornby achieved great success, have become equally successful films, and in many ways are seen to embody the laddish male ethos of the 1990s embodied in the television series *Men Behaving Badly*, which derived from a novel of 1991 by Simon Nye. Hornby acknowledges both Martin Amis and Roddy Doyle as major influences on his writing and, in fact, these debts are visible in his works. All Hornby's main characters are men who are self-absorbed, if not self-obsessed. Their lists and obsessions become a kind of objective correlative, as revenge was for Hamlet, giving a spurious meaning to a life devoid of taxonomy. The obsessions take many forms: with football (*Fever Pitch*, 1992), with old records and lists (*High Fidelity*, 1995), with love life and paternity (*About a Boy*, 1998), and with changing the world (*How To Be Good*, 2001). Although his novels are witty and perceptive accounts of the concerns of 1990s England, they essentially also reflect the selfish individualism of what emerges more and more clearly as a rather sad and empty society. This moment in the record shop in *High Fidelity* is something of a classic:

> 'Have you got any soul?' a woman asks the next afternoon. That depends, I feel like saying; some days yes, some days no. A few days ago I was right out; now I've got loads, too much, more than I can handle. I wish I could spread it a bit more evenly, I want to tell her, get a better balance, but I can't seem to get it sorted. I can see she wouldn't be interested in my internal stock control problems though, I simply point to where I keep the soul I have, right by the exit, just next to the blues.
>
> **Nick Hornby, *High Fidelity***

Hornby describes his fiction as 'comedy of depression'. His characters are filling in the emptiness of their lives with their obsessions and passions, and seem to be loutish lads, unredeemable and, of course, unsympathetic to women. *How To Be Good* attempts to redress the balance with a female narrator, married to 'the angriest man in Holloway'. The conversion to altruism, like the mid-life crisis of the father in *About a Boy*, is a paradigm of the responsibility/irresponsibility, success/failure, fulfilment/emptiness dichotomies that Hornby uses as the basis of all his comedy.

Will Self has set himself up as something of an *enfant terrible* of modern letters. But now aged over 40, the coke-snorting iconoclast has to be judged on his writing rather than his TV image – and the novels, stories and satires stand up well. *Cock and Bull* (1992) is an archetypal satire in a long tradition going back to Swift and Sterne – a woman grows a penis and a man develops a vagina: a simple reversal of roles and equipment which allows the novelist plenty of scope for satirical observation of the rampant sexuality and greed of modern society. *My Idea of Fun*, his 'cautionary tale' of 1993, is one of the funniest books about the junk society. The stories in *Grey Area* and the raunchy but ultimately rather cynical and sad *Junk Male* (1995) may now be seen as among the sharpest observations of what was wrong with the greed society of the 1990s. Self's laboured modern retelling of Wilde's *The Picture of Dorian Gray*, called *Dorian: an Imitation* (2002), caused some controversy by rendering explicit some of the sex and drug-related possibilities of the original ('druggery and buggery' as the narrator calls it), much as the gay novel *Teleny*, fully published only in the new social climate of 1986, had opened up the specifically sexual aspects of the story Wilde very deliberately left to the original readers' imagination.

Voices and devolutions

Varieties of Scots have given great vitality and inventiveness to contemporary Scottish fiction, and writers have been generally successful in creating believable characters with their own clear identity who speak a created version of Scots which can be understood relatively readily by all readers of English. Such writers draw inspiration from a long history of Scots writing as well as from more recent models such as Lewis Grassic Gibbon in prose and Hugh MacDiarmid and William Soutar in poetry, and more recently Alasdair Gray, James Kelman and Irvine Welsh.

Writing such as this signals a kind of linguistic devolution to match the increasing political devolutions of the period with the establishment of Assemblies for Scotland and Wales in 1998 to 1999. Such writers as these, together with a large band of Irish writers, typified by Roddy Doyle and Bernard MacLaverty, would, however, doubtless argue that political devolutions are no more than developments with no real material consequences for the dispossessed and disempowered voices they write into their work. (See also Note on 'What is Standard, Who is Standard, What is English?', pp. 96–97.)

The state of Wales and Welsh provides a contrast, however. There are more distinct oppositions to the English language throughout Wales than there are in either Scotland or Ireland but this is due above all to the existence and the constant promotion of the Welsh language through the schools and institutions of the country. This situation has led furthermore to the development of writing in Welsh to the point where interrogation of English voices takes on much less significance than in other devolved and decentred contexts.

FLOWERS OF SCOTLAND

In recent years Alasdair Gray and James Kelman have contributed greatly to the revival of Scottish literature in the vernacular accents of Glasgow. Indeed the Irish novelist Colm Tóibín is on record as saying that 'only in Scotland (Kelman, Gray, Welsh,), and in the United States, has the true torch of modernism in fiction been carried'. Gray's *Lanark* (1981) was one of the great fictional works of the 1980s, and has established its lasting reputation as one of the texts of the times. It is partly magic realism, partly social fantasy, perhaps best described as a phantasmagoria of writing and illustration, as outrageous as Blake, as inventive as Rushdie. Gray's later work can be equally zany, or, as in *Janine 1982* (1984), fairly straightforward story-telling. The prize-winning *Poor Things* (1992) looks at the medical profession in Victorian Scotland, and provides a comic critique of the age. The author himself describes it as 'the funniest book I have ever written'. He then goes on to say: 'it's also the most socialist, really . . . but people don't need to notice that.'

Gray's *Mavis Belfrage* (1996) continues his idiosyncratic progress with a series of stories linked by themes of alienation and loss of identity. Gray, as ever, provides his own cover design and page embellishments, making the presence of the creative writer evident at all stages of the book's production. He has given considerable impetus to a new wave of Scottish writing which put Glasgow, and to a lesser extent Edinburgh, very much on the literary map of writing in the 1990s. His language is Scottish English, and his concerns are both realistic (social problems, unemployment) and artistic (the nature of creative endeavour, critical attitude, the role of the artist). *A History Maker* (1994) moves into the future of Scottish history, telling a story of border wars in 2220, echoing and subverting the kind of official Scottish history found in the novels of Sir Walter Scott from the nineteenth century.

The vitality and humour of Gray are found in many of the new generation of Scottish writers. Janice Galloway and Alison (A.L.) Kennedy have brought women's voices fully to the forefront of the recent flourishing of Scottish writing. Galloway, in *The Trick Is to Keep Breathing* (1989), uses her own training to describe vividly the mind of a woman living alone in a state of psychological collapse. In *Female Friends* (1994) her two heroines travel abroad (to France) in a search for adventure, reality and friendship. Galloway's short stories, in *Blood* (1991) and *Where You Find It* (1996), range through a spectrum of experience, often with undertones of psychological violence. A.L. Kennedy's stories, in *Night Geometry and the Garscadden Trains* (1990) and *Now That You're Back* (1994), share this undercurrent of violence and social concern. Her first novel, *Looking for the Possible Dance* (1993), is a narrative of a train journey from Glasgow to London (literal and metaphorical references to trains recur in modern Scottish writing – perhaps because there seem to be fewer and fewer of them but also perhaps as a reversal of the positive images of trains as emblems of progress in the mid-Victorian novel). The journey is also one of memory, of the heroine's relationships and hopes for the future. The climax is among the most violent in modern writing. *So I Am Glad* (1995), a further collection of stories, *Original Bliss* (1998), a short novel widely acclaimed as her best, and a documentary book on the controversial subject of bullfighting have continued to keep Alison Kennedy at the forefront of recent Scottish writing. *Everything You Need* (1999) is a novel very much of, for and about the 1990s. It is an ambitious, long and very involving year-by-year depiction of its hero's painful search for, or rediscovery of, love. *Indelible Acts* (2002) is a collection of interlinked stories on her favourite theme of the longing for love.

This is a complete chapter from *Looking for the Possible Dance*, giving us the train journey and the mix of voices of a casual encounter:

It's odd in the train without James. The carriage windows seem to have run out of countryside and Margaret watches one dull town smirr into another.

When they pass into sun the graffiti she sees by the track is unfamiliar, definitely English now. A foreign country opens ahead and then closes behind her and she can imagine the white light on the lines, pushing all the way to London on her behalf.

A thick black marker pen was left on James's seat. Now it is in Margaret's pocket; something she feels will keep to remind her of a friend.

DIFFRENT

'Yes, but I still don't understand that.'

NO ME

'How can you not be you?'

EASY

'Actually, now you say it, yes, I do it all the time.'

NOW?

'No, not now.'

?

'Because – '

???

'Alright, alright. Because it's different on trains. I was told. Worries on board and off they go without you. They go on ahead, or in the guard's van or something. I was told. I mean, you can relax here – this isn't anywhere. Whatever happens outside, there's nothing we can do about it right now. and you meet people that – '

. Margaret remembers that she stopped herself from saying they were people you would never see again; that it didn't matter what you told them. She wanted to see James again. That was important.

PEOPLE CAN TALK TO

She had the impression he wrote that very quickly, as if he were hurrying to save her from embarrassment. The way a friend would.

PEOPLE CAN TALK TO

'Yes. You meet people you can talk to and be yourself with. Not often, but you do. Are you yourself now?'

YES NO PILLS NO JAGS ALL MEEEE

'One-hundred percent James Watt. I'm honoured.'

FUC

'Away you go. You should learn to take compliments better, then you'll get more.'

FUC WON HUNNER PERCEN MEEEEEE

Which was all that seemed to matter at the time. She hopes no one manages to change that.

A.L. Kennedy, *Looking for the Possible Dance*

Jackie Kay is a Scottish poet of Nigerian descent whose first novel *Trumpet* (1998) won several prizes. It is the story of a female musician who pretended to be a man, and the consequences for her wife and son. Questions of gender and identity, family and social recognition are handled with finesse. Here the wife is coping with the bureaucratic aspects of the funeral of her partner:

Mohammad did not even have to impose his moment on this woman. The woman took it for herself, completely aware of the significance of the certificate. That woman would not take his lovely handwriting for granted. She would be happy she had a beautiful death certificate. He did not want it spoiled. He said nothing to her. He dipped his marbled fountain pen in the black Indian ink and wrote the name *Joss Moody* on the death certificate. He wrote the date. He paused before he ticked 'female' on the death certificate, then handed the pen to her; it was as if the pen was asking her to dance. She took the pen carefully and looked at it, twirling it around slowly as she did so. Then she wrote her name in the registrar's entries of deaths book on the anointed line. She looked as if she was praying as she wrote. He looked over to see if her writing was as lovely as he was expecting it to be. It was; she had a beautiful hand.

The woman smiled at him. The intimacy between them had been like love. Mohammad would miss her. She said, 'Thank you' to him. She put her certificate and official papers in the Please Do Not Bend envelope that she had brought with her. She paid the fee for her own copy of the death certificate which she looked at before putting it away, as if to check that everything was all right. She picked up her brown leather handbag, putting the strap over her shoulder. She said, 'Thank you, thank you', opened his door and closed it quietly behind her.

Jackie Kay, *Trumpet*

Ali Smith is also Scottish, and is a very adventurous writer. Her first volume of stories was called *Free Love* (1995) and was followed by a novel, *Like* (1997) and the gloriously entitled volume *Other Stories and Other Stories* in 1999. It was her complex, rich, allusive and strange novel *Hotel World* (2001) which finally brought her to a wide readership: it was nominated for both the Orange Prize for Fiction and the Booker Prize.

It follows five characters in and around the Global Hotel, somewhere in northern England. It is a self-contained world which is 'not functioning properly', and thus can easily become a metaphor for a wider society. But that would be to simplify it, because this is a novel which plays with modern literary theory, with concepts such as 'story' and 'character' and with perceptions, with reality and illusion, with reading and seeing, in ways which pioneers like John Fowles were experimenting with in the 1960s and which are now coming to be seen more widely in all kinds of fiction. There is a journalist with a broken PowerBook, which nicely echoes Jeanette Winterson's novel *The.Powerbook* and has possible echoes too of the completely different sister novel *Hotel du Lac* by Anita Brookner. Ali Smith is very aware of her sources and her echoes, and revels in wordplay while having the confidence to tackle big political and social themes. She is a writer of otherness in every sense: fractured language, fractured fictional devices, fractured realities, go, in the postmodern world of fiction, to make up new realities. Some readers find this difficult, others have found it stimulating. Here is a sample of how *Hotel World* tells its 'story' – her use of a variation on the diary form is quite different from Helen Fielding's:

> **The clock on the computer:** The clock is at present running 12.33 seconds ahead of GMT.
>
> The computer can provide information on hotel guests, staff, international tariffs and more general Global matters. It lists in its staff files (to which only certain members of staff have access) the payment details and home addresses of all members of the Global staff, including those of Joyce Davies, chambermaid, who lives at 27 Vale Rise, Wordsworth Estate, and will first thing tomorrow morning be fired from this branch of Global Hotels by Mrs Bell, who believes (having been assured first by Lynda Alexander and Lise

O'Brien, day and evening shift Reception, that Room12 has been unoccupied) that Davies has neglected to attend to Room 12 over a period of two days and is therefore directly or indirectly to blame, in the absence of any responsible hotel guest, for damage caused to the hotel by a bath left to overflow. The cost of damages, £373.90 for replacement and drying, will be removed from Davies's final pay-check.

Lise, behind Reception, is at work: There she is, Lise, behind Reception, at work. The lobby is empty.

In a moment, she will glance at the clock on the computer and see the moment when the number changes on it, from a 1 to a 2. She will be pleased to see it happen. It will feel meant.

That was then. This was now.

Lise was lying in bed. She was falling. There wasn't any story like the one you've just read, or at least, if there was, she hadn't remembered it. All of the above had been un-remembered; it was sunk somewhere, half in, half out of sand at the bottom of a sea. Weeds wavered over it. Small stragglers from floating shoals of fish darted in and out of it open-mouthed, breathing water.

Ali Smith, *Hotel World*

'THAS THI TRUBL': NEW SCOTTISH ENGLISH

Jeff Torrington's *Swing Hammer Swing!* (1992), set in the poorest area of Glasgow, the Gorbals, attracted a lot of attention, and has been talked of as the ultimate Glasgow novel, 'doing for Glasgow what Joyce did for Dublin'. One of the recurring phrases in the novel caught on in a big way, as it gives a local slant on one of the big multi-cultural presences in the modern world: 'Disney exist' in Glasgow dialect means 'it doesn't exist'. Torrington followed this, his first novel, one that was some thirty years in the writing, with *The Devil's Carousel* in 1996.

James Kelman's novels are unrelentingly naturalistic pictures of inner-city desolation, portrayed with a vivid humour and empathy. *The Bus Conductor Hines* (1984) was his first success, and *A Disaffection* (1989), about the frustration of a man on the edge of middle age, enjoyed wide acclaim. *Not Not While the Giro* (1983) is a collection of stories, which was followed by a second collection, *The Burn* (1991). Kelman's *How Late It Was, How Late* (1994) won the Booker Prize, and that achievement perhaps marked the arrival of the Glasgow novel. It is a long monologue, famously full of violent, vernacular language which depicts the despair of one of society's victims, Sammy. Close to Beckett's novels in style, it has also evoked comparison with Kafka in its picture of frustration; but the music and humour of the language raise it from despair into an affirmation of survival, despite all the odds.

The Good Times (1998) explored this masculine working-class voice further, with twenty first-person monologues covering all sorts and ages of masculinity. In a post-feminist age, Kelman is one of the few writers giving voice to the formerly excluded, ill-educated, marginalised male. The theme is continued in *Translated Accounts* (2001), where the style of the novel is deliberately compressed, ironed out, an experiment in finding a new 'translation' of fictional language that is both challenging and rewarding. Kelman's collected journalism and essays, *And the Judges Said . . .* (2002), are full of political passion and a necessary scepticism about the society he grew up in and now lives in and writes about. He is consistently good on how censorship continues to flourish in various disguises in the superficially tolerant and liberal modern world: his own works' use of taboo words has led to several hilarious confrontations with the media. Righteous anger is very much a part of his non-fiction, as it is in the voices of the characters in his fiction.

Irvine Welsh's novel *Trainspotting* (1993) achieved huge popularity and cult status (also as a play and film) in the mid-1990s, despite being written in broad Edinburgh (Leith) dialect (noticeably different from Kelman's Glaswegian). It is about a group of drug addicts, their pain and pleasure, and owes a great deal of its success to its accurate and sympathetic depiction of the concerns of a disaffected generation.

> Whin the auld man shot the craw, ah managed tae cajole ma Ma intae giein us a couple ay her valium. She wis oan them fir six months after Davie died. The thing is, because she kicked them, she now regards hersel as an expert oan drug rehabilitation. This is smack, fir fuck's sake, mother dear.

I am tae be under house arrest.

The morning wisnae pleasant, but it wis a picnic compared tae the efternin. The auld man came back fae his fact-finding mission. Libraries, health-board establishments and social-work offices had been visited. Research hud been undertaken, advice hud been sought, leaflets procured.

He wanted tae take us tae git tested fir HIV. Ah don't want tae go through aw that shite again.

Ah git up fir ma tea, frail, bent and brittle as ah struggle doon the stairs. Every move makes ma blood soar tae ma throbbing heid. At one stage ah thought that it wid just burst open, like a balloon, sending blood, skull fragments and grey matter splattering oantae Ma's cream woodchip.

The auld girl sticks us in the comfy chair by the fire in front ay the telly, and puts a tray oan ma lap. Ah'm convulsing inside anyway, but the mince looks revolting.

– Ah've telt ye ah dinnae eat meat Ma, ah sais.

– Ye eywis liked yir mince n tatties. That's whair ye've gone wrong son, no eating the right things. Ye need meat.

Now there is apparently a causal link between heroin addiction and vegetarianism.

– It's good steak mince. Ye'll eat it, ma faither says. This is fuckin ridiculous. Ah thought there and then about making for the door, even though ah'm wearing a tracksuit and slippers. As if reading ma mind, the auld man produces a set ay keys.

– The door stays locked. Ah'm fittin a lock oan yir room as well.

– This is fuckin fascism, ah sais, wi feelin.

Irvine Welsh, *Trainspotting*

Welsh's later works, *The Acid House* (1994), *Marabou Stork Nightmares* (1995) and *Ecstasy* (1996) continue in a similar vein but with a broader range of locales and experiences. *Marabou Stork Nightmares* takes the reader inside the mind of a man in a coma. It relates his experiences and recollections from childhood in Scotland and South Africa through sexual and drug-related traumas to a conclusion of considerable ambiguity between life and death, and between past, present and future. *Filth* (1998) is about police corruption in Edinburgh and is in many ways a parody of the successful detective novels of Ian Rankin, which are also set in that city. *Filth* was not well received, perhaps because of its unsympathetic leading character. *Glue* (2001) returned to the territory of *Trainspotting* and brought Welsh back to what he does best. The glue represents the ties that bind four young men growing up in deprived circumstances in Edinburgh, and the novel is humane and very funny, using again the balance of dialect and standard language for comic effect and for sharp social satire. Two of the characters from *Trainspotting*, Begbie and Renton, make brief appearances. *Porno* (2002) again reunites several of these characters ten years on, as they try one last chance at avoiding the failure that has beset them – returning to Edinburgh and making pornographic movies. It is a multi-voiced novel, giving an insight into disillusion, not only with the drug culture, but with the perceived failures of capitalism as a system.

In the introduction to the theatrical adaptation of *Trainspotting*, which was highly successful, Welsh says that his writing is informed by the belief that 'the deliberate fostering of political, social and economic inequities (has) altered our various cultures in Britain. . . . The increasing marginalisation and criminalisation of people by the state has resulted in the development of a particular "alternative" culture and attendant sub-cultures. These cultures are now no longer the preserve of a bohemian few.' In many ways Welsh tries to encapsulate in his novels the experience of alienation of the younger generation of the 1980s and 1990s, with its concomitant democratisation of an indie culture which purports to be independent and outside the system. This is perhaps why his novels have achieved some kind of cult status, although their commercial success and exploitation has been enormous, from the Edinburgh Fringe to London's West End, on to Hollywood and back again. Cults often go out of fashion quicker than they came in, but Irvine Welsh's graphic use of demotic language marks a significant broadening of the scope of local English in the context of a new generation of writers and new subject matter. Like many writers before him, he forges a new English for the stories he has to tell.

Iain Banks is also a prolific Scottish novelist with a wide range of styles and subjects, from science-fiction to pop. *Espedair Street* (1987) is one of the very few novels to use the world of pop music successfully to examine modern solitude, success and values. *The Wasp Factory*

(1984) is an obsessive fantasy which aroused both critical revulsion and acclaim. *Feersum Endjinn* (1994) continues Banks's fantastic vein, using a wonderful kind of Scots Internet language which works phonetically: 'Thas thi trubl wif sparos; they got a veri limitid tenshun span & r inclind 2 go witterin on 4 ages b4 they get 2 thi poynt, always flutterin off @ tanjints. . . .'

The Crow Road (1992) became very successful on television – again it is a story of modern Scotland. *The Business* (1999) is a wide-ranging story about the power of money and business, and *Looking to Westward* (2000) marks a return to his favoured science-fiction mode, and *Dead Air* (2002) takes its place as one of the first novels that is a serious reaction to 11 September 2001.

George Mackay Brown's novels were set largely in his native Orkney Islands, the birthplace also of Edwin Muir, and are concerned with the lives of the fishing people in Hamnavoe, which is Stromness. *Greenvoe* (1972) is a novel which anticipates the late twentieth-century concern with the environment, examining the effects on an island community of industrial invasion and exploitation, then the abandonment of what was an idyllic society. *Beside the Ocean of Time* (1994), a story of a Viking boy who is reborn in several centuries, was nominated for the Booker Prize. Mackay Brown was also a poet and short-story writer, and was influenced and encouraged by Muir, but, unlike him, decided to return to his native islands for his inspiration. *Magnus* (1973) goes into the history of the islands, showing the influences of folklore, the Norse sagas, history and legend in the culture of one of the northernmost areas of British culture.

Allan Massie is one of the liveliest Scottish novelists writing today. His range has covered Ancient Rome in *Augustus* (1986) and *Tiberius* (1987), Scottish history in the John Buchan mode in *The Hanging Tree* (1990), and novels which explore the related themes of guilt and responsibility in the context of the Second World War, *The Sins of the Father* (1991) and *A Question of Loyalties* (1989). *Change and Decay In All Around I See* (1978) is a very indicative title, given the preoccupations of a lot of modern fiction.

THE CONTEMPORARY IRISH NOVEL

Brian Moore is of an earlier generation. His early novels, such as *The Lonely Passion of Judith Hearne* (1955), are set in Belfast and *The Emperor of Ice-Cream* (1965) uses the bombing of that city as its background. Moore moved to Canada, then to California, and his later works exploit similar tensions on a more international scale. *I Am Mary Dunne* (1968) uses Molly Bloom's monologue in *Ulysses* as a starting point for a woman's search for her true identity, and *Catholics* (1972) shows the author's constant concern with problems of Catholicism. Moore's *The Colour of Blood* (1987) is set in an imaginary 'Eastern bloc' country with a cardinal as the central character. With David Lodge, Moore is one of the few writers to explore the subject of Catholicism in the modern world throughout his work. He returned to an Irish setting with *Lies of Silence* (1993).

Bernard MacLaverty's novel of the Northern Ireland troubles, *Cal* (1983), reached a wide readership and became a successful film. *Lamb* (1980) starts off in a monastery off the Irish coast, but then Brother Lamb escapes to England with one of his 12-year-old charges. Much of MacLaverty's writing uses the perspective of childhood and young adulthood to examine rites of passage and adult experience. *Grace Notes* (1997) was also widely acclaimed. It and the poet Seamus Deane's moving novel of growing up in Ireland, *Reading in the Dark* (1996), were both nominated for the Booker Prize.

William Trevor is a writer from Ireland whose stories, *The News from Ireland* (1986), return frequently to Ireland, but their subject matter is loneliness, love and loss, rather than a concentration of specifically Irish problems. Trevor's novel *Fools of Fortune* (1983) achieves a similar balance of sympathy to Bowen's classic pre-war Irish novel *The Last September* (1929), moving the story backwards and forwards in time to show the period of the Troubles, and its consequences more than half a century later. Of Trevor's later novels on these themes, *Felicia's Journey* (1994) is probably the best known. It won the Whitbread Prize and became a successful film. It tells the story of a young Irish girl who has been abandoned by the father of her child – her journey is the search to try to find him in England. *Death in Summer* (1998) is a novel about the return of figures from the past and their influence on the present.

His 2002 novel *The Story of Lucy Gault* is one of his most acclaimed, and made the Booker Prize list, his first to do so since *Reading Turgenev*, from *Two Lives* in 1991. It is typical Trevor territory, looking back to the Ireland of the early 1920s through the eyes of its young heroine.

John McGahern's first new novel in twelve years, the wonderfully titled *That They May Face the Rising Sun* (2002), brought back to notice one of the most characteristic of Irish fictional voices. A gentle, happy story set in County Leitrim and full of gossip, talk and character, it is a year in the life of a community and, like all McGahern's work, is deceptive in its simplicity, and ultimately profound and moving in its depiction of aspirations, dreams and failures. McGahern's first novel was *The Barracks* (1963), which established his territory of village life contrasting with the outside world. His second novel *The Dark* (1965) was banned for several years by the Catholic Church as 'indecent and obscene', but *Amongst Women* achieved widespread recognition and made the 1990 Booker Prize list. It is a deceptively gentle piece, set in Monaghan, again aiming towards a balance of happiness. *The Pornographer* (1979) is something of a classic, its hero being a writer of pornography who, of course, cannot get his own love life in order. McGahern's are novels of equilibrium and the difficulty of reaching it. His *Collected Stories* (1992) are among the best from Ireland in recent years. McGahern's influence on writers such as Conor McPherson (*The Weir*) is clear – in many ways he could be representative of a certain kind of perceived Irishness, unworldly, soft-spoken, humane, easy to undervalue in its impact.

For many critics, John Banville is the major Irish novelist currently writing. His novels tend not to be easy reading, and his subject matter is often immensely intellectual, but few novelists write with such care, elegance and intelligence. *The Book of Evidence* (1989) was shortlisted for the Booker Prize and is possibly his most accessible novel. It uses the crime genre with great technical assurance in the slow revelation of its hero/speaker's soul. *The Newton Letter* is a short *tour de force* of historical imagining. *Ghosts* (1993) is a mysterious and disturbing tale of guilty souls on an anonymous island. *Athena* (1995) is a Dublin novel of art and passion. Every Banville novel breaks new ground, takes risks, and experiments with form and content, always in stunningly elegant and well-rhythmed prose. *Eclipse* (2000) heralded a new departure: Banville's current work tends to be looking back, a mature artistic hero assessing his life and coming to terms with his ghosts. In his atmospheric new novel *Shroud* (2002) secrets are again catching up with the hero, past is meeting present after many years, and the city of Turin gives the novel its context and title.

Colm Tóibín has emerged as a major novelist, with a range of subjects which takes him from his native Ireland as far as Argentina and Spain. His first novel *The South* (1990) explored love and loss between Spain and rural Ireland. It opens up Tóibín's particular area of concern – human emotional identity and the courage of the affirmation of that identity. He uses religion, sexuality and historical memory as the background to an increasing body of work, from *The Heather Blazing* (1992) through *The Story of the Night* (1997) to *The Blackwater Lightship* (1999), which was also Booker nominated. The range of Tóibín's writing is wide – he has written vivid journalistic examinations of the Irish problem, and more recently a book about the city of Barcelona, *Homage to Barcelona*.

The voice of Ireland and, in particular, working-class Dublin has reached a worldwide audience through the works of Roddy Doyle. His novels are bleakly comic descriptions of working-class life in Dublin and are told frequently through conversations. *The Commitments* (1988) is about a white band trying to make its name singing black American music; *The Snapper* (1990) is about the Rabbitte family's reactions to a daughter's pregnancy; and *The Van* (1991) is about a 'mobile' chip-shop van as a solution to the problem of unemployment. These novels, known as the Barrytown Trilogy – from the area of Dublin in which they are set – were all made into successful films.

The comic tone takes on a more serious note in *Paddy Clarke Ha Ha Ha* (1993) which won the Booker Prize, and *The Woman Who Walked Into Doors* (1996). Paddy Clarke is a 10-year-old schoolboy and the story follows his own views of his parents' marital breakup – it is close to Nick Hornby's later novel *About a Boy* in its perceptions, but rather more powerful in its impact: it would not make a successful Hollywood movie, as did the Hornby novel. In *The Woman Who Walked Into Doors*, the story is told by a semi-literate alcoholic woman, Paula Spencer, and traces her own marital difficulties. At the end her husband turns out to be a murderer as well as a wife-beater.

Doyle's huge popular success has also brought controversy: he is accused of being uncompromisingly negative about lower-class life in Ireland, but his social observation, authentic dialogue and portrayal of modern Irish humour in increasingly desperate circumstances mark him out as the true successor of Sean O'Casey and Flann O'Brien. A *Star Called Henry* (1999) marked a change of direction for Doyle. It is a historical examination of the Irish fight for independence in the early years of the twentieth century – it is the first of a projected trilogy. In the meantime he has written a detailed and vivid memoir of his parents' life in Dublin in *Rory and Ita* (2002).

Titles of the times

The titles of the earliest novels written in English are designed to suggest a certain solidity. The names of people predominate; for example, *Tom Jones*, *Joseph Andrews*, *Roderick Random*, *Moll Flanders* all indicate the writer's attempt to blur a distinction between fiction and real-life biography at a time when there were suspicions that a novel was merely something invented, a fiction or romance which need not be taken seriously. Similarly, the names of 'real' places serve as titles, reflecting a not dissimilar realist pretension to truth; for example, *Mansfield Park*, *Wuthering Heights*, *Cranford*, *Middlemarch*. As moral concerns come increasingly to the fore, so the titles signal the seriousness of the issues which the novelist sets out to explore; for example, *Sense and Sensibility*, *Pride and Prejudice*.

By contrast, Modernist writers generally prefer titles which are more oblique and symbolic and which require an act of interpretation from the reader. They do not always provide the reader with any definite anchor in recognisably realistic people and places; for example, *Ulysses*, *The Rainbow*, *Heart of Darkness*, *To The Lighthouse*.

In the titles of a number of post-war British novels another trend may be seen. Some titles carry a clearly marked imprint of the speaking voice. The voice may or may not be that of the author, suggesting in turn that the author's voice may only be one among several voices in the novel and may not necessarily be the most authoritative or the one which offers a secure and stable vantage point. The voice may also not represent the moral centre from which the world of the novel can be interpreted. Here are some typical titles from this period:

An Awfully Big Adventure (1990) Beryl Bainbridge
How Late It Was, How Late (1994) James Kelman
Now That You're Back (1994) A.L. Kennedy
Take A Girl Like You (1960) Kingsley Amis
You Can't Do Both (1994) Kingsley Amis
Ginger, You're Barmy (1962) David Lodge
How Far Can You Go? (1980) David Lodge
Burning Your Boats (1995) Angela Carter
A Far Cry From Kensington (1988) Muriel Spark
What a Carve Up! (1994) Jonathan Coe

The titles are marked stylistically by features which recur more frequently in spoken than in written discourse. Personal pronouns, in particular, set up a more direct tone of involvement and the use of imperatives and interrogatives explicitly establishes dialogue and interaction with the reader. Titles such as these also draw, however, on formulaic, idiomatic phrases ('a far cry from . . .'; 'burn your boats') and everyday spoken lexis ('barmy', 'awfully big', 'a carve up') in ways which suggest a direct and evaluative tone of voice. It is not immediately clear where the voice is coming from and a point of view cannot be established easily. Such voices are, however, deliberately intrusive and are a little unsettling.

More recently still, some titles have been constructed from present participles or from single dependent clauses with no main clause, conveying greater expressions of tentativeness. Titles such as *Looking for the Possible Dance* (1993) and *So I Am Glad* (1995) by A.L. Kennedy, *That They May Face The Rising Sun* by John McGahern (2002) and *If Nobody Speaks Of Remarkable Things* (2002) by Jon McGregor convey a sense of events which are ongoing but incomplete. They contrast even more sharply with the greater certainty and definiteness of the eighteenth and

nineteenth centuries and are in their own way also unsettling. Titles such
as these do not seek to lead readers, leaving them with greater semantic
space within which to make their own interpretations and to find their own
endings and outcomes.

THE WORLD SONG, I AM!

Bruce Chatwin was very much an outsider. A traveller both in the
physical and spiritual sense, he explores regions of the world and of
human sensibility which other writers never even approached. His
best works are evocations of travel with the heightened response of
the imaginative writer, as in *The Viceroy of Ouidah* (1980), based
on the slave-trade in Dahomey (Benin), and *In Patagonia* (1977) which
continues the long tradition of the voyage of wonder started by
Mandeville in the fourteenth century. Chatwin's novels *On the Black
Hill* (1982), set in the Wales associated more closely with the poetry
of R. S. Thomas, and *Utz* (1988), set in eastern Europe, are studies of
resilience and survival, a theme which resonates through *The Songlines*
(1987), which traces the invisible pathways of aboriginal culture in
Australia.

> Trade means friendship and co-operation; and for the Aboriginal the principal
> object of trade was song. Song, therefore, brought peace. Yet I felt the
> Songlines were not necessarily an Australian phenomenon, but universal:
> that they were the means by which man marked out his territory, and so
> organized his social life. All other successive systems were variants – or
> perversions – of this original model.
>
> The main Songlines in Australia appear to enter the country from the
> north or the north-west – from across the Timor Sea or the Torres Strait – and
> from there weave their way southwards across the continent. One has the
> impression that they represent the routes of the first Australians – and that they
> have come from *somewhere else.*
>
> How long ago? Fifty thousand years? Eighty or a hundred thousand years?
> The dates are insignificant compared to those from African prehistory.

> And here I must take a leap into faith: into regions I would not expect anyone to follow. I have a vision of the Songlines stretching across the continents and ages; that wherever men have trodden they have left a trail of song (of which we may, now and then, catch an echo); and that these trails must reach back, in time and space, to an isolated pocket in the African savannah, where the First Man opening his mouth in defiance of the terrors that surrounded him, shouted the opening stanza of the World Song, 'I AM!'
>
> **Bruce Chatwin, *The Songlines***

Chatwin was a nomad himself, and fascinated by nomads; a wanderer who questioned modern society in a way that is quite different from other writers. His early death, in 1989, meant that his selection of essays and reflections in *What Am I Doing Here?* (1989) became the last testament of this adventurer and romantic's lifelong 'search for the miraculous'. The myth of Chatwin has continued to grow, with the publication of a volume of 'uncollected writings', *Anatomy of Restlessness*, in 1996, and of an excellent full-scale biography by the novelist Nicholas Shakespeare in 1999. More than any other writer, Chatwin used his travels to the remotest parts of the globe as a means to search for the truths of humanity, *pre-* as well as post-Darwin. A writer such as Bruce Chatwin actually blurs the distinction between fiction and non-fiction, between oral story-telling traditions and modern scientific discourse.

Like Chatwin, Angela Carter was a genre bender: her essays, stories and novels are all-encompassing in their verve, imagination and polemic. Like many modern (or, indeed, postmodern) writers, she had a great fondness for the intertextuality that pastiche and a wide range of allusions permit. *The Magic Toyshop* (1967), one of the very first magic realist novels in English, was her earliest success: it uses myth and magic to tell the story of a young girl's sexual awakening, and the ruining of her mother's carefully preserved wedding dress. Death and destruction, magic and creativity coexist in this world. Angela Carter brings together magic realism, postmodernism, feminism, the Gothic, the real and the surreal. If that all seems a heady mixture, let the final paragraphs of her last novel – *Wise Children* (1991) – speak for her: the twins Dora and Nora Chance (the Chances, illegitimate daughters of Melchior Hazard) celebrate with their own double offspring.

> We put our handbags in the pram, for safety's sake. Then and there, we couldn't wait, we broke into harmony, we serenaded the new arrivals:
> 'We can't give you anything but love, babies,
> That's the only thing we've plenty of, babies –'
> The window on the second-floor front window of 41 Bard Road went up, a head came out. Dreadlocks. That Rastafarian.
> 'You two, again,' he said.
> 'Have a heart!' we said. 'We've got something to celebrate, tonight!'
> 'Well, you just watch it, in case a squad car comes by,' he said. 'Drunk in charge of a baby carriage, at your age.'
> We'd got so many songs to sing to our babies, all our old songs, that we didn't pay him any attention. 'Gee, we'd like to see you looking swell, babies!' and the Hazard theme song, 'Is You Is or Is You Ain't'. Then there were songs from the show that nobody else remembers. '2b or not 2b', 'Hey nonny bloody no', 'Mistress Mine', and Broadway tunes, and paper moons, and lilacs in the spring, again. We went on dancing and singing. 'Diamond bracelets Woolworths doesn't sell.' Besides, it was our birthday, wasn't it, we'd got to sing them the silly old song about Charlie Chaplin and his comedy boots all the little kids were singing and dancing in the street the day we were born. There was dancing and singing all along Bard Road that day and we'll go on singing and dancing until we drop in our tracks, won't we, kids.
> What a joy it is to dance and sing!

Angela Carter, *Wise Children*

The death of Angela Carter in 1992 robbed modern writing of one of its major and most distinctive figures. Feminist and iconoclastic, humorous and passionate, her writing ranges from the retelling of fables in *The Bloody Chamber* (1979) to extravagant magic realism in *Nights at the Circus* (1984); from a disturbing examination of love, in *Love* (1971), to the battle between reason and emotion in *The Infernal Desire Machine of Doctor Hoffman* (1972). Her novels illustrate her range and daring, as characters change sex, grow wings, move between reality and fantasy, and explore beyond the range of normal human experience. Her short stories were collected posthumously in *Burning Your Boats* (1995). Like many of her contemporaries, Angela Carter looked back to the traditions which inform all story-telling, and rewrote the history of our own times in her own style.

Drama and the novel have expanded and developed over the decades in terms of language, scope, voices and subject-matter. In the final chapter poetry will be seen to have had its movements too, from 'the Movement' through as many parallel strands as its sister genres, always with the individual voices speaking out in the most personal, as well as very public ways.

CHAPTER 5

Poetry

Old pasts, new presents

IN MY END . . .

The 1960s was a new beginning in many ways, but of the poets who were writing, some were nearing the end of their careers, and some had just started.

John Betjeman was particularly popular as a poet and a public figure; he had been popular since the late 1940s, but it was in the early 1960s that he became a best-seller and a television star. A passionate defender of Victorian architecture and heritage, on which he broadcast frequently, he wrote witty poetry which had wide public appeal and dealt with everyday subjects (for example, 'Sudden Illness at the Bus-Stop') with sympathy and concern. He came to be identified as a representative cultured middle-brow voice, perhaps the last voice of the past, just as the raucous, younger, sexier voices of the present were beginning to make themselves heard. His verse autobiography *Summoned by Bells* (1960) became a best-seller and was followed by his *Collected Poems* (1962). There is an underlying melancholy in Betjeman's best work which relates him closely to Philip Larkin, who was one of his greatest admirers, and in many ways his successor in the depiction of modern urban life.

The 1950s was known as the decade when the 'angry young man' first appeared in novels and plays; poetry also took on a new tone with a group which came to be known as The Movement. Although it was short-lived, and was never very homogeneous as a group, its aim to liberate poetry of high-flown Romanticism and bring it down to earth may be seen to have been realised in the work (most notably) of Philip Larkin, and of Donald Davie, D.J. Enright and Elizabeth Jennings.

It was a female poet rather than an angry young man who gave the key to the perceptions that were to become the taste of the times: A *Way of Looking* (1955) by Elizabeth Jennings contains in its title something of what the group represented – a different way of perceiving the world – but she cannot really be grouped with the others. Most of her poetry is of personal suffering and struggle, rather than the detached, slightly ironic writing of the more socially acute poets such as Larkin. Her *Collected Poems* was published in 1987, and that volume was followed by *Familiar Spirits* (1994) and *Praises* (1998). A devout Catholic, she was a glowing example of the mystical and religious traditions of English poetry. *New and Collected Poems* (2002) show her lyric gift and her graceful range over such diverse, and often unfashionable, genres as the love elegy and the verse epistle.

Norman MacCaig, a Scot, wrote in English, unlike some of his contemporaries who used Gaelic, or experimented with Scots, which has now been rehabilitated in the Scottish educational system. Although he uses both the Highlands and the city of Edinburgh for his inspiration, he has a wider sphere of reference than many. A prolific poet since the 1940s, the 1960s was his most fruitful decade, including the popular *Measures* (1965) and *Surroundings* (1966); MacCaig's *Collected Poems* were published in 1990. One of his poems is about his 'Aunt Julia' who 'spoke Gaelic very loud and very fast. I could not understand her.' This was a familiar problem for many Scots during the time when Gaelic was officially neglected. The one poetic voice which kept the language alive was that of Sorley MacLean (Somhairle MacGill-Eain). He translated his work into English, but wrote first in Gaelic. He published his first volume in 1943, the same year as MacCaig, and, like MacCaig, wrote much of his best work in the 1960s and 1970s. His *O Choille gu Bearradh/From Wood to Ridge* (*Collected Poems in Gaelic and English*) was published in 1989 and achieved wide acclaim.

D.J. Enright, whose *Collected Poems* were published in 1981, taught English literature, largely in the Far East, and his view of cultural difference and misunderstanding is a distinctive and ironic one. Donald Davie's work is more obscurely erudite and philosophical, moving, as he put it, 'among abstractions'. Like Enright he was a critic and academic, using his poetry to express a world view rather than the provincial English view associated with a great deal of writing in the 1950s and 1960s.

For many, W.H. Auden was one the greatest poets of the twentieth century. By the 1960s he was living in America, although he returned to Oxford in the early 1970s. In the 1960s he was of an age that his poems were being collected in tomes, such as *Collected Shorter Poems* and *Collected Longer Poems* (1966 and 1968), but he also continued to produce strong and original work in volumes such as *City Without Walls* (1969) and *Academic Graffiti* (1971). Perhaps the most unexpected success of any poetry in the entire century came in the mid-1990s when his gay elegy from the 1930s, 'Stop all the Clocks', was used in the movie *Four Weddings and a Funeral* – suddenly Auden was a best-seller more than twenty years after his death.

LARKIN AND GUNN

Philip Larkin more than any other poet was the voice of his time. As the critic Richard Eyre reminds us: 'Larkin feared that he'd be memorialised by thousands of schoolchildren in the Albert Hall intoning "They fuck you up, your mum and Dad."' This image is appositely hilarious and outrageous. For that line, from the poem 'This Be the Verse', written in 1971 and published in 1974, must be his best known and most frequently quoted. But it includes the f—— word, which until the 1960s had been very much a taboo word, not just in polite society, but in almost any context (see pp. 41–42). It was first uttered on British television in 1963, it was admitted into fictional acceptance through *Lady Chatterley's Lover*, and, through Larkin, came to be accepted as a recognisable semantic element, with a clear and precise meaning, in poetry. Compare its function here to the desemanticised function the word still has in Irvine Welsh's *Trainspotting* on p. 184.

In the Introduction to his controversial anthology *The Oxford Book of Twentieth-Century English Verse* (1973), Larkin underlines the importance of a native English tradition, as opposed to the Modernist influence, and gives considerable space to Chaucer, Wordsworth, Hardy and Auden, with Hardy being seen as the major poet of the Modern period. Larkin's speaking voice, his 'I' persona, is quiet and unsentimental; he represents and records his experience with fidelity and with great sensitivity. Larkin has to be seen, as he saw himself, as part of a long tradition of English poetry.

His poetry plays both with and against the Romantic tradition in poetry. Larkin has a clear and easily identifiable view of the world but does not assert the importance of his own personal experience. His vision is realistic and unsentimental, preferring to be indirect and ironic. He continues the tradition of Romantic poets in exploring eternal themes of death and change using established rhythms and syntax, and he generally uses traditional rather than innovative poetic forms. Like Hardy, he writes about what appears to be normal and everyday, while exploring the paradox that the mundane is both familiar and limited, presenting experiences which many readers recognise and feel they can share. He is also a social poet, commenting on the tawdry, superficial aspects of modern urban living. Although his poetry can seem patronising in tone, the intention is always to see things as honestly as possible.

There are many single lines and images which Larkin has given to modern perception: the solitary character in 'Mr Bleaney' living in his bleak room, the travellers on the train in 'The Whitsun Weddings' (both published in 1964), the couple of effigies on the tomb in 'An Arundel Tomb' to whom Larkin gave the epitaph 'what will survive of us is love'.

Larkin was a very domestic observer of the everyday: 'The Daily Things We Do' is the title of one of his later poems. He manages to combine a cynical world-weariness with a celebration of a very English status quo. Above all, Larkin is funny, emotionally direct, and linguistically clear, vivid and to the point. His last poems look bleakly at the processes of life again and begin to face the reality of death in an unemotional way: 'Death is no different whined at than withstood', he wrote in 'Aubade', written and published in 1977. In what is a seeming contradiction of the tradition of Wordsworth and Hardy mentioned above, his language seems often very 'unpoetic'.

He caught the spirit of the 1960s in 'Annus Mirabilis', which as we have already seen celebrates the lifting of the *Lady Chatterley* ban and the Beatles' first LP, and proclaims the optimism of the decade:

> Everyone felt the same,
> And every life became
> A brilliant breaking of the bank,
> A quite unlosable game.
>
> **Philip Larkin, 'Annus Mirabilis'**

The different languages in his poetry, from colloquial slang through plain speaking and on to occasionally high-flown images, embody the differences in lifestyle, behaviour and social ambitions he portrays. His rhymes can be simple, as in the extract above, and unexpectedly clever – he rhymes 'sex' and 'cheques' in one poem. He creates characters who have come to represent the age. In 'The Whitsun Weddings' (1964) he describes various couples attempting to give their lives some happiness and order, but concludes that happiness is something which only 'happens elsewhere', outside our lives, in the past rather than in the present. It was ten years before he published his next collection, *High Windows* (1974), which was to be the last complete collection published in his lifetime, so he was certainly not prolific. Yet his writing reached a very wide audience, and he became a well-known public figure, notably as a jazz critic. His critical pieces were collected in *Required Writing* in 1983.

This new flux of language which we can see in Larkin is vital to modern poetry. Between the 1950s and the turn of the millennium there was a shift towards post-Empire, postcolonial, less class-oriented, more pluralist societies and communities. Whereas in the 1940s T.S. Eliot was able to pronounce in *Four Quartets* on the role and indeed the mission of the poet as being 'to purify the dialect of the tribe', there was from the 1960s onward an explosion of Englishes, going beyond class and social status, beyond geographical, educational or gender boundaries, and beyond ethnicity. What Seamus Heaney called 'the mud flowers' of dialect flourished as never before, and 'the notion of a hieratic voice of authority (whether that of received pronunciation, the BBC, the Irish Catholic priest, the Oxford don, or the patriarchal male) was rejected', as Simon Armitage and Robert Crawford put it in their Introduction to a major 1990s anthology.

Thom Gunn's early work also appeared in the 1950s, in *New Lines*, and already he had a distinctive voice in his depiction of the new young culture of leather-clad motorbikers, their attitudes and passions. His later poems, in such volumes as *My Sad Captains* (1961), *The Passages of Joy* (1982) and *The Man with Night Sweats* (1992), show a growing technical mastery and an ever more uninhibited expression of gay themes. Gunn has lived in San Francisco since 1960, and is one of the few English poets to have moved west; while retaining the detached ironic viewpoint of The Movement, he has a touch of American verve, to which his poetry on AIDS brings a note of sadness.

> My thoughts are crowded with death
> and it draws so oddly on the sexual
> that I am confused
> confused to be attracted
> by, in effect, my own annihilation.
> Who are these two, these fiercely attractive men
> who want me to stick their needle in my arm?
> They tell me they are called Brad and John,
> one from here, one from Denver, sitting the same
> on the bench as they talk to me,
> their legs spread apart, their eyes attentive.
> I love their daring, their looks, their jargon,
> and what they have in mind.
>
> **Thom Gunn, 'In Time of Plague', from *The Man with Night Sweats***

Boss Cupid (2000) is a collection about survival and triumph, tempered with sadness and memory, inspired by Cupid 'the devious master of our bodies'. With it Thom Gunn has gone beyond the AIDS tragedy and on to the everlasting affirmation of human passions and desires.

LIVERPOOL POETS

In the 1960s a wave of pop poetry reached a wide audience, and writers such as Roger McGough, Brian Patten and Adrian Henri, all from the Beatles' home city of Liverpool, produced a great deal of popular light verse, considered unworthy of serious comment by some critics, but using language, imagery and contemporary reference in ways which many British readers find accessible, enjoyable and significant. The democratisation of poetry which the Liverpool poets brought about, at exactly the same time as pop music was making its biggest ever impact, with colloquial speech, everyday themes and humour, is not always recognised as a major influence on poetry, and indeed on pop song lyrics, over the next decades. All these poets have continued to write and perform, and Roger McGough in particular has established himself as one of the major popular poets of our time.

> He wakes when the sun rises
> Gets up   Exercises
> Breakfasts with one whom he despises
> Chooses one of his disguises
> and his gun   Fires his
> first bullet   It paralyses
> Drives into town   Terrorizes
> Armed police in vizors
> materialize   His demise is
> swift   No surprises.
>
> **Roger McGough, 'No Surprises', from Defying Gravity**

Defying Gravity (1992) is one of his most significant volumes; *Bad Bad Cats* (1997) one of his funniest. *The Way Things Are* (2000) is his most recent collection. McGough has been instrumental in making poetry attractive to younger readers: many of his collections are directed at children, and his work, alongside that of others such as Michael Rosen and Benjamin Zephaniah, has taken the performance and the reading and writing of poetry into classrooms and other spaces where poetry had made little impact before.

READING AND HUGHES

Peter Reading is one of the more original and most politically concerned of poets currently writing. He frequently publishes 'found' poetry, using texts he has discovered as graffiti, slogans, conversations overheard, and so on. But he can also be immensely serious: the volume

C (1984) takes cancer as its subject matter, and uses a hundred 100-word units to discuss it. His other volumes include *For the Municipality's Elderly* (1974), *Fiction* (1979), *Ukulele Music* (1985), *Stet* (1986), *Final Demands* (1988), *Perduta Gente* (1989), and *Work in Regress* (1997), in which, to take one example, he takes as the title and inspiration for one poem the Prime Minister Tony Blair's statement as reported in the headline 'Clear Beggars from Streets, says Blair'. His *Faunal* (2002) meditates on death and extinction, especially of the planet's creatures: as he says in one poem, 'we are all members of the Wildlife Trust'. He is one of the most concerned and innovative of poets currently writing.

One of the lasting images to come through poetry in the 1970s was of Ted Hughes's savage and menacing bird figure, the crow, which emphasised the pitiless and violent forces of nature. In *Crow* (1971) Hughes retells the creation story from the point of view of a violent, anarchic consciousness – the crow himself – who emerges as a kind of anti-Christ. The 'I'/'eye' is all-seeing: 'I kill where I please because it is all mine/. . . . I am going to keep things like this.' Many critics have equated this state of mind with the psychology of a totalitarian dictator. The poems in this volume, and in *Gaudete* (1977), are sparse dramas in which traditional metrical patterning and realistic presentation are abandoned. Hughes was much attracted to the dark and surreal work of European more than British poets, and like them he explored a post-Holocaust awareness of what it felt like to live in the spiritual chasm at the end of the twentieth century. The darkness of Ted Hughes's poetry is often contrasted with Larkin's seemingly more gentle, very English, urbane and introspective manner.

At the time of his death in 1998 Ted Hughes was enjoying considerable popularity. Two volumes, *Birthday Letters* and *Tales from Ovid*, became best-sellers and confirmed his status as a unique individual poetic voice who could reach a very wide audience. *Birthday Letters* courageously explored the relationship with his late wife, the American poet and novelist Sylvia Plath. Her suicide in 1963 had always marked out their relationship, but Hughes's reflective, elegiac, deeply personal late volume helped redress the balance, and struck a chord with a large number of readers. The very first poem in the book goes right back to before the couple even met:

Where was it, in the Strand? A display
Of news items, in photographs,
For some reason I noticed it.
Of Fulbright Scholars. Just arriving –
Or arrived. Or some of them.
Were you among them? I studied it.
Not too minutely, wondering
Which of them I might meet.
I remember that thought. Not
Your face. No doubt I scanned particularly
The girls. Maybe I noticed you.
Maybe I weighed you up, feeling unlikely,
Noted your long hair, loose waves –
Your Veronica Lake bang. Not what it hid.
It would appear blond. And your grin.
Your exaggerated American
Grin for the cameras, the judges, the strangers, the frighteners.
Then I forgot. Yet I remember
The picture: the Fulbright Scholars.
With their luggage? It seems unlikely.
Could they have come as a team? I was walking
Sore-footed, under the hot sun, hot pavements.
Was it then I bought a peach? That's as I remember
From a stall near Charing Cross Station.
It was the first fresh peach I had ever tasted.
I could hardly believe how delicious.
At twenty-five I was dumbfounded afresh
By my ignorance of the simplest things.

Ted Hughes, 'Fulbright Scholars', from Birthday Letters

The combination of very personal memory (compare how much he uses the pronoun 'I' with how rarely Larkin used it), closely observed detail, and then sensation through nature is characteristic of the best of Hughes, here with very personal reflection, which shows the poet at his most moving. Sylvia Plath herself, after her death, came to be one of the most widely studied and influential female poets of the whole century on the strength of her two volumes *Ariel* (1960) and *Colossus* (1965).

ENGLANDS OF THE MIND

Charles Tomlinson and Geoffrey Hill share a concern with time, history, tradition and place. Tomlinson's *The Way of the World* (1969) and *The Shaft* (1978) are direct examinations of continuity and change: this goes against the notion that most contemporary poetry is about chaos and disorder. Some poets do indeed concentrate on breakdown, Sylvia Plath in particular. But Tomlinson, Hill and others take the constants of their landscape as the basis of their work. For Hill, this means the landscape of Mercia, as in *Mercian Hymns* (1971), which celebrate, in a kind of prose poetry, Offa, 'the presiding genius of the West Midlands' in early English history. Where Sylvia Plath's violence, for example, is emotional, personal, suicidal – see her *Collected Poems* (1981) – Hill's is latent, hidden in the past and brooding, to produce perhaps the most complex and allusive of recent poetry.

Geoffrey Hill admits 'though with some reluctance, that my poetry is generally regarded as difficult'. He goes on to say, 'I think that legitimate difficulty (difficulty of course can be faked) is essentially democratic.' He has been engaged in a four-part project, begining with *Canaan* and *The Triumph of Love*, which many critics have seen as a modern rewriting of Dante's *The Divine Comedy*. Hill wants *Speech! Speech!* (2001) to be considered as more accessible than much of his other work, to be taken as 'the equivalent' of a tragic farce, to be read quickly. It is a theatre of voices in 120 twelve-line poems, a musical exploration inside the mind of its speaker, a new-century soliloquy full of memorable images and word-games. With its exclamation marks *Speech! Speech!* echoes an invitation to an unscheduled speech, usually in a company of admirers, while at the same time undermining the conviviality of the occasion by indicating a frustration with the world of unendingly empty talk. It is an almost ironic statement by Hill that he is not sure how to respond to the modern world. Despite reference in the volume to a range of public and popular artists and heroes ('Great singer Elton John though') Hill remains ambitious, admirable, but hardly the most accessible of modern poets. *The Orchards of Syon* (2002) concludes the project – a collection of seventy-two poems of twenty-four lines, in which he says 'I write/to astonish myself' and uses what he calls 'indigent word play, stubborn, isolate/language of inner exile'. It is a magisterial language which repays close attention, and the volume has received considerable acclaim. But Hill remains a defiantly difficult poet.

In an essay entitled 'Englands of the Mind', Seamus Heaney discusses the poetry of Ted Hughes, Philip Larkin and Geoffrey Hill. He contrasts Hill's primitive landscapes and Larkin's city-scapes. Hill is a poet of another England; he searches for the roots of English identity, in historical, linguistic and cultural terms, in the region of Mercia – the West Midlands. Hill's search is not far removed from Heaney's own digging into the depths of his own Irishness. In this extract from 'Mercian Hymns', Geoffrey Hill celebrates the work of English needleworkers, in echoes of the Victorian celebration of medieval work found in the works of Thomas Carlyle and William Morris:

> In tapestries, in dreams, they gathered, as
> it was enacted, the re-entry of
> transcendence into this sublunary world.
> *Opus Anglicanum*, their stringent mystery
> riddled by needles: the silver veining, the
> gold leaf, voluted grape-vine, masterworks
> of treacherous thread.
>
> They trudged out of the dark, scraping their
> boots free from lime-splodges and phlegm.
> They munched cold bacon. The lamps grew
> plump with oily reliable light.
>
> **Geoffrey Hill from *Mercian Hymns***

C.H. Sisson shares Hill's fascination with the genius of the past, especially distant English and classical history. His *Collected Poems* (1984) show a wide span of reference, a concern with the fallen nature of man, and a rich range of cultural images.

. . . AND SCOTTISH VOICES

Edwin Morgan is one of the foremost Scottish poets of the twentieth century. Noted for experimental 'concrete' poetry, which makes visual images of words and letters, he is also a lyric poet, and acute observer of the city of Glasgow, where he has lived and worked for most of his life – he was even named the Glasgow Laureate. Like many poets he is also an academic, and his volume of essays, interviews and observations, *Nothing Not Sending Messages* (1992), gives useful insights into his *Collected Poems*, published in 1990.

> When love comes late, but fated,
> the very ground seems on fire with tongues of running time,
> and conscious hearts are speaking
> of the long vistas closed in clouds
> by lonely waters, all goodbyes
> where the swallow is a shadow
> swooping back, like youth, to silence,
>
> If all goodbyes could be drowned in one welcome,
> and the pains of waiting be washed from a hundred street-corners,
> and dry rebuffs and grey regrets, backs marching into rain
> slip like a film from the soiled spirit made new –
> I'd take that late gift, and those tongues
> of fire would burn out in our
> thankful fountains, to the sea.

Edwin Morgan, 'The Welcome', from *Collected Poems*

Edwin Morgan's career has continued to flourish with *Virtual and Other Realities* (1997), for which he won the Scottish Writer of the Year award, and *New Selected Poems* (2000). He continues his prolific and accessible work in *Cathures* (2002).

Douglas Dunn, with *Terry Street* (1969), *Elegies* (1985), *Northlight* (1988) and *Dante's Drum Kit* (1993), has been called the major Scottish poet of his generation. Strongly political in much of his work, he challenges Sir Walter Scott's turning 'our country round upon its name/And time'. Dunn's nationalist sentiment is concerned with common, popular experience, underlying recorded history. The elegies written on the death of his wife – *Elegies* (1985) – display an emotional range allied with a technical mastery which has taken Dunn's work on to new levels of achievement.

HEANEY DIGGING

Seamus Heaney is far and away the most significant poet writing in English. He is a poet who writes both directly and obliquely about politics, speaking in a clearly personal voice; he is a poet of nature, a poet of the countryside, a poet of his own land and a poet of the wider world. As an Irishman, many of his poems deal with the horrors which continue to afflict Northern Ireland. In his early poems, Heaney writes of the countryside and the natural world in ways which suggest the influence of D. H. Lawrence and Ted Hughes. In one of his earliest poems, 'Digging' (1966), he establishes a metaphor which recurs in different ways in several subsequent poems.

> Between my finger and my thumb
> The squat pen rests.
> I'll dig with it.

He digs into his own memory, into the lives of his family, into the past of Irish history and into the deeper levels of legend and myth which shape the character of the people of his country. Heaney attempts to go beyond the terrible daily events of life in Northern Ireland to discover the forces beneath the history of that country which might restore hope and comfort. But he does not hide the deep-rooted tribal passions of revenge and honour which endure in contemporary society.

The award of the Nobel Prize for Literature to Seamus Heaney in 1995 set the seal on his worldwide reputation. It was the volume of poems *North* (1975) which established Heaney's fame and popularity, after *Door Into the Dark* (1969). In that first volume the poem that has come to be best known is 'Digging', which is very characteristic of Heaney – he moves from present to past, as he sees his grandfather cultivating potatoes, which are the main crop of Ireland, and historically potent because of the potato famine of the nineteenth century. But Heaney's twist on the theme of digging is that he has a pen in his hand, not a gun, recalling Shelley's dictum that the pen is mightier than the sword. And Heaney has continued to dig, in history, in Irishness and in humanity, ever since.

More recent collections of verse have examined the 'bog people', the poet's own relationships, and the complex relationships between individual and society, cult and history. In these lines from the poem 'North', the poet looks back to the hidden imperial roots of the English language in Viking Ireland and Norse culture:

> 'Lie down
> in the word-hoard, burrow
> in the coil and gleam
> of your furrowed brain.
>
> Compose in darkness.
> Expect aurora borealis
> In the long foray
>
> But no cascade of light.
> Keep your eye clear
> As the bleb of the icicle,
> Trust the feel of what nubbed treasure
> Your hands have known.'

In his essays and academic writings, Seamus Heaney is perceptive and polemical. He is particularly acute in his writings on poets and poetry. His early lecture 'Yeats as an Example?' ends with words of praise for one of Yeats's last poems, 'Cuchulain Comforted': words which might, in some way, also stand for Heaney's own creative work:

> It is a poem deeply at one with the weak and the strong of this earth, full of a motherly kindness towards life, but also unflinching in its belief in the propriety and beauty of life transcended into art, song, words.

Much of the major poetry of recent years focuses on place, and the language used to evoke its setting. Seamus Heaney has described Ted Hughes's sensibility as 'pagan in the original sense; a heath-dweller', in direct contrast with the urban concerns of Larkin. Heaney, himself attracted to the peat bog, its wildness and its capacity to preserve, celebrates his contemporaries, saying, 'all that I really knew about the art [of poetry] was derived from whatever poetry I had written'. His observations on Hughes, Larkin and Geoffrey Hill focus on their sense of place: Hughes's heath is as much 'England as King Lear's heath', Larkin's 'landscape . . . is dominated by the civic prospects' and the poet a 'humane and civilised member of the . . . civil service'; Hill's Mercia is seen with 'a historian and school's eye', with the poet seeming, to the Irishman's objective eye, to be 'celebrating his own indomitable Englishry'. When Seamus Heaney's poems were included in the 1982 *Penguin Book of Contemporary British Poetry*, Heaney riposted, in 'An Open Letter' (1983), that 'My anxious muse . . . Has to refuse/The adjective' – concluding, 'British, no, the name's not right'. This is a crucial assertion of the Irishness of modern writing in Ireland, whether in the North (Ulster) or in Eire.

Heaney's first volume after winning the Nobel Prize was *The Spirit Level* (1996). The title brings together his spiritual side and his practical nature, and the volume consolidates his position as a poet of nature, politics and humanity who can make major poetry out of the essentially mundane. It is interesting that, although Heaney rejected the label 'British', he has always written in English rather than using any regional Irish dialect. In *The Spirit Level* he illustrates how, growing up a Catholic in a divided province, then becoming an emblematic exile in England and America, has given him the capacity to voice images of universal healing rather than division, to find 'personal solutions to a shared crisis, momentary stays against confusion'. Like Samuel Beckett, his vision is to 'gain an inch against the darkness'. *Opened Ground* (1998) collected his poems from between 1966 and 1996, and the translation of *Beowulf* (1999) brought him great popular and critical acclaim, followed by *Electric Light* (2001).

Heaney travels widely and his poetry and myth-making are international: Tollund in Denmark features frequently in his poems (it is where the 'Bog People' were found); America, Africa and Ancient Greece are visited and imaginatively revisited. To this international experience Heaney brings a deep awareness of English linguistic and poetic traditions. From Anglo-Saxon poetry through the metaphysicals, Wordsworth, Gerard Manley Hopkins and W.H. Auden, to Yeats and Ted Hughes, Heaney revels in the historical voices to which he is now compared.

> You are like a rich man entering heaven
> Through the ear of a raindrop.
> Listen now again.
>
> **Seamus Heaney, 'The Rain Stick', from *The Spirit Level***

Electric Light is a rich volume, with influences from the classics to recent poetry, philosophical musings, jokey memories and a glorious range of inventive verse forms, versions and voices. The second part of the book is elegiac in much of its tone of memory, celebrating many of his contemporaries and antecedents in the history of poetic tradition. Of George Mackay Brown he speaks of

> Allegory hard as a figured shield
> Smithied in Orkney for Christ's sake and Crusades.

Heaney also alludes again to *Beowulf*, confirming himself and Ted Hughes in the great tradition of poetry, 'things for keeping', in the ode to the late Poet Laureate called *On His Work in the English Tongue*.

The title poem in this wide-ranging collection returns to Heaney's semi-autobiographical mode, where his own memories (or the recollections of the authorial 'I') bring together the coming of 'the magic' of electricity and the wireless to the static society of timeless memory. 'Keep' is a key word throughout: cherishing, lasting, memory and presence are Heaney's concerns. *Electric Light* continues to prove him a poet of modern race-memory, and reaffirms his status as a major figure in world poetry. *Finders Keepers* (2002) collects Heaney's essays and prose from the past thirty years.

MORE IRISH VOICES

Poets such as Tom Paulin, Medhb McGuckian, Paul Muldoon, Paul Durcan, Eavan Boland, Michael Longley and Derek Mahon – together with Heaney, and the older generation of Pearse Hutchinson, Brendan

Kennelly and Thomas Kinsella – have given Irish poetry a new vitality, which brings North and South together in common concern. Ciaran Carson emerged as one of Ulster's foremost poets when he won the T.S. Eliot Prize in 1993 for *First Language*. In *Opera Et Cetera* (1996) he uses long-lined rhyming couplets to echo Irish ballad rhythms, and writes sequences of poems, telling a range of stories, and examining the very nature of language. He returned to this way of working in the prose work *Fishing for Amber* (1999) which uses similar A to Z alphabetical sections to examine how we see art, light and words. Carson uses local terms of reference in many of his poems, from 'The Irish for No' (1987) and 'Belfast Confetti' (1990) to 'The Ballad of HMS *Belfast*' (1999) and 'Shamrock Tea' (2001). But his artistic aims and concerns go far beyond local issues, and he is one of the most intellectually engaged poets working today.

Tom Paulin also uses his Ulster background in many of his poems, although he has lived in England for most of his life. In one of the very personal poems in *The Wind Dog* (1999) he apologises for this in the line 'Forgive me Lord that I only skip back now and then to this city', Belfast. His other volumes since *The Strange Museum* (1980) include *Walking a Line* (1994) and *Selected Poems 1972–1990* (1991). Tom Paulin is also a polemical critic, writing on such figures as Thomas Hardy and William Hazlitt. *Minotaur: Poetry and the Nation State* (1992) is an important collection of his critical writings.

Tom Paulin's *The Invasion Handbook* (2002) is an original and provocative mix of poetry interspersed with prose, full of dark and different voices, full of horror and pain. The subject is basically the Second World War, but it is of course, being Paulin, an examination of the politics of disrupted societies, a patchwork of pain, indifference and survival. In its piecemeal way it constitutes a war epic, and as such is a most unusual achievement, and one which, although some readers find it controversial, stands as a major exploration of what we know and how we know about it, between reading, experiencing and empathising.

Paul Durcan's titles show much of his spirited attitude to his work (for example, *Daddy Daddy* and *Crazy About Women*). *A Snail in My Prime* (1993) is a retrospective of his work. He uses poetry as a vehicle for story-telling, lyricism and the exploration of feelings. Roger McGough has this to say about him: 'For him poetry is story-telling and his stories are told in a direct fashion that makes them totally accessible.' Durcan has been a prolific and original poet for many years – *Cries of an Irish Caveman* (2001) is his eighteenth volume. His poetry has always contained a mix of very serious and seemingly frivolous work, which has meant that the critical response has been mixed. But his work is always entertaining, individual and idiosyncratic.

Eavan Boland has emerged as one of Ireland's foremost poets: volumes such as *Outside History* (1990) and *In a Time of Violence* (1994) show, like Seamus Heaney, an awareness of history, a sense of national pride, and, in Boland's case, a feminist sense of the potential for the growth of her country.

> we will live, we have lived
> where language is concealed. Is perilous.
> We will be – we have been – citizens
> of its hiding place. But it is too late
> to shut the book of satin phrases,
> to refuse to enter
> an evening bitter with peat smoke,
> where newspaper sellers shout headlines
> and friends call out their farewells in
> a city of whispers
> and interiors where
> the dear vowels
> *Irish Ireland ours* are
> absorbed into Autumn air,
> are out of earshot in the distances
> we are stepping into where we never
> imagine words such as *hate*
> and *territory* and the like – unbanished still
> as they always would be – wait
> and are waiting under
> beautiful speech. To strike.
>
> **Eavan Boland, 'Beautiful Speech', from *In a Time of Violence* (1994)**

Eavan Boland handles themes of love and marriage in *Code* (2001) with strong narrative force in a poem about working women called 'Making Money', one of the outstanding poems in a very distinguished collection.

Michael Longley's resonant poems from Northern Ireland have been described by another contemporary poet, Ruth Padel, as having 'helped to shape the sensibility of all British poetry of the last quarter-century'. His *Selected Poems* of 1998 was followed by the entertaining *Weather in Japan* (2000).

Contemporary Irish poetry can be urban working-class, polemical, feminist, occupied with history and tradition, and at the same time open to international influences and concerns. Poets such as Pearse Hutchinson and Michael Davitt, to name only two, are reinvestigating the tradition of poetry in the Irish language, bringing together the strands of history, legend, literature and language, which give Ireland its modern identity and heritage.

MARTIANS AND GORGONS

In the late 1970s Craig Raine came to be known as leader of the 'Martian' school of poetry. It was not so much a 'school' as a defamiliarising mode of perception which derived from the poem 'A Martian Sends a Postcard Home' (1979). This plays with ways of seeing; books are 'Caxtons', the toilet is 'a punishment room' where 'everyone's pain has a different smell'. From *The Onion Memory* (1978) through to *Clay: Whereabouts Unknown* (1996), Raine continued in this vein, bringing unexpected perspectives to everyday things: 'a pug like a car crash' and the moon fading in the morning 'like fat in a frying pan'. He is, more than any other, the poet who sees likes in unlikes. More ambitious projects such as the long poem *History* (1995) have less of this distinctive characteristic and have enjoyed less success.

Tony Harrison regards poetry as 'the supreme form of articulation' and sees part of the poet's role as to 'reclaim poetry's public function'. His writing, often set in his home county of Yorkshire, as in *v* (1985 to 1988), uses colloquial forms, natural speech and local dialect in perfectly scanning rhymes to explore matters such as education and class, violence and language, questions of social conflict. The letter v stands for 'versus', punning on 'verses', and the traditional V for Victory; the poem was written during the miners' strike of the mid-1980s, causing scandal when it was broadcast on television. Harrison's work, often for theatrical performance, is a vital assertion of poetry and language, with none of the safe, ironic detachment of some of his contemporaries: Harrison's is committed, dramatic poetry which is never comfortable and always challenging.

The Gaze of the Gorgon (1992), a long poem for television written in the wake of the First Gulf War, has shown that Tony Harrison's energy and creativity are constantly developing, making him both accessible and exciting. He is also an accomplished translator, especially from classical Latin and Greek. The range of poetic and dramatic reference in his works is immense. *A Kumquat for John Keats* (1981) finds the fruit to celebrate the famous poet; *U.S. Martial* (1981) punningly transposes the Latin epigrammatist Martial into 1980s New York. 'The Pomegranates of Patmos' (from the 1992 volume *The Gaze of the Gorgon*) is an apocalyptic vision:

> I'm so weary of all metaphorers.
> From now on my most pressing ambition's
> to debrainwash all like Prochorus
> made Moonies by metaphysicians.
> But my poor brother could never respond.
> I couldn't undermine his defences.
> His brain went before him to the Beyond.
> He took all leave of his senses.
> My brother's heart was turned to stone.
> So my revenge on St John's to instil
> in lovers like these, who think they're alone,
> the joy John and his ilk want to kill,
> and try any charm or trick
> to help frightened humans affirm
> small moments against the rhetoric
> of St Cosmocankerworm.

> **Tony Harrison, 'The Pomegranates of Patmos',**
> **from *The Gaze of the Gorgon* (1992)**

Few modern poets are as observant as Harrison about how England is still preoccupied with class distinction, and about how speech reflects class. 'Them and Uz' (phonetic rendering (uːz)) recalls his schooldays, when his accent 'murdered' the words of Keats: at least, according to his English master. Later, the poem 'Y' (the initial stands for the cheapest form of airline travel) shows the same perception on a flight across the Atlantic:

> the First Class can pay
> while the Y class gapes
> *pour encourager* . . .
> any man can fly
> Premium if he can pay
> (or his company).
>
> We curtain the classes
> while they eat,
> the plastics from glasses,
> we are so discreet!
> **Tony Harrison, 'Y'**

Tony Harrison refused to be considered for the appointment as Poet Laureate after the death of Ted Hughes, and wrote polemically about it, describing the role as 'rat-catcher to our present Queen'. His most recent collection takes its title from that text: *'Laureate's Block' and Other Occasional Poems* (2000).

After the emotionally charged verses of Sylvia Plath, there was talk of 'women's poetry', but in a post-feminist world a writer's gender has come to be less remarked upon, and his or her work considered rather for what it is and does. If we group some writers together it is because they have all tended to mix emotion with humour, passion with acute observation, penetration with pleasure rather than with pain. Jenny Joseph, Anne Stevenson, U.A. Fanthorpe, and Scottish-born Carol Ann Duffy are particularly noteworthy. Ursula Fanthorpe's volumes include *Safe as Houses* (1995), *Consequences* (2000) and *Queuing for the Sun* (2003), and demonstrate a wry perception of attitudes, subversive and witty. This kind of subversion is demonstrated neatly in Carol Ann Duffy's unromantic version of a Valentine:

> Not a red rose or a satin heart.
> I give you an onion.
> It is a moon wrapped in brown paper.
> It promises light
> like the careful undressing of love,
>
> Here.
> It will blind you with tears
> like a lover.
>
> **Carol Ann Duffy, 'A Valentine',**
> **from *Mean Time* (1993)**

Her collection of poems representing female voices through the ages, *The World's Wife* (1999), was a critical and popular success, and was followed in 2002 by *Feminine Gospels*. Duffy's poems are always witty, pungent and provocative: she writes a lot for children, and she feels that this has given her more adult work a myth-like quality: 'I write them white, words on the wind.'

Of the younger generation, the Scottish-born Jackie Kay, who writes memorably about being adopted in *The Adoption Papers* (1991), Kathleen Jamie (*The Way We Live*, 1987), and London-born Lavinia Greenlaw have established themselves as favourites. Kathleen Jamie is Scottish, and her poems are precise, profound and lyrical, mixing the mundane and the mysterious with wit and originality. Her collection *Mr and Mrs Scotland Are Dead: Poems 1980–1994* (2002) brings together poems from no fewer than five collections. She moves through standard English and Scottish English and a wide range of subject matter: nationhood is a theme, as it is in most Scottish writers of the time, when independence, the state of the nation and its culture, and the return of a Scottish Parliament were burning topics. The title poem reads 'Mr and Mrs Scotland, here is the hand you were dealt', and is unflinching in its depiction of urban degradation combined with the things that make a culture worth cherishing. Politics, sex, history and poverty all find their place in Jamie's poetry. She is an accomplished, versatile and enjoyable poet.

The award-winning title poem in Lavinia Greenlaw's collection *A World Where News Travelled Slowly* (1997) bids fair to become one of the most widely anthologised poems of its decade. Her first volume of poetry was *Night Photograph* (1993), and her first novel *Mary George of Allnorthover* (2001) was also well received. It is a vision of the troubled England of the 1970s and a fascinating fictional portrait of that decade. Wendy Cope has also reached a wide audience with a form of witty and pungent light verse, such as *Making Cocoa for Kingsley Amis* (1986). Her latest volume is *If I Didn't Know* (2001).

Stevie Smith was something of an outsider; she wrote spare, inventive, often humorous verse with 'a particular emotional weather between the words', as Seamus Heaney put it. She was a very popular reader of her own poetry in the burgeoning poetry-reading market of the late 1960s and 1970s. She was a compassionate observer of the modern tragedy of isolation, memorably in the much anthologised poem 'Not Waving but Drowning' (1957). Her *Collected Poems* were published in 1975.

Nobody heard him, the dead man,
But still he lay moaning:
I was much further out than you thought
And not waving but drowning.

Poor chap, he always loved larking
And now he's dead
It must have been too cold for him his heart gave way,
They said.

Oh no no no, it was too cold always
(Still the dead one lay moaning)
I was much too far out all my life
And not waving but drowning.

Stevie Smith, 'Not Waving but Drowning'

ANDREW MOTION

Andrew Motion quotes Stevie Smith in one of his own poems: 'Close', in *Love in a Life* (1991). The title covers both the close escape and the feelings for his family.

> The afternoon I was killed
> I strolled up the beach from the sea
> where the big wave had hit me, . . .
> Nobody spoke about me
> or how I was no longer there.
> It was odd, but I understood why:
> when I had drowned I was only
> a matter of yards out to sea
> (not *too far out* – too close),
> still able to hear the talk
> and have everything safe in view.
> **Andrew Motion, 'Close'**

Motion is a poet of contrasts, working with that kind of intimacy: he also writes larger-scale, longer poems, such as 'Bathing at Glymenopoulo', in *Dangerous Play: Poems 1974–1984* (1985), and 'Scripture', in *Natural Causes* (1987).

Motion is also an important and innovative biographer. Biography, especially literary biography, has gained best-seller status in recent years, and figures such as Andrew Motion, Nicholas Shakespeare and Richard Holmes have made major contributions to the genre. Motion has written biographies on a range of subjects covering art to pop music. He wrote important biographies of the poets Philip Larkin (1993) and John Keats (1997). Experimentation with the ways in which lives are presented has now changed the traditional face of biography, and *Wainewright the Poisoner* (2000) is an innovative variation on the theme. It examines a near-forgotten figure from the early nineteenth century who was discussed by Oscar Wilde in his 1891 essay 'Pen, Pencil and Poison', and the book turns out to be more than a life – it is an examination of time, truth and how words can represent these intangibles. Biography and fiction continue to be fascinatingly intertwined in the novel *The Invention of Dr Cake* (2003) which came out of Motion's research into Keats – what if the poet had not in fact died in Rome . . .?

Motion's poetry, like his biographies, is constantly teasing out the relationships between art and life, reality and imagination, and the essence of creativity. His own poetry has frequently reflected the pain and emotion of his own life, from the tragic long drawn-out death of his mother to an operation on a life-threatening condition which afflicted him, in a poem entitled 'A Free Man'. This concern with private pain and public emotion fits him well for the public role of Poet Laureate, to which he was appointed in 1999, and suggests the title to his most recent volume *Public Property* (2002). This is a collection of elegiac idylls recalling a country childhood and questioning how much of a writer's feelings, thoughts and emotions can, indeed, be made public property through his work. Motion used his Laureate's voice to take a stand against the war against Iraq in 2003, describing the motivations for such a war memorably as 'Elections, money, empire, oil, and Dad' – a reference to George Bush's father, and the previous war in the Gulf.

This extract from the long poem 'Scripture' shows something of the immediacy of a private moment of discovery: the line 'with its secret self laid bare' perhaps sums up the way Motion's poetry creates its effects.

> Out of bounds too was the swimming pool,
> laid like sugary glass in its privet enclosure.
> My afternoon's chance companion,
> Jonathan,
> pressed back the hedge and beckoned me in,
> all innocence, simply because it was there.
> Close up, it was not as we'd thought.
> The glass was rucked – the pool whipped into waves
> and frozen.
> So when I skimmed a stone across,
> instead of an iron tinkle and hiss
> there was one crack and the stone stuck,
> though its echo creaked and pinged for nearly a minute,

trapped in the liquid heart.
It was as though the face of a living thing
had been brushed by the wings of death,
and killed with its secret self laid bare –
a white, wild, bitter grimace
where we had expected steadiness, flatness,
the sheen of a distant summer.
It wasn't for this it was out of bounds,
but it was why, easing our way through the privet
and back to the school,
I carefully slid my hand into Jonathan's hand
and asked: *We won't tell anyone, will we? Are you my friend?*

Andrew Motion, 'Scripture', from *Natural Causes* (1987)

VOICES AND REGIONS

Basil Bunting, whose *Collected Poems* appeared in 1978, was for many
years the forgotten man of modern English poetry. He had been a
disciple of Pound in the 1920s, but his achievement was not widely
recognised until the publication of his lengthy autobiographical poem
Briggflatts in 1966. Set in his home county of Northumberland, it is
an account of the county and the century, bringing Pound's influence
up to our own day.

For many, J.H. Prynne is the leading experimental poet of his time,
a priest of High Modernism. His poetry makes great use of free verse,
is lyrical, dense and hermetic. Much of his work was available only in
pamphlets, but in 1983 a collected volume entitled *Poems* brought his
work to a wider audience. Another collected *Poems* was published in
1999.

R.S. Thomas was the most significant Welsh poet since Dylan
Thomas. He used to be described as 'our best living religious poet', and
there was some truth in this, although many poets discuss religion in
their works. Thomas was, in fact, a clergyman, and his work in a rural
parish imbued his poetry with a harsh, bleak, pastoral quality, reflecting
the landscape and the history of Wales. 'There is no present in Wales/
And no future;/There is only the past', he affirmed, contradicting T.S.

Eliot. His poetry has a roughness to it, a challenge to 'the English/ Scavenging among the remains/of our culture'. *Pietà* (1966) and *Selected Poems 1946–68* (published in 1973) are representative of his work. After his death *Residues* was published in 2002.

> What's living but courage?
> Paunch full of hot porridge,
> Nerves strengthened with tea,
> Peat-black, dawn found me
> Mowing where the grass grew,
> Bearded with golden dew.
> Rhythm of the long scythe
> Kept this tall frame lithe.
> **R.S. Thomas, 'Lore', from *Tares* (1961)**

Dannie Abse, by profession a doctor, is a consistent and prolific Welsh poet. The title of his collected poems from 1948 to 1988 hints at his double identity: *White Coat, Purple Coat*. He also edited the indispensable volume *Twentieth Century Anglo-Welsh Poetry* (1997). In his Introduction he writes: 'it is evident that many poets in Wales, rightly or wrongly, believe themselves to be members of a defeated nation. That awareness leads them, in the signature of their poems, to side with the losers of history and of life's procession – the underdogs, the outsiders, the downtrodden.' It is interesting how both Ireland and Scotland have responded to any possible threat of being considered 'inferior' or downtrodden by producing strong, clear affirmations of literary identity: Wales less evidently so, despite the flourishing of the Welsh language and of writing in Welsh. That double identity theme recurs in Abse's acclaimed 2002 novel *The Strange Case of Dr Simmonds & Dr Glass*, where a doctor falls in love with his patient.

MIXES AND MATCHES

There is no lack of variety in English poetry. Craig Raine's 'Martian' school, after *A Martian Sends a Postcard Home* (1979), enjoyed a great vogue, but more recently the vivid urban expression of Simon Armitage, in *Zoom!* (1989), *Kid* (1992), *The Dead Sea Poems* (1995)

The city and the country

> And that will be England gone,
> The shadows, the meadows, the lanes,
> The guildhalls, the carved choirs,
> There'll be books; it will linger on
> In galleries, but all that remains
> For us will be concrete and tyres.
>
> **Philip Larkin 'Going, Going' (1972)**

Literature in English has long explored the tensions between the country and the city and the rhythms of rural and urban living, and has faced the social and cultural changes brought about by ever-increasing urbanisation. In the post-Second World War years, the changes have accelerated and the gradual passing of a way of life recorded as landscapes become townscapes. H.E. Bates's novels represent almost the end of a line with his pastoral novel *The Darling Buds of May* (1958) depicting the acceptance and to some degree celebration by the Larkin family of the existing order and their own place within it. Angus Wilson's *Late Call* (1964) is, however, a sustained lament at the growth of new towns which do more than encroach on the countryside but which represent an attempt to create a homogenous modern world which does not cohere because it lacks any real spirit of community and where the countryside has become no more than a playground escape from urban living.

The theme of the limits and loss of community and the creation of new worlds with new values echoes through many writings in this period, through the poetry of Basil Bunting's *Briggflatts*, Geoffrey Hill's *Mercian Hymns*, Martin Amis's depiction of an anonymous and atomised modern world in the ironically entitled *London Fields* through to Simon Armitage's analysis of the end-of-century and millennium dystopia represented by the soulless 'Millennium Dome' in London in *Killing Time* (1999). These and many other writers take a centuries-old theme and give it its modern inflections, chief among which is a record of the increasing inability in contemporary Britain to distinguish where, if anywhere, the city stops and the country begins.

and *CloudCuckooLand* (1997), and Glyn Maxwell, in *Tale of the Mayor's Son* (1990) and *Out of the Rain* (1992), have attracted considerable acclaim. Their technical accomplishment, in the tradition of Larkin and Harrison, has become a vital part of poetic achievement. Simon Armitage's *Xanadu* (1992) is a film poem, set in Lancashire, using twenty-six alphabetically named blocks of flats – being demolished – as the background for his reflections on social deprivation.

> I have to say I'd never thought
> of this place as a ski resort.
> Ashfield Valley
> and its thousand chalets,
> a case of the half-light
> making me snow-blind.
>
> In any case,
> this house of cards, these Meccano apartments
> thirty years ago were the cat's pyjamas.
>
> So instead
> of putting the cart before the horse
> I should trace this rumour back to its source;
>
> the place: perhaps a council chamber,
> the date: nineteen-sixty something or other . . .
> **Simon Armitage, *Xanadu* (1992)**

Simon Armitage's most distinctive volume is perhaps *Book of Matches* (1993). His imagery is remarkably simple, making poetry out of such things as changing the brake fluid in a car, or dying in a car trapped in a snowdrift. The image in the title poem of a match burning out, as an image of the transitory nature of all things, is one of the simplest and most vivid of metaphors in all modern poetry. His *Killing Time* was a 1000-line poem for the millennium, covering one thousand years in that extent. Like several other writers of the 1990s he has gone back to the Greek dramatist Euripides for inspiration, reworking the Greek dramatist's work in *Mister Heracles* (2000). *All Points North* (1999) is a prose work, 'a declaration of Northernness', examining the essence of what it means to belong to the North of England, and confirming the decentring that has taken place, away from universities and from London in current poetry.

Simon Armitage's *Selected Poems* (2001) brings together an excellent range of his work. It is a questioning of poetry and its purpose (he famously compares it to shouting down a lavatory in its wasteful lack of audience). But it is also a grand affirmation of language, of imagery and of the popular appeal of poetry at the beginning of the new century. His latest volume is *The Universal Home Doctor* (2002), which demonstrates his story-telling gifts and sharp imagery: the Amazon Rain Forest turns out to be a cashpoint-free zone. His gift for portraying present-day emotional failure is acute and pungent: 'those who have suffered least feel the most pain.'

With his *Selected Poems* (2002) Matthew Sweeney finally achieved some of the recognition he had been slow in reaching despite producing ten volumes over twenty fruitful years of writing. His vision is dark and disturbing, and his subject matter has been well described as 'being undermined by your own existence'. This view of the human condition is handled gently and often humorously: 'I sent you a postcard of a hanging', for example.

Robert Crawford has affirmed his Scottishness both in his poetry and in his critical and academic writings. His volumes of verse are in no way parochial, however – the modern poet is both local and universal. *A Scottish Assembly*, published in 1990, anticipated the creation of the new Scottish Parliament by almost a decade. His other volumes include *Talkies* (1992), *Masculinity* (1996) and *The Tip of My Tongue* (2003). His critical works, *Devolving English Literature* (1992) and *The Scottish Invention of English Literature* (1998), are important contributions to the debate on the status of the subject.

Don Paterson has made an enormous impact with a couple of spare, beautifully textured volumes speaking from present-day Scotland about emotions of now and always. *Nil Nil* (1993) was his first volume, and was followed by the equally impressive *God's Gift to Women* (1997) and *The Landing Light* (2003).

DANCE TO DE RIDDIMS

Writers such as Ben Okri, born in Nigeria – where his Booker Prize-winning novel *The Famished Road* is set – Grace Nichols, and John Agard, born in Guyana, and Benjamin Zephaniah, born in Birmingham but brought up in Jamaica and the UK, are bringing new rhythms, performance styles, social and racial concerns into current British poetry. Zephaniah's *The Dread Affair* (1985) and his nomination for the post of Professor of Poetry at Oxford University confirm his status as a new voice in the multi-faceted revitalisation of poetry in English. *Talking Turkeys* (1995) and *Funky Chickens* (1996), and his novels *Face* (1998) and *Refugee Boy* (2001), are addressed to young adults. *Refugee Boy* (2001) is set in today's Africa and again presents urgent social concerns in a very readable novel.

'I think poetry should be alive,' he has said. 'You should be able to dance to it.' 'As a African' shows something of the range of minorities Benjamin Zephaniah is speaking for in his poetry.

As a African a plastic bullet hit me in Northern Ireland,
But my children overstood and dey grew strong.
As a African I was a woman in a man's world,
A man in a computer world,
A fly on the wall of China,
A Rastafarian diplomat
And a miner in Wales.

I was a red hot Eskimo
A peace loving hippie
A honest newscaster
A city dwelling peasant,
I was a Arawak
A unwanted baby
A circumcised lady,
I was all of dis
And still a African.

Benjamin Zephaniah, 'As a African'

His latest volume is the best-selling *Too Black, Too Strong* (2001). It contains a rewriting of Larkin's 'This Be the Verse' under the title of 'This Be the Worst', starting with the line 'They fuck you up, those lords and priests' – and in this case they *do* mean to. As always his new work is committed, and urgently political. The initial description of it as 'dub' poetry is not enough: Zephaniah writes about British society as he sees it, with affection, but with stinging criticism of racism, hypocrisy and the things he sees as wrong in today's world where he says 'we have to stand back/and watch them bomb Iraq' and where he asks 'how did these lefties reach dis Tory place?' He describes himself as 'an angry, illiterate, undereducated, ex-hustler, rebellious Rastafarian' but he is one of the most significant and vital voices in modern British writing. Anger has always been a force in literature – poetry does not have to be comforting to be good. Benjamin Zephaniah and a few others such as Valerie Bloom bring that anger into the open, with force, wit and a hugely positive impact on audiences and readers alike.

The new generation of writers, many from the Caribbean, have followed the novelist Sam Selvon in making wondrous use of 'rotten' English to write literature which both affirms identity and subverts language at the same time. Linton Kwesi Johnson's reggae texts such as 'Reggae Sounds' and 'Reggae fi Dada' bring oral culture and pop culture closer together: as he says in the first of these, 'bass history is a moving is a hurting black story'.

Poets such as Grace Nichols and Amryl Johnson, Fred D'Aguiar and Benjamin Zephaniah, who have moved from the West Indies or Guyana to Britain, have necessarily written about the cultural and linguistic mixes, confusions and difficulties they have experienced, and have developed new linguistic techniques to do so. Fred D'Aguiar, for example, wrote a poetry collection entitled *British Subjects* (1993) as well as volumes celebrating his Guyanese roots, such as *Mama Dot* (1985), *Bill of Rights* (1998) and *Bloodlines* (2001). His novel *The Longest Memory* (1994) tells the story of Whitechapel, an eighteenth-century slave working on a Virginia plantation, to explore questions of history, racial memory and identity. The language the slave had to learn was, of course, English.

Grace Nichols wittily challenges British preconceptions in such lines as 'Is Black British dey call we', and 'we come back inna kinda reverse' (in 'Beverley's Saga'). Her poems in *I Is a Long-memoried Woman* (1983), which was later filmed, tell a moving story of slavery. Amryl Johnson in her poem 'The Loaded Dice' reminds us (and we) it was 'pure chance wha' bring we here. . . . When dey divided Africa, who getting where.' And John Agard challenges stereotyping in a poem called 'Stereotype', running through many traditional British ways of seeing 'a full-blooded West Indian stereotype' until concluding that yes he is:

> that's why I
> graduated from Oxford University
> with a degree
> in anthropology

The challenge is often met with humour. Grace Nichols's *The Fat Black Woman's Poems* (1984) and *Lazy Thoughts of a Lazy Woman* (1989) use the voice of a Third World woman in the big city, and as such become a linguistic and cultural satire on value systems and cultural presuppositions. Her novel *Whole of a Morning Sky* (1986), although written in England, is set in Guyana, and uses the time-honoured move from village to city to explore the nation's history before independence. As E.A. Markham has said, Grace Nichols's skill at slipping in and out of modes of English is as good as any and she manages to make 'nation language' seem not a duty, not a deliberate act of 'rooting', but a gift joyfully received. Humour and a certain necessary subversiveness are part of this process: for example, Linton Kwesi Johnson called one of his volumes of poetry *Inglan Is a Bitch* (1980). This is postcolonial 'writing back', and is an example of how the English language has always been a magpie language, and British culture a magpie culture, ready to absorb influences from any source. Outsiders do not easily become insiders, but the language and humour allow what Nichols has called an 'act of spiritual revival' which gives the excluded new voices.

Of course, many other UK-based writers from Commonwealth countries have written in more standard forms of English – E.A. Markham himself is one major writer of Caribbean origin (from Montserrat) whose writings are largely in standard English, although the themes are frequently 'from the island'. In one poem, 'Late Return', about going back to Montserrat, Markham uses references to the Old English *Exeter Book* poems, 'The Wanderer' and 'The Seafarer', pointing out their 'powerful elegiac sense of exile from the pleasures of life'. His latest volume is *John Lewis & Co.* (2003). Exile and belonging have always been strong themes in literature. The new diasporas have simply renewed their vigour, as the novels of the time also conclusively demonstrate.

CODA 'News that stays news'

We have covered about forty years of recent writing, from the Cold War to the war on terrorism, through several changes of government and even of world order, no change in the monarch, but many changes in society: material changes, superficial changes, and some deeper, lasting changes.

The writing of these decades mirrors and often anticipates these changes. As Ezra Pound once put it, 'literature is news that stays news.'

Literature is one of the constants, as is language. Constantly evolving, constantly changing. More words, more books, more songs, more images have been produced and consumed in the past forty years than probably in all the centuries before. Every continent has been used as a setting in English literature, and there are now fewer barriers than ever in terms of who is writing and for whom. In times of tragedy it is the artist who helps us recover our balance; in happier times it is the writer who shows us the tears on the edge of the laughter.

For many readers and critics, none of the writers we have looked at in this book is more emblematic of his age than Samuel Beckett. He is one of the constants, from the 1950s till his death in the late 1980s, and his words resonate far beyond then.

'YOU MUST GO ON, I CAN'T GO ON, I'LL GO ON.'

The note of continuity is the triumph of the writer in the face of eternity. Literature is the triumph of the imagination. As such, it will only die if or when imagination dies. In the early 1950s Samuel Beckett, a towering figure in both drama and prose, had written a novel called *The Unnamable* which contains the line quoted above: past, present and future are the subject of all literature, and his 1965 novel was called *How It Is*, underlining the importance of the present in his work. His vision of how things are, bleak and unsparing, Irish and humorous, sad and comic, went on to find more and more reduced and concentrated expression throughout the 1960s and 1970s: as if in response to those critics who had seen something of *King Lear* in his plays, Beckett picks up on lines from that play – 'The worst is not so long as one can say, This is the worst.' This led him to *Worstword Ho* (1981), a multiple-punning title which moves on from other prose pieces such as *Lessness* (1970). The vision is not as negative as it might appear – where failure is the norm, the motto has to be 'Fail better'. But the process is one of reduction of the text just as much as it is one of expansion of the imagination, of the world, and of humanity's terms of reference. Against all the odds, literature and the imagination keep surviving, just as the characters in all of Beckett's works survive, and just as Beckett himself kept producing short, graphic, concise pieces of prose to the end of his life: *Company* (1979) and *Ill Seen, Ill Said* (1982) are two of the finest of these late works.

In a novel of only seven-and-a-half short pages, Samuel Beckett takes us to that furthest extreme in *Imagination Dead Imagine*, first published in 1965. It is the most concisely existential of Beckett's prose works, describing a profoundly simple but eternal human relationship, set in an eternal void. There is a narrator, and someone listening to him or her as the story begins, about this world with no life in it. It is a primordial vision, beyond science-fiction, almost beyond creation. The title is the climax of the opening sentence – and all human stories, from the beginning of time to the end of time resonate through this story, and through these positive/negative deathless/lifeless opening words:

> No trace anywhere of life, you say, pah, no difficulty there, imagination not
> dead yet, yes, dead, good, imagination dead imagine.

Authors and prizes

1. THE GRANTA LISTS

In each of the past three decades the magazine *Granta* has published a list of the most important young British writers.

THE 1983 GRANTA LIST

This list defined a generation . . . but whatever happened to Christopher Priest and Ursula Bentley?

Martin Amis
Pat Barker
Julian Barnes
Ursula Bentley
William Boyd
Buchi Emecheta
Maggie Gee
Kazuo Ishiguro
Alan Judd
Adam Mars-Jones
Ian McEwan
Shiva Naipaul
Philip Norman
Christopher Priest
Salman Rushdie
Lisa St Aubin de Terán
Clive Sinclair
Graham Swift
Rose Tremain
A.N. Wilson

THE 1993 GRANTA LIST

Time has proven that Rushdie and the other 1993 judges were right. No one asks nowadays, 'who is Louis de Bernières?' – though they may well enquire after Adam Lively.

Iain Banks
Louis de Bernières
Anne Billson
Tibor Fischer
Esther Freud
Alan Hollinghurst
Kazuo Ishiguro
A.L. Kennedy
Philip Kerr
Hanif Kureishi
Adam Lively
Adam Mars-Jones
Candia McWilliam
Lawrence Norfolk
Ben Okri
Caryl Phillips
Will Self
Nicholas Shakespeare
Helen Simpson
Jeanette Winterson

THE 2003 GRANTA LIST

Rising stars of literature and their age in 2003.

Monica Ali, 35
Nicola Barker, 36
Rachel Cusk, 35
Susan Elderkin, 34
Philip Hensher, 37

Peter Ho Davies, 36
A.L. Kennedy, 37
Hari Kunzru, 33
Toby Litt, 34
Robert McLiam Wilson, 38
David Mitchell, 33
Andrew O'Hagan, 34
David Peace, 35
Dan Rhodes, 30
Ben Rice, 30
Rachel Sieffert, 31
Zadie Smith, 27
Adam Thirlwell, 24
Alan Warner, 38
Sarah Waters, 36

2. THE ORANGE PRIZE

This prize has been awarded for women's writing since 1996.

1996 Helen Dunmore, *A Spell of Winter*
1997 Anne Michaels, *Fugitive Places*
1998 Carol Shields, *Larry's Party*
1999 Suzanne Berne, *A Crime in the Neighborhood*
2000 Linda Grant, *When I Lived in Modern Times*
2001 Kate Grenville, *The Idea of Perfecton*
2002 Ann Patchett, *Bel Canto*

3. THE BOOKER PRIZE

The Booker Prize is awarded by a panel of judges to the best novel by a citizen of the United Kingdom, the British Commonwealth or the Republic of Ireland. It was first awarded in 1969, and after twenty-five years a 'Booker of Bookers' prize was given to *Midnight's Children* by Salman Rushdie, the Booker Prize-winner in 1981. There were joint winners in 1974 and 1992. Up to 2002 there had been only twelve female winners out of thirty-six.

Authors marked * are mentioned in the text of *The Routledge Guide*. (Tr) Trinidad, (Ire) Ireland, (SA) South Africa, (In) India, (Aus) Australia, (NZ) New Zealand, (Nig) Nigeria, (Can) Canada.

Year	Author	Title
1969	P.H. Newby	*Something to Answer*
1970	Bernice Rubens	*The Elected Member*
1971	V.S. Naipaul*	*In A Free State* (Tr)
1972	John Berger	*G*
1973	J.G. Farrell*	*The Siege of Krishnapur* (Ire)
1974	(joint winners)	
	Nadine Gordimer	*The Conservationist* (SA)
	Stanley Middleton	*Holiday*
1975	Ruth Prawer Jhabvala	*Heat and Dust* (In)
1976	David Storey	*Saville*
1977	Paul Scott*	*Staying On*
1978	Iris Murdoch*	*The Sea, The Sea*
1979	Penelope Fitzgerald	*Off Shore*
1980	William Golding*	*Rites of Passage*
1981	Salman Rushdie*	*Midnight's Children* (In)
1982	Thomas Kenneally	*Schindler's Ark* (Aus)
1983	J.M. Coetzee	*Life and Times of Michael K* (SA)
1984	Anita Brookner*	*Hotel du Lac*
1985	Keri Hulme	*The Bone People* (NZ)
1986	Kingsley Amis*	*The Old Devils*
1987	Penelope Lively*	*Moon Tiger*
1988	Peter Carey	*Oscar and Lucinda* (Aus)
1989	Kazuo Ishiguro*	*The Remains of the Day*
1990	A.S. Byatt*	*Possession*
1991	Ben Okri*	*The Famished Road* (Nig)
1992	(joint winners)	
	Michael Ondaatje	*The English Patient* (Can)
	Barry Unsworth*	*Sacred Hunger*
1993	Roddy Doyle*	*Paddy Clarke Ha Ha Ha* (Ire)
1994	James Kelman*	*How Late It Was, How Late*

1995	Pat Barker*	*The Ghost Road*
1996	Graham Swift*	*Last Orders*
1997	Arundhati Roy*	*The God of Small Things* (In)
1998	Ian McEwan*	*Amsterdam*
1999	J.M. Coetzee	*Disgrace* (SA)
2000	Margaret Atwood	*The Blind Assassin* (Can)
2001	Peter Carey	*True History of the Kelly Gang* (Aus)
2002	Yann Martel	*Life of Pi* (Can)
2003	D.B.C. Pierre	*Vernon God Little* (Aus/Ire)

4. THE WHITBREAD PRIZE

The Whitbread Prize is awarded to writers who have been resident in the UK or the Republic of Ireland for three years. The Book of the Year is chosen from five awards: first novel, novel, biography, poetry, and children's book. The winners of each of these are then candidates for the overall award. Authors marked * are mentioned in the text of *The Routledge Guide*.

1971	Gerda Charles	*The Destiny Waltz*
1972	Susan Hill*	*The Bird of Night*
1973	Shiva Naipaul	*The Chip Chip Gatherers*
1974	Iris Murdoch*	*The Sacred & Profane Love Machine*
1975	William McIlvanney	*Docherty*
1976	William Trevor*	*The Children of Dynmouth*
1977	Beryl Bainbridge*	*Injury Time*
1978	Paul Theroux	*Picture Palace*
1979	Jennifer Johnston	*The Old Jest*
1980	David Lodge*	*How Far Can You Go?*
1981	William Boyd*	*A Good Man in Africa*
1982	Bruce Chatwin*	*On the Black Hill*
1983	John Fuller	*Flying to Nowhere*
1984	James Buchan	*A Parish of Rich Women*
1985	Douglas Dunn*	*Elegies*
1986	Kazuo Ishiguro*	*An Artist of the Floating World*
1987	Christopher Nolan	*Under the Eye of the Clock*
1988	Paul Sayer	*The Comforts of Madness*

1989	Richard Holmes*	*Coleridge: Early Visions*
1990	Nicholas Mosley	*Hopeful Monsters*
1991	John Richardson	*A Life of Picasso*
1992	Jeff Torrington*	*Swing Hammer Swing!*
1993	Joan Brady	*Theory of War*
1994	William Trevor*	*Felicia's Journey*
1995	Kate Atkinson	*Behind the Scenes at the Museum*
1996	Seamus Heaney*	*The Spirit Level*
1997	Ted Hughes*	*Tales From Ovid*
1998	Ted Hughes*	*Birthday Letters*
1999	Seamus Heaney*	*Beowulf*
2000	Matthew Kneale*	*English Passengers*
2001	Philip Pullman*	*The Amber Spyglass*
2002	Michael Frayn*	*Spies*

Novel of the Year when not Book of the Year.

1981	Maurice Leitch	*Silver's City*
1982	John Wain*	*Young Shoulders*
1983	William Trevor*	*Fools of Fortune*
1984	Christopher Hope	*Kruger's Alp*
1985	Peter Ackroyd*	*Hawksmoor*
1987	Ian McEwan*	*The Child in Time*
1988	Salman Rushdie*	*The Satanic Verses*
1989	Lindsay Clarke	*The Chymical Wedding*
1991	Jane Gardam	*The Queen of the Tambourine*
1992	Alasdair Gray*	*Poor Things*
1995	Salman Rushdie*	*The Moor's Last Sigh*
1996	Beryl Bainbridge*	*Every Man for Himself*
1997	Jim Crace*	*Quarantine*
1998	Justin Cartwright	*Leading the Cheers*
1999	Rose Tremain*	*Music and Silence*

First Novel of the Year by authors mentioned in *The Routledge Guide*.

1981	William Boyd	*A Good Man in Africa*
1985	Jeanette Winterson	*Oranges Are Not the Only Fruit*
1986	Jim Crace	*Continent*
1990	Hanif Kureishi	*The Buddha of Suburbia*
1994	Fred D'Aguiar	*The Longest Memory*
1996	John Lanchester	*The Debt to Pleasure*

5. THE NOBEL PRIZE FOR LITERATURE

British and Irish winners of the Nobel Prize for Literature 1963 to 2003.

The Nobel Prize is awarded annually by the Swedish Nobel Academy to 'the person who shall have produced in the field of literature the most outstanding work of an idealistic tendency'. It honours a major lifetime contribution to literature from any country and in any language. All authors are mentioned in the text of *The Routledge Guide*.

1969	Samuel Beckett (1906–1989)	*Waiting for Godot, Endgame, How It Is*
1983	William Golding (1911–1993)	*Lord of the Flies, Rites of Passage*
1995	Seamus Heaney (1939–)	*Death of a Naturalist, North, The Spirit Level*
2001	V.S. Naipaul (1932–)	*A House for Mr Biswas, The Enigma of Arrival, Half a Life*

Timeline

THE 1960s

Beginning with a great fear of world crisis, notably the 'Cold War' and rivalry between the communist USSR and the anti-communist USA, in Britain this decade was characterised by optimism and a youth-led culture ('the swinging sixties' – when Britain led the world in fashion and music). Many laws were liberalised, especially after the Labour Party took power in 1964.

The dissolution of the British Empire was accelerated, and the post-colonial 'Commonwealth of Nations' firmly established. Meanwhile, Northern Ireland began to cause political problems, as Irish Republicans fought to integrate Ulster into the predominantly Catholic state of Eire, established in 1922.

Immigration to Britain from former colonies peaked in this decade.

Events

1960 With the independence of Nigeria, Britain's withdrawal as a colonial power from Africa increased. The democratisation of Britain's former colonies in Africa was not always easy; the process in the white-dominated states of Rhodesia (independent Zimbabwe from 1980) and South Africa was especially difficult.

Lady Chatterley's Lover, a 1928 novel by D.H. Lawrence, previously banned in the UK, was cleared in court of charges of obscenity.

The young John F. Kennedy was elected President of the United States.

1961 Building of the Berlin Wall, across Germany's largest city. The wall was the ultimate symbol of the Cold War, separating the communist and non-communist worlds. (It was demolished in 1989.)

1962	Jamaica, with Trinidad & Tobago, were the first Caribbean states to gain independence.
	President Kennedy of the USA came into conflict with Soviet leader Khrushchev over the installation of nuclear warheads in the communist Caribbean state of Cuba. This was the height of the Cold War.
	First hit single for the Beatles. Their first LP was *Please Please Me*, in 1963.
1963	A new wave of satirical comedy began on British television.
	Dependence on road traffic increased in Britain, following the Beeching Report, recommending closure of most rural railways. Motorway building increased dramatically.
	The assassination of President Kennedy shocked the western world.
1964–1970	The Labour Party, under Harold Wilson, held the majority in Britain, after thirteen years of Conservative government.
1964	First Race Relations Act in Britain.
1966	England hosted the World Cup of football, and won the championship.
1967	The summer of 'peace and love' was based particularly in San Francisco, California, as a protest against US aggression in Vietnam (ended in 1973; war concluded 1975).
	The act known popularly as the Homosexual Bill decriminalised consensual gay sex in private for men over 21 in England and Wales. (Lesbianism was never a criminal offence.)
1968	Colour TV was introduced in Britain.
	Theatres Act abolished state censorship of drama (in place for 231 years).
1969	US astronauts Armstrong and Aldrin landed on the moon. This was the end of a 'space race' with the USSR, begun with the Soviet cosmonaut Yuri Gagarin being the first man to travel in space (in 1961).
	Beginning of the 'Troubles' in Northern Ireland.

J.R.R. Tolkien's *The Lord of the Rings* became a best-seller. (First published 1954–1955.)

1969–1974 The TV comedy show *Monty Python's Flying Circus* achieved huge success.

TEXTS OF THE TIME

1960   D.H. Lawrence, *Lady Chatterley's Lover*
1961   Samuel Beckett, *Happy Days*
1963   John Le Carré, *The Spy Who Came in from the Cold*
1964   Philip Larkin, *The Whitsun Weddings*
         Roald Dahl, *Charlie and the Chocolate Factory*
1965   Harold Pinter, *The Homecoming*
1966   Tom Stoppard, *Rosencrantz and Guildenstern Are Dead*
1969   John Fowles, *The French Lieutenant's Woman*

THE 1970s

The national mood slowed in this decade. Strikes affected both Conservative and Labour governments. With a rapid rise in oil prices, currency inflation throughout Europe became very high. Issues of energy conservation began to become important.

Prime Minister Edward Heath brought the UK into the European Economic Community in 1971 (ratified, with the Irish Republic and Denmark, on 1 January 1973). Trade expanded within Europe, with some disadvantages for former colonial nations.

Industrial disputes led to an increasing awareness in society between the 'haves' and the 'have nots'. Rejection of the pragmatism of James Callaghan's Labour Party government in the winter of 1978 to 1979 led to the election of a new Conservative government under Margaret Thatcher.

Events

1970   The age of becoming an 'adult' in Britain was reduced from 21 to 18. Voting rights were thus extended.

Australian author Germaine Greer's *The Female Eunuch* raised feminist consciousness.

Invention of computer 'floppy' disks.

The Beatles played together for the last time.

1971–2 Britain negotiated entry to the EEC (now the European Union).

President Idi Amin expelled Asians from Uganda (a British colony in central Africa until 1962): many refugees settled in the UK.

1973 European and American demand for oil precipitated a financial crisis, leading to great wealth for oil-rich states in the Middle East, when prices were greatly inflated.

1975 Discrimination Act passed by Labour government.

Inflation in Britain reached 25 per cent.

1977 'Punk rock' music became fashionable: it reflected antisocial youth culture, typified by the phrase 'sex and drugs and rock'n'roll'.

Silver Jubilee of Queen Elizabeth II.

1979 Mrs Thatcher's first (Conservative) government elected to power.

TEXTS OF THE TIME

1970 Ted Hughes, *Crow*
Germaine Greer, *The Female Eunuch*
1971 Frederick Forsyth, *The Day of the Jackal*
1973 Peter Shaffer, *Equus*
1975 Shirley Conran, *Superwoman*
Malcolm Bradbury, *The History Man*
1978 Iris Murdoch, *The Sea, the Sea*
Andrew Motion, *The Pleasure Steamers*
1979 Craig Raine, *A Martian Sends a Postcard Home*
Douglas Adams, *The Hitch-hiker's Guide to the Galaxy*

THE 1980s

Generally, a renewed optimism accompanied the premiership of Margaret Thatcher, which lasted throughout this decade. Youth was again highly valued, and the creation of money became a principal goal. (In this respect, Thatcher was in tune with Ronald Reagan, US President from 1981 to 1989.) Scepticism about playing a role in Europe became widespread. Mrs Thatcher was also criticised widely for causing new divisions in British society.

A second generation of African, Asian and Caribbean immigrants began to be heard and seen: those born in Britain to immigrant parents in the 1950s and 1960s. Often there was a culture clash (as among poor and better-off white-skinned people) over the question of social status. Immigrant families often looked to their 'roots' and questions of 'displacement'.

Elsewhere in Europe, at the end of the decade, communist states began to collapse with the initiatives of Soviet leader Gorbachev, who dissolved the 'Warsaw Pact' – a military alliance of East against West. Removed from the threat of Soviet domination (exercised in Hungary in 1956 and the former Czechoslovakia in 1968), many constituent parts of some European countries opted for self-determination and reversion to former ethnic boundaries. However, the Cold War with America was over, though it hotted up in some areas.

Events

1981 Marriage of Charles, Prince of Wales and heir to the throne, to Lady Diana Spencer.

Scientists identified a new sexually transmitted virus, HIV, which leads fatally to AIDS (Acquired Immuno-Deficiency Syndrome). A high proportion of early victims were gay men.

Splits in the Labour Party, when the moderate Callaghan was replaced as leader by the more strident Michael Foot, led to the formation of the SDP (Social Democratic Party). In 1988, this merged with the Liberals, Britain's third largest party in recent years (but frequently in government before 1922), and whose name was changed to Liberal Democrats.

1982	The Falklands War. The UK reasserted authority in its South Atlantic dependency following aggressive claims to sovereignty from Argentina. A few months later, in 1983, Mrs Thatcher was re-elected as Prime Minister.
1984–1985	A long-lasting strike by British coal-miners heightened class divisions in society. The 'Me' generation of young urban professionals ('Yuppies'), centred on London, was contrasted with an impoverished working class based largely in northern Britain.
1985	The reforming Mikhail Gorbachev became First Secretary of the USSR Communist Party. His concentration on foreign policy up to 1991 led to difficulties in Russia, when he was replaced that year by Boris Yeltsin.
	Unemployment in Britain reached its highest peak, at about three and a half million.
1987	Margaret Thatcher formed her third government after another election victory.
1989–1991	Blind devotion to communism in Central and Eastern Europe was removed, with Gorbachev's policies of 'perestroika' and 'glasnost' (reform and openness). Communist régimes in the region all broke down with the new openness, but not without some ethnic conflicts in the next decade.

TEXTS OF THE TIME

1980 William Golding, *Rites of Passage*
Howard Brenton, *The Romans in Britain*
1981 Salman Rushdie, *Midnight's Children*
1982 Sue Townsend, *The Secret Diary of Adrian Mole, Aged 13¾*
1983 Terry Pratchett, *The Colour of Magic*
1985 Jeanette Winterson, *Oranges Are Not the Only Fruit*
1987 Peter Wright, *Spycatcher*
1989 Kazuo Ishiguro, *The Remains of the Day*

THE 1990s AND INTO THE TWENTY-FIRST CENTURY

The period from 1990 brought anxiety and disillusionment in Britain. A Prime Minister, equally admired and detested, had gone. Eventually, the Conservative government was beaten comprehensively in the election of 1 May 1997, though it had survived narrowly in 1992. So, Tony Blair's New Labour assumed power after eighteen years of Tory government.

The greed of ambitious young people in the 1980s turned to reflection on being over 30 and largely unsatisfied. A slightly younger age group was represented in 'chick' and 'lad' culture.

It was accusations of impropriety and shady financial dealing – both denied – which brought down John Major's government so overwhelmingly in 1997: the media word was 'sleaze'. Throughout the 1990s, all areas of the media enormously increased their influence on public opinion. Blair is very aware of this, and thus has advisers on presentation and so on, popularly called 'spin doctors'. There is a message, undeniably, but you must make it sound good! 'Spin', therefore, is often seen as media manipulation for political advantage.

The multi-cultural nature of Britain is now taken for granted, and is usually seen as an advantage. Unlike Ireland, however, the UK failed to join the Euro currency, launched into people's pockets elsewhere in the European Union from January 2002.

Events

1990 Mrs Thatcher replaced as Prime Minister by John Major (to 1997).

1991 Gulf War. Iraq's invasion of Kuwait led to rapid military intervention by the USA, under President George Bush senior, and was joined by the UK.

1990s Ethnic wars in the former Yugoslavia – particularly Bosnia and Kosovo – were the major European problem of the decade. These followed the dissolution of the USSR in 1991, with the three Baltic states seceding, and the other twelve republics forming a loose 'Commonwealth of Independent States'. (Russia remains the largest country in the world in terms of land area.)

1991–1992 Satellite-based communications became established in Britain and Ireland for both TV and Internet. Personal computer ownership was expanding rapidly in these years.

1992 With the end of the Cold War, a series of arms limitation talks was concluded between the USA and Russia. START 2 (Strategic Arms Reduction Talks 2) marked a significant agreement between Yeltsin of Russia and recently elected President Clinton of the USA to cut dangerous weapons of war, bilaterally, by about 70 per cent.

1994 Ceasefire agreed in Northern Ireland; however, this broke down in early 1996 but a new accord was reached on Good Friday 1998. Troubles in Ulster nevertheless continue to rumble on.

1996 The great symbol of Scottish national identity, the Stone of Destiny, was returned to Scotland, after being in England for six centuries.

1997 Tony Blair's New Labour Party won a landslide election victory.

Britain returned sovereignty over Hong Kong to the Chinese.

The accidental death of Diana, Princess of Wales, caused an unprecedented public expression of grief.

1998–2001 The use of mobile phones and Internet became commonplace. In addition, digital technology was widely introduced in the broadcast media.

1999 Scottish Parliament and Welsh Assembly created.

2000 Legal age for consensual gay sex reduced to 16 – the same as for heterosexual partners. (By coincidence, this judgement was made on the exact hundredth anniversary of Oscar Wilde's death – 30 November.)

2001 Blair's Labour Party re-elected with another huge majority.

Britain joined the USA in the Afghan War, which followed the terrorist attack on (and destruction of) the twin towers of New York City's World Trade Center and on government buildings in Washington DC on 11 September.

Rowling's *Harry Potter* books and Tolkien's *Lord of the Rings* first released as films in the cinema, with huge success.

2002   Golden Jubilee of Queen Elizabeth (fifty years as monarch).

2003   Invasion of Iraq toppling Saddam Hussein's regime.

TEXTS OF THE TIME

1990 Derek Walcott, *Omeros*
1991 Angela Carter, *Wise Children*
1992 Thom Gunn, *The Man with Night Sweats*
      Andrew Morton, *Diana: Her True Story*
1995 Martin Amis, *The Information*
      Sarah Kane, *Blasted*
1996 Helen Fielding, *Bridget Jones's Diary*
1997 J.K. Rowling, *Harry Potter and the Philosopher's Stone*
      Ian McEwan, *Enduring Love*
1999 Joanne Harris, *Chocolat*
2000 Germaine Greer, *The Whole Woman*
2001 Zadie Smith, *White Teeth*
2002 Yann Martel, *Life of Pi*
2003 Mark Hadden, *The Curious Incident of the Dog in the Night-Time*
      Monica Ali, *Brick Lane*

Select bibliography:
further reading and resources

Abse, Dannie, *Twentieth Century Anglo-Welsh Poetry* (Bridgend, Seren, 1997).

Alexander, Flora, *Contemporary Women Novelists* (London, Arnold, 1989).

Armitage, Simon and Robert Crawford (eds), *The Penguin Book of Poetry from Britain and Ireland since 1945* (London, Penguin, 1998).

Bloom, Clive, *Bestsellers: Popular Fiction Since 1900* (Basingstoke, Palgrave/Macmillan, 2002).

Booker 30: A Celebration of 30 Years of the Booker Prize for Fiction 1969–1998 (London, Booker, 1998).

Brannigan, John, *Orwell to the Present: Literature in England, 1945–2000* (Basingstoke, Palgrave/Macmillan, 2003).

Callil, Carmen and Colm Tóibín, *The Modern Library: The 200 Best Novels in English Since 1950* (London, Picador, 1999).

Connor, Steven, *The English Novel in History: 1950 to the Present* (London, Routledge, 1995).

Davies, Alastair and Alan Sinfield (eds), *British Culture of the Post-War: An Introduction to Literature and Society 1945–1999* (London, Routledge, 2000).

Eccleshare, Julia, *British Literature for Young People: A Bibliography, 1999–2000* (London, British Council, 2001).

Ferguson, Catriona, *Eyes Wide Open: A Select Bibliography of New Fiction from the UK, 1999–2001* (London, British Council, 2002).

Gordon, Lois (ed.), *Pinter at 70: A Casebook* (London, Routledge, 2001).

Head, Dominic, *The Cambridge Introduction to Modern British Fiction 1950–2000* (Cambridge, Cambridge University Press, 2002).

Leggatt, Alexander, *English Stage Comedy 1490–1990: Five Centuries of a Genre* (London, Routledge, 1998).

Longley, Michael (ed.), *Twentieth Century Irish Poems* (London, Faber, 2002).

Maroula, Joannou, *Contemporary Women's Writing: From 'The Golden Notebook' to 'The Colour Purple'* (Manchester, Manchester University Press, 2000).

Parker, Peter (ed.), *The Reader's Companion to Twentieth Century Writers* (London, Fourth Estate/Helicon, 1995).

Harold Pinter: A Celebration (London, Faber, 2000).

Prentice, Penelope, *The Pinter Ethic: The Erotic Aesthetic* (London, Garland Science, 1994).

Shellard, Dominic, *British Theatre Since the War* (London and New Haven, CT, Yale University Press, 1999).

Roberts, Neil, *Narrative and Voice in Postwar Poetry* (London, Longman, 1999).

Sierz, Aleks, *In-Yer-Face Theatre: British Drama Today* (London, Faber, 2000).

Sinfield, Alan, *Literature, Politics and Culture in Postwar Britain* (London, Athlone Press, 1997).

Sutherland, John, *Reading the Decades* (London, BBC, 2002).

Tynan, Kenneth, ed. by John Lahr, *The Diaries of Kenneth Tynan*, London, Bloomsbury, 2001.

Wandor, Michelene, *Post-War British Drama: Looking Back in Gender* (London, Routledge, 2001).

Waugh, Patricia, *Feminine Fictions: Revisiting the Postmodern* (London, Routledge, 1989).

Waugh, Patricia, *Harvest of the Sixties: English Literature and its Background 1960–1990* (Oxford, Oxford University Press, 1995).

WEBSITES

Arts Council www.liveliterature.net

BBC/British Council linked websites: www.britishcouncil.org/arts/literature

www.contemporarywriters.com 250 writers. Twenty are added each month.

www.poetrybooks.co.uk
www.poetrylibrary.org.uk
www.poetrysoc.com
www.thewomen'slibrary.ac.uk
www.booktrust.org.uk

Many writers also have their own websites or can be searched using a variety of web search engines. For example,

www.benjaminzephaniah.com
www.jim-crace.com

This book is updated with regular reviews, commentaries, reports on the annual Booker prize on the authors' personal pages at www. nottingham.ac.uk/english

Index

crime novels *see* detective fiction

critical writing 64, 131, 157, 166–7, 169

Crow Road, The (Iain Banks) 143

cult novels 68–9, 142

cultural events *see* political and cultural events

Dabydeen, David (b. 1955) 2, 108

D'Aguiar, Fred (b. 1960) 184

Dahl, Roald (1916–1990) 65, 66, 68

Dancing at Lughnasa (Brian Friel) 30

Davie, Donald (1922–1995) 153, 154–5

Davies, Andrew (b.1936) 2

Davitt, Michael (b.1950) 171

Deane, Seamus (b.1940)144

de Bernières, Louis (b. 1954) 115, 189

Debt to Pleasure, The (John Lanchester) 120

De Quincey, Thomas (1785–1859) 120

Desai, Anita (b. 1937) 2, 104–5

detective fiction 2, 61, 68, 83–6, 145; imitations of classic form 57, 99

Dexter, Colin (b.1930) 85, 86

Dialogues of the Dead (Reginald Hill) 85, 86

diaries, fictional 124–6

'Digging' (Seamus Heaney) 165

Din, Ayub Khan, *see* Khan Din, Ayub

Donne, John (1572–1631) 88

Doyle, Arthur Conan (1859–1930) 117–18

Doyle, Roddy (b.1958) 64, 131, 133, 146–7

Drabble, Margaret (b.1939) 28, 76–7, 78

drama 1, 7–42, 64, 74, 124

Duffy, Carol Ann (b.1955) 173, 174

Dunmore, Helen (b.1952) 88

Dunn, Douglas (b.1942) 164–5

Durcan, Paul (b.1944) 168, 169–70

Durrell, Lawrence ((1912–1990) 46

East is East (Ayub Khan Din) 34

Eco, Umberto, (b. 1932) 112

Eliot, George (1819–1880) 2, 15, 125

Eliot, T(homas) S(tearns) (1888–1965) 157, 179

Elyot, Kevin (b.1951) 35

Emecheta, Buchi (b.1944) 2, 106–7

Enduring Love (Ian McEwan) 89–90, 91

English Passengers (Matthew Kneale) 118–19

Enright, D(ennis) J(oseph) (1920–2002) 58, 153, 154

Equal Music, An (Vikram Seth) 103–4

Equus (Peter Shaffer) 21–2

Euripides (5th century B.C.) 29

Exeter Book poems 186

Experience (Martin Amis) 128, 130, 131

Eyre, Richard (b.1943) 155

Face (Benjamin Zephaniah) 67

Fairly Honourable Defeat, A (Iris Murdoch) 54–5

Falling Slowly (Anita Brookner) 82, 83

fantasy writing 68–9, 117, 134, 150–1

Fanthorpe, U(rsula) A(skham) (b.1929) 173

Far Cry from Kensington, A (Muriel Spark) 51–2, 148

Farquhar, George (c.1677–1707) 29

Farrell, J(ames) G(ordon) 50, 92, 121

'Fat Black Woman Goes Shopping, The' (Grace Nichols) 97

Faulks, Sebastian (b.1953) 50, 59, 114

Fielding, Helen (b.1960) 1, 124–6, 128

Fielding, Henry (1707–1754) 127

Filth (Irvine Welsh) 141–2

Fine, Anne 66–7

Flaubert, Gustave (1821–1890) 123

Flaubert's Parrot (Julian Barnes) 113